IMAGES
of America
FORGOTTEN HOUMA

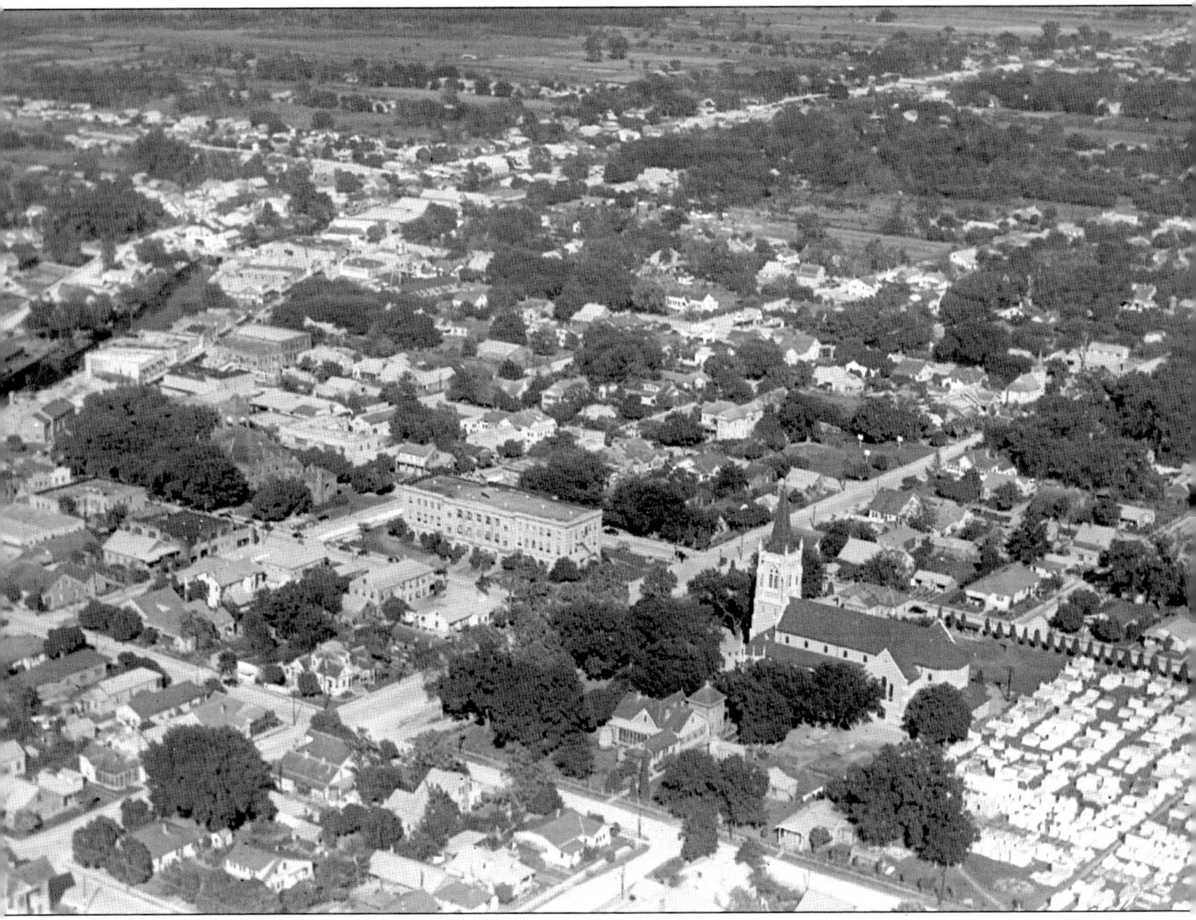

An aerial view of Houma from 1936 shows the center of town. In the middle of the image is the original Terrebonne Parish High School, which is no longer standing. The houses to the west of St. Francis Cathedral and cemetery (below the cathedral and cemetery) are now gone to make way for the Allen J. Ellender Federal Building, which houses federal courts and the post office on Lafayette Street. (Dr. Christopher Cenac Sr. collection.)

On the Cover: This image shows a shrimping boat unloading at the docks in Houma. (Terrebonne Historical and Cultural Society.)

IMAGES
of America

FORGOTTEN HOUMA

Rachel E. Cherry

ARCADIA
PUBLISHING

ISBN 978-1-4671-1312-0

Published by Arcadia Publishing
Charleston, South Carolina

Printed in the United States of America

Library of Congress Control Number: 2014941886

For all general information, please contact Arcadia Publishing:
Telephone 843-853-2070
Fax 843-853-0044
E-mail sales@arcadiapublishing.com
For customer service and orders:
Toll-Free 1-888-313-2665

Visit us on the Internet at www.arcadiapublishing.com

Forgotten Houma *is dedicated to the Terrebonne Historical and Cultural Society, the United Houma Nation, and the individuals who keep history alive in Terrebonne Parish.*

Contents

ACKNOWLEDGMENTS

The materials in this book come from many different sources in the community. Special thanks go to Corrine Paulk of the United Houma Nation (UHN) for the images she put together for me that make this volume unique.

Dr. Chris Cenac Sr.'s collection was of great help with capturing alternative industries, such as logging and oil and gas, and providing the images of old downtown Houma.

Photographs also came from the Edward Lyons and Ellender family collections, though the images from the Ellenders are housed in exhibit at Southdown Plantation House and Museum.

This book would not be possible without the extensive collections of photographs within the Terrebonne Historical and Cultural Society (THACS) at Southdown Planation House and Museum. A special thanks goes out to the dedicated, hardworking, and creative men and women who have kept the dream of Southdown Plantation alive for more than 30 years, and to the first incorporators of the THACS who made it all possible. These members were Gerald J. Bridges Sr., Louise Dupont, William L. Manning, Ellen McCollam, Margaret Shaffer, M.L. Shaffer Jr., and Betty Wurzlow (first board president).

Special dedication goes to Edward Borne, docent, tour guide, and historian at Southdown Plantation House and Museum. It was under his tutelage that I was able to learn so much of the history and culture of Houma and to unlock some of the other stories therein.

INTRODUCTION

When I think about the history of Houma, Louisiana, I see diversity. Each group of people that came to call this land their own brought unique cultures with different customs, traditions, skills, and views. What may have started as a culture of isolation would survive for a time, but with the increasing number of people and cultures that shared a geographic area, life had to change.

For centuries, French and Spanish explorers reached the coast of Louisiana and explored the course of the Mississippi River. Spanish explorers, as early as 1519, had an interest in Louisiana. In 1528, Pánfilo de Narváez navigated coastal Louisiana waters for Spain.

René-Robert Cavelier, Sieur de La Salle, was sent by King Louis XIV to travel south from Canada and sail down the Mississippi River to the Gulf of Mexico. He was the first European to travel the length of the Mississippi River. His mission was to explore and establish fur-trade routes along the waterway in 1679.

Pierre Le Moyne, Sieur d'Iberville, and his brother Jean-Baptiste Le Moyne, Sieur de Bienville, arrived to explore Louisiana and the Mississippi River in 1699. Antoine de Lamothe Cadillac arrived in Mobile in May 1713 and was the first person to officially be called the governor of Louisiana. Bienville stayed in the colony as the military commander of French troops.

In 1682, the French explorer Brinson noted existence of the Houmas in Louisiana. Later, explorers such as d'Iberville detailed their village to be six to eight miles inland from the east bank of the Mississippi River near the mouth of the Red River. Because of increasing tension with the French, Spanish, and English colonists, the Houmas moved farther south to an area near modern-day Houma. The people of the United Houma Nation are a vital and integral part of the history and heritage of the community of Terrebonne Parish and the south Louisiana region.

The Acadians, or French colonists, arrived from Nova Scotia to the area starting in 1749. People of the two cultures—Acadians, or what came to be known as Cajuns, and Houmas—found many similarities in their lifestyles, morals, and skills, and they bonded by intermarrying. Eventually, the dominant language of the Houmas was Cajun French.

With the arrival of the Anglo-Saxon wealthy landowners, the landscape of agriculture started to change. Although there were Spanish and French land grants given in the area, the new landowners bought out many of these grants and created a system of plantations that were mostly owned by families such as the Barrows, Shaffers, Minors, McCollums, Ellenders, and others.

French- and Anglo-Saxon–owned plantations were equal in number in 1860 according to the US census, but the number of French-owned plantations plummeted shortly after the Civil War. Fishing, shrimping, fur trading, oystering, and other water-based endeavors took over for the people down the bayou. The wealthier French colonists started canneries and packing and processing companies for the seafood industry.

Sugarcane plantations, mills, and refineries took hold in Houma starting in the late 1820s. The first mill at Southdown was built in 1846, with alterations and improvements made every year until 1854. In 1846, a steam-driven engine was installed in the mill, and it remained in use until 1869. The engine was built by Messrs. Leeds & Company of New Orleans, Louisiana. Improvements in the mill proper continued over the years, and extensive improvements were made in 1920 under the administration of David W. Pipes, husband of Mary Minor, and Charles C. Krumbhaar, husband of Margaret Minor. In 1928, the Fulton Iron Works Company of St. Louis, Missouri, installed a modern sugar mill with the capacity of 2,000 tons of sugar per day. At this time, the most troubled period of the Louisiana sugar industry was beginning, and Southdown Plantation would become a leader in the sugar industry.

During the heyday of cane farming in Louisiana, most cane was moved by mule-drawn wagon to narrow-gauge rail lines that ran from central locations in the fields to the mill. In Terrebonne Parish, however, the bayous and waterways that were nearly equal in area to the land were a main source of transportation. Still, most mills had their own railroads, or "dummy lines." The name *dummy* refers generally to the engine portion of the line, which had a muted or otherwise distinct noisemaker to avoid confusion with commercial lines. In later years, mules were replaced by tractors, and still later, by 18-wheeler trucks.

Other industries, such as logging, raising livestock, and other agricultural endeavors, continued to change land and occupations. Truck farms, as they were called, did not necessarily transport the quick-crop goods by truck; the name refers to the verb *to truck* ("to exchange" or "to barter"). Other methods of transporting garden goods in Houma—like corn, potatoes, strawberries, and even day lilies—to either farmer's markets or ports of sale included waterway, truck, wagon, or railcar.

It was the discovery of oil and gas that brought on the most significant changes in Houma and the surrounding areas. The oil and gas industry took its foothold in Houma in the early 1900s, and both oil wells and gas wells were present in the area. Lirette Well No. 4 was owned by the Terrebonne Gas Company of Houma; in 1917, it was the largest six-inch gas well in the world. Natural gas wells enabled the existing industries in the area to grow, change, and become more efficient as the gas was piped to these facilities to be used as an alternative power source. The discovery of oil and gas also changed the physical landscape as sugarcane plantations were sold off in parcels for the discovery and production of oil and gas. It was also at this time that old plantation homes were torn down and many businesses in Houma started to build metal warehouses in place of the older buildings.

Of course, no story of Houma would be complete without including the recreational, cultural, and traditional activities of south Louisiana. Travelers from around the world still visit for swamp tours, hunting and fishing expeditions, festivals and food celebrations, and the preserved treasures of the original plantation era.

The many changes in Houma are seen throughout this volume, but none is more apparent and important than that of the changing coastline. Once-beloved locations have disappeared from the coast completely. The effects of floods, hurricanes, industry, and coastal erosion are evident in the images of the 1927 Mississippi River flood and the hurricane of 1926. Yet, it is the vanishing coast that brings the alarm to a state that is losing the equivalent of one football field of coastline every 15 minutes.

The images within may have some resemblance to the Houma of today, but for the most part, they capture a forgotten Houma.

One

About the Town

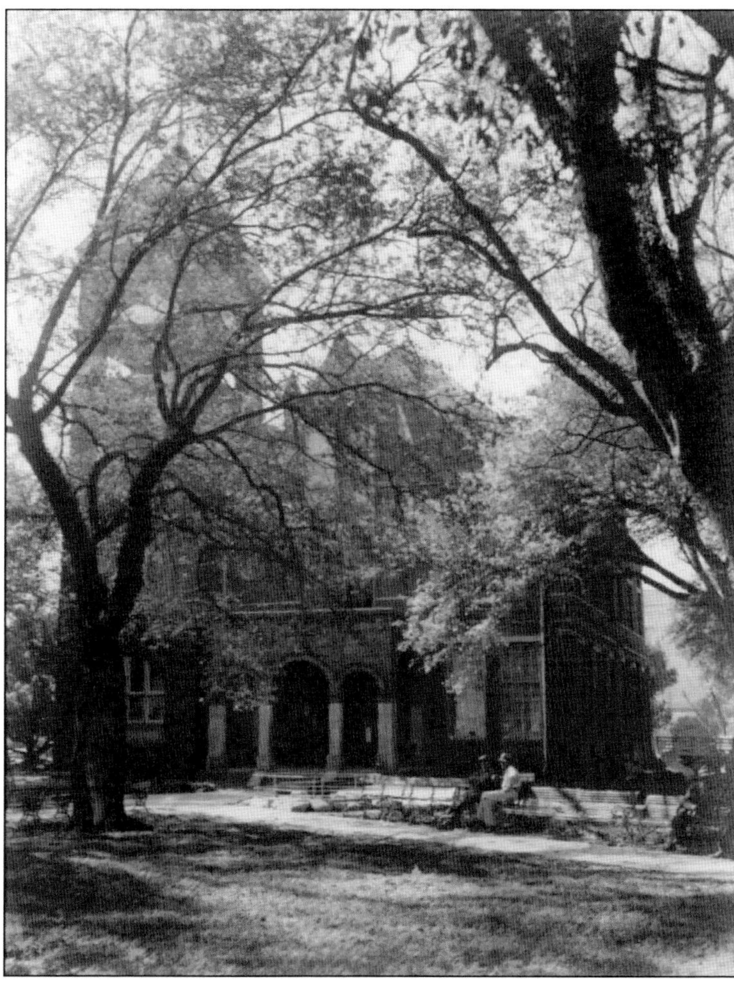

The courthouse in downtown Houma was completed in 1860 and remodeled in 1892, as seen in this 1898 image. The tower boasts a clock face on all sides. The courthouse square is adorned with old live oak trees. The square is also the original burial site of two Union soldiers who were murdered by an angry group of Confederate sympathizers. (Nicholls State University.)

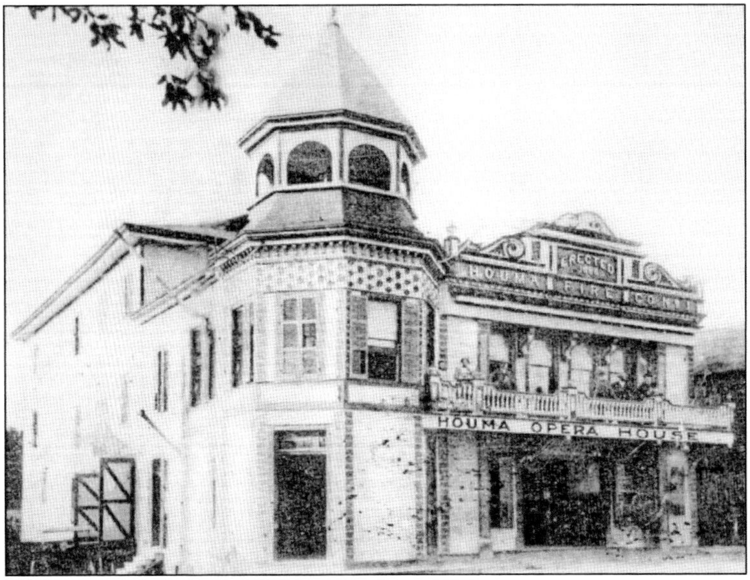

The opera house built it 1896 boasted a distinctive spire and once housed the city clerk's office. The two-storied, wooden structure had balconies and a six-sided tower. Below the tower was the belfry. High steps led from the banquette (wooden sidewalk) to the structure. The belfry housed a bell that was sounded in the event of a fire. Silent films were shown, accompanied by a piano. (THACS.)

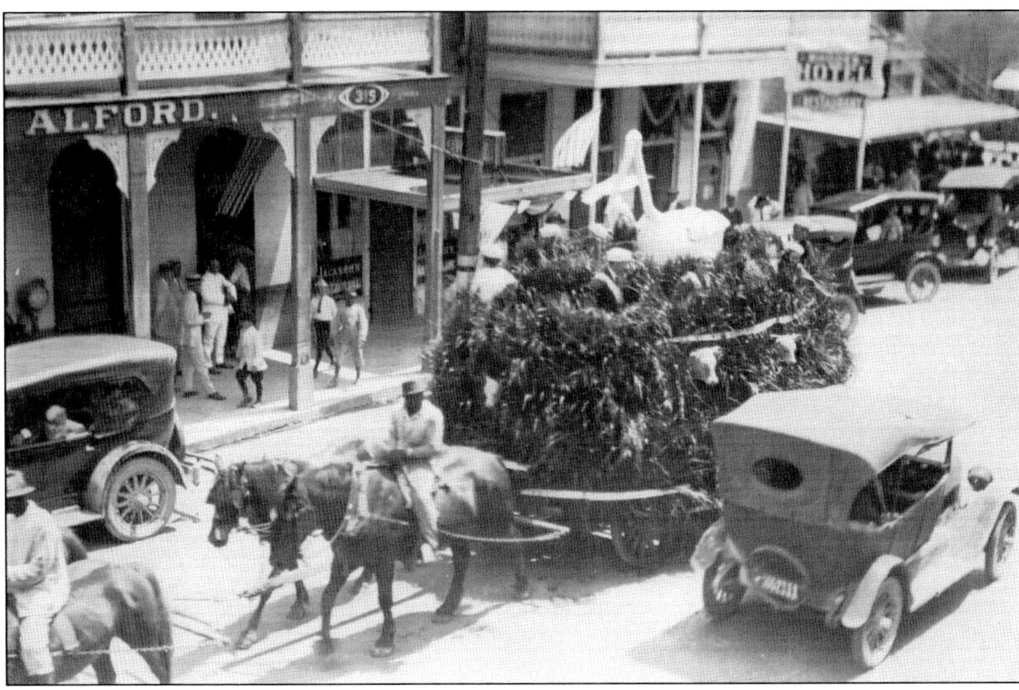

Started in 1914 by Tican Duplantis, a butcher and planter in Houma, the annual Mardi Gras carnival and parade passed down Main and Park Streets. Planters would decorate their wagons, throw treats to the children, and "pass a good time" on Fat Tuesday each year. Shown here is the float of the H.C. Minor Company in 1929. (THACS.)

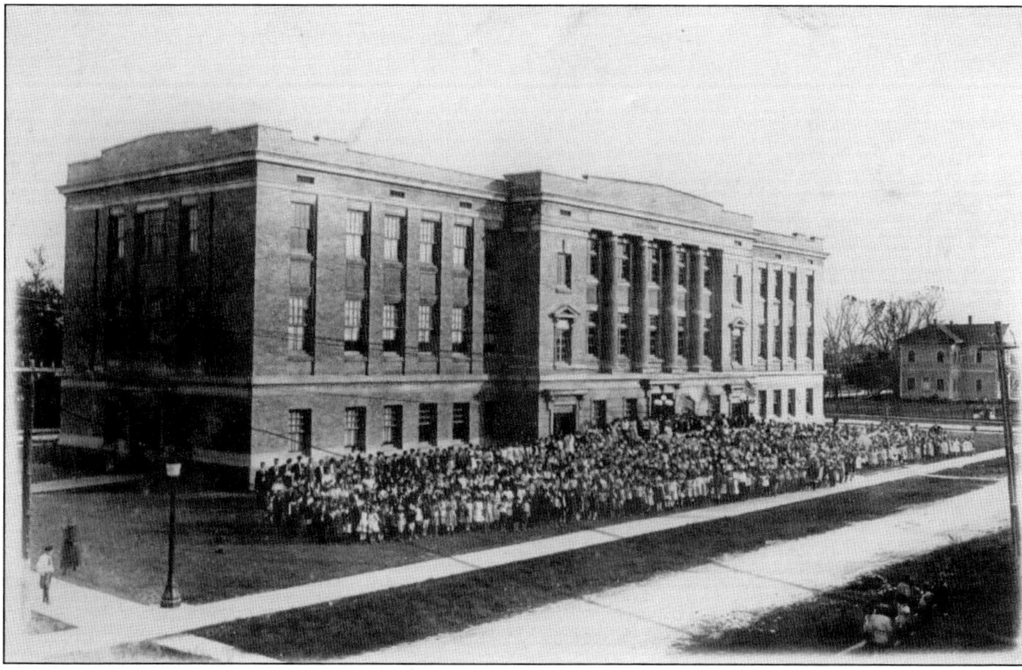

Terrebonne High School, erected in 1909, was the first built in the parish. Located at Goode and Point Streets, it was constructed to house 400 students. In 1898–1999, the High School Auxiliary and High School Association had been formed to promote the idea of a high school for the parish. Prior to the building of the high school, the students attended classes at the fire station. (THACS.)

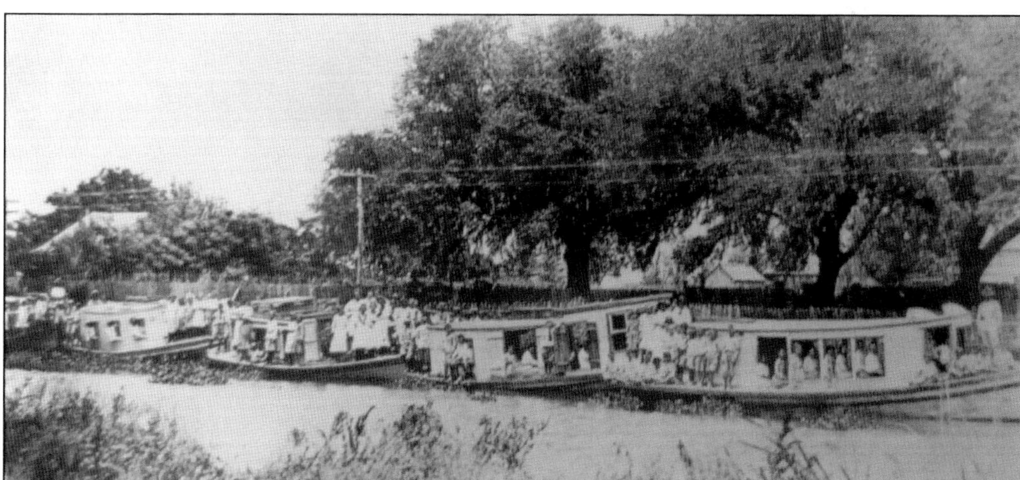

Due to the many waterways and bayous, it could be difficult to transport students to Houma for school. Boats were utilized instead of busses in areas "down the bayou." To be hired by the Terrebonne Parish School Board, it was best to be a bus driver and a boat captain. (THACS.)

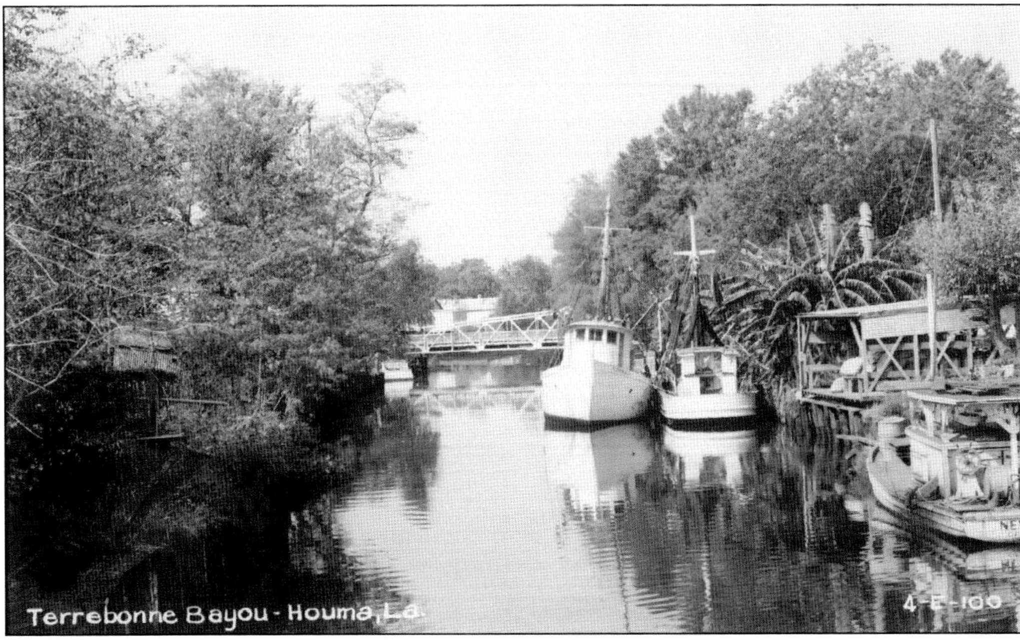

Bayou Terrebonne was one of two main "streets" (one of water and one of dirt) in Houma. The waterway that runs through Houma was at times busier that the dirt road named Main Street. Bayou Terrebonne once ran 60 miles from Thibodaux to Callou Island in the Gulf of Mexico. Out of the 2,080 square miles that make up the Parish of Terrebonne, 1,255 square miles is land, and 825 square miles is water. The average low temperature for Houma is 44 degrees, but there have been times, on a frozen Bayou Terrebonne, that transportation on the waterways was halted until the thaw. (Above, CENAC; below, THACS.)

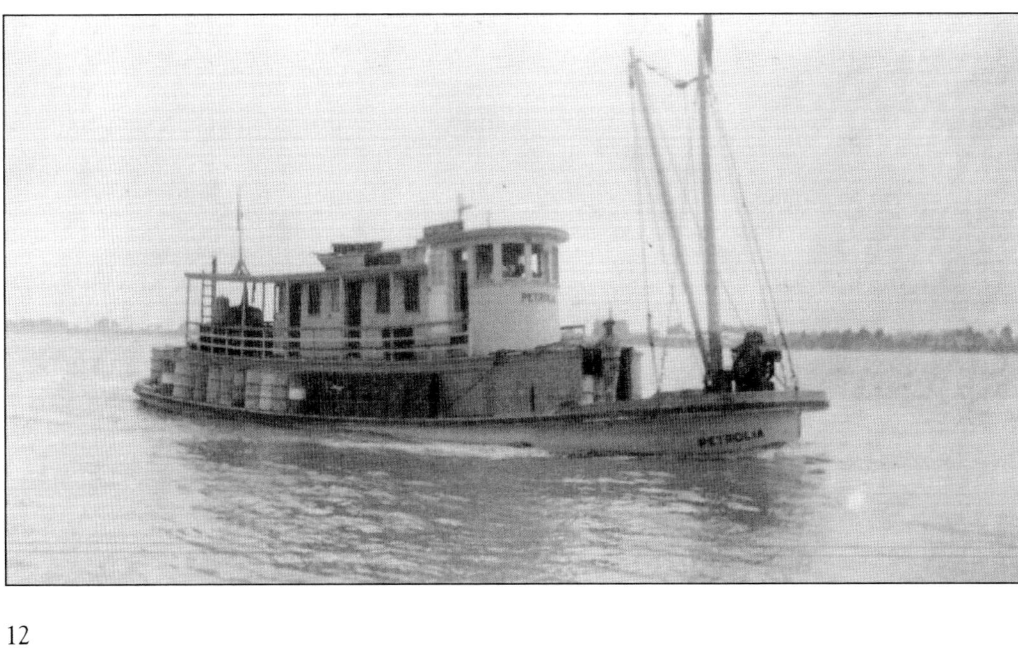

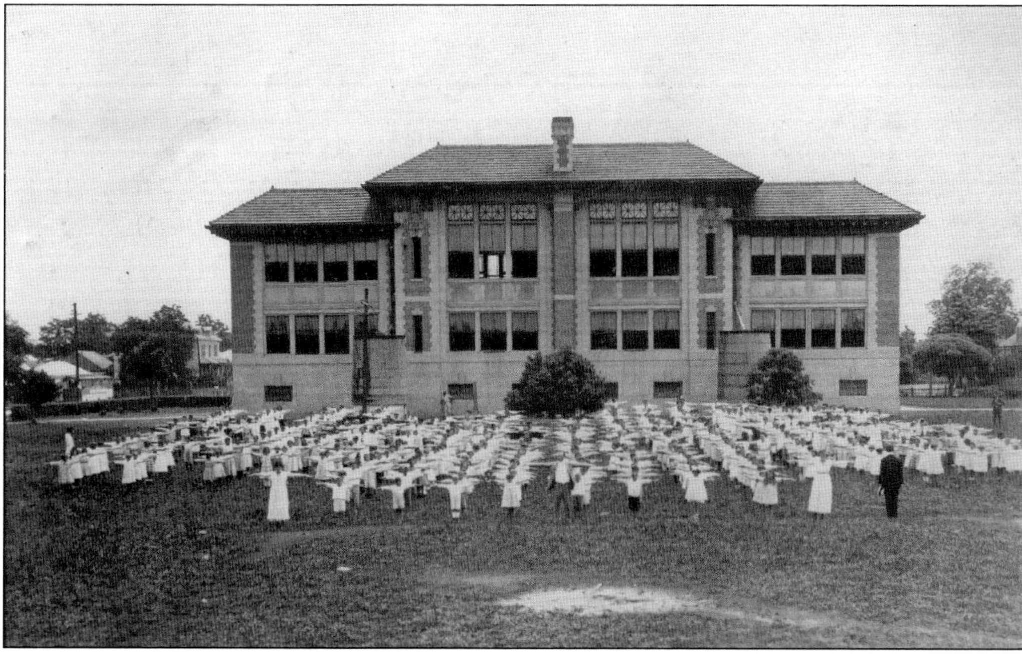

After the Civil War, the Constitutional Convention of 1868 passed an article saying students would be admitted to class without distinction of race, color, or previous condition. This led to many parents pulling their children out of the two-room schoolhouse that stood behind the courthouse. A new school for white children, shown here, was built in 1872. In 1878, Governor Nicholls reinstated segregation, and many children returned to the classrooms. (THACS.)

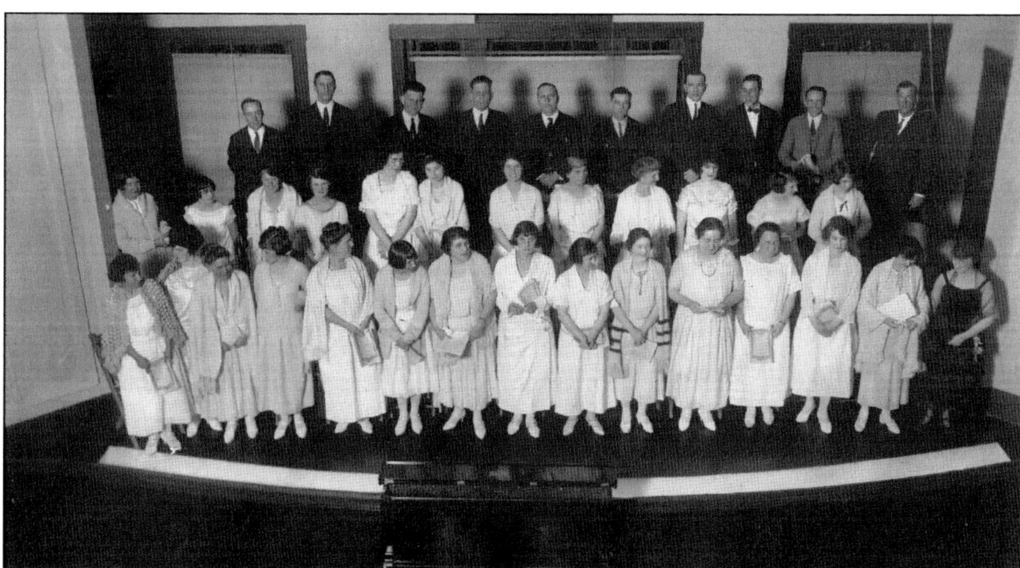

The Houma Community Chorus was led by Dora (Sutliff) Thatcher. The hundreds of voices of the chorus were heard in concerts of classical music twice a year for a period of five years, from 1923 to 1928. Thatcher was presented a silver loving cup as a token of appreciation from the people of Houma. (THACS.)

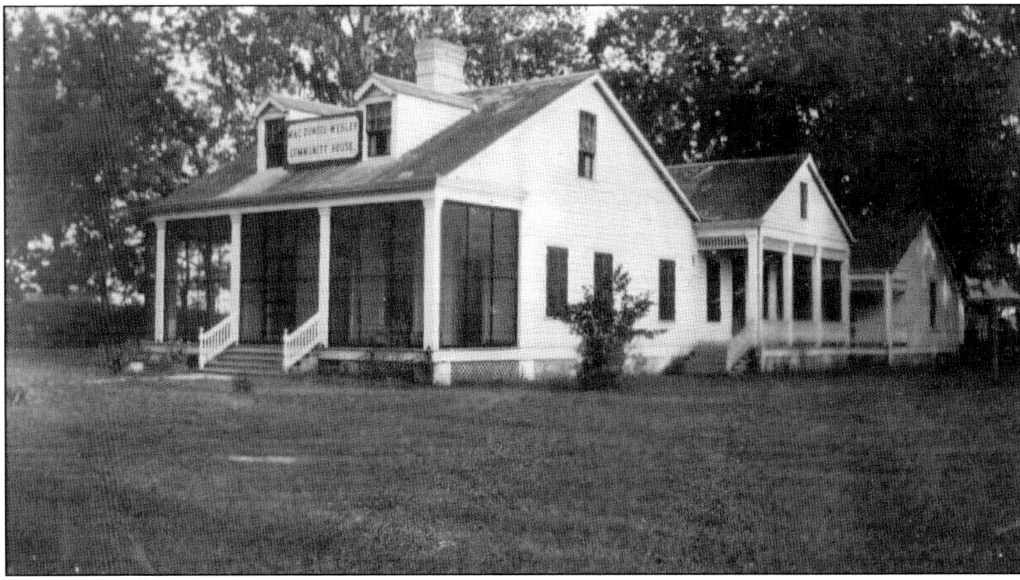

Originally the home of Joseph Gagne, the MacDonell-Wesley Methodist School stands on East Main Street in Houma. It was reported to be haunted by the ghost of Sarah Gagne, who told a later tenant, "I want my house. Get out!" The school was later used as a home for indigent children. It still stands today, surrounded by old oak trees. (THACS.)

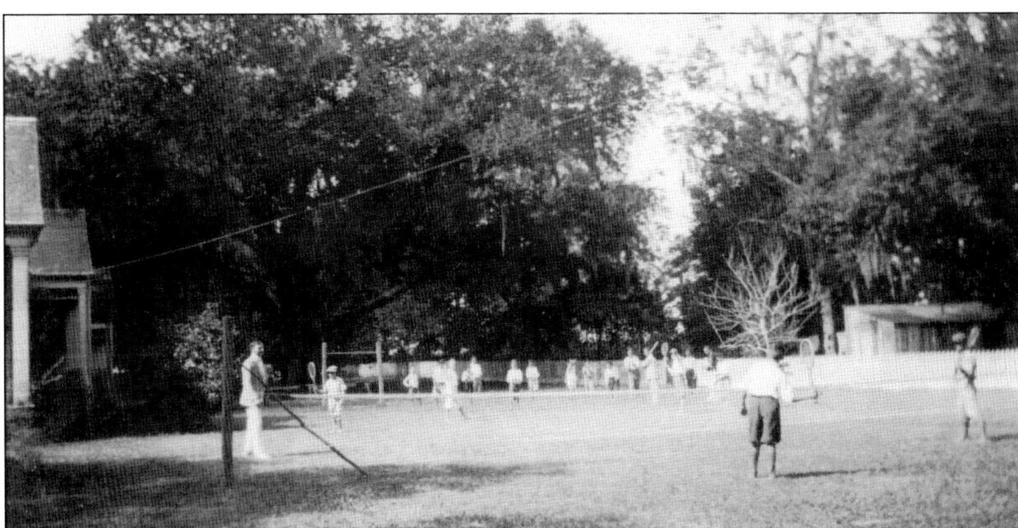

Students of the MacDonell-Wesley Methodist School are pictured playing a tennis match on the lawn in the 1920s. The building in the background served as the dining hall for students and then was used as a community center. It was also home to the Women's Division of the Board of Global Ministries of the United Methodist Church. (THACS.)

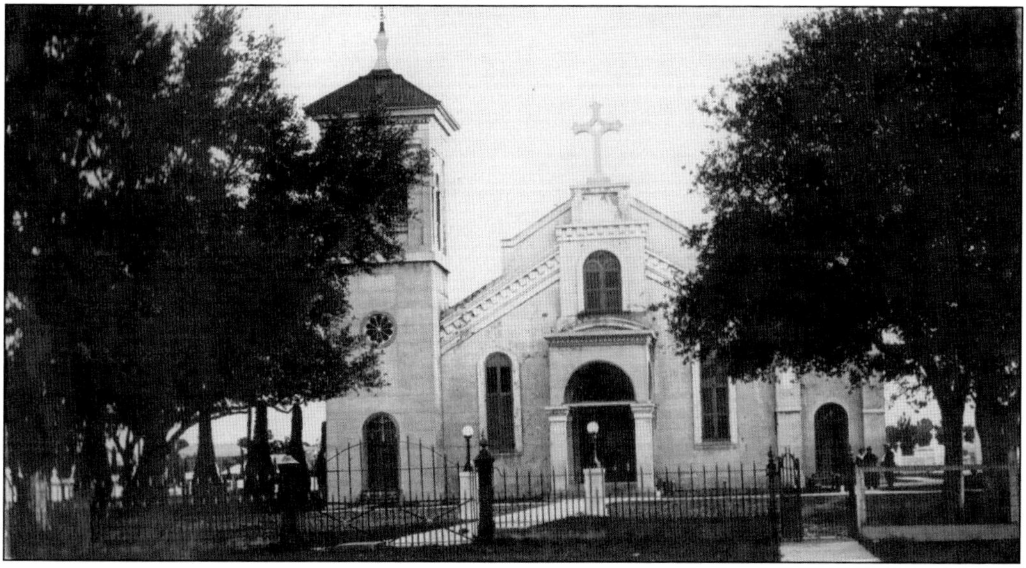

The tradition of Roman Catholicism in Houma is long, starting with the Acadians who arrived from Nova Scotia and the French and Spanish settlers with land grants from their respective kings. The main church in Houma was St. Francis de Sales, first built in 1847 on property donated by Robert Ruffin Barrow Sr. (THACS.)

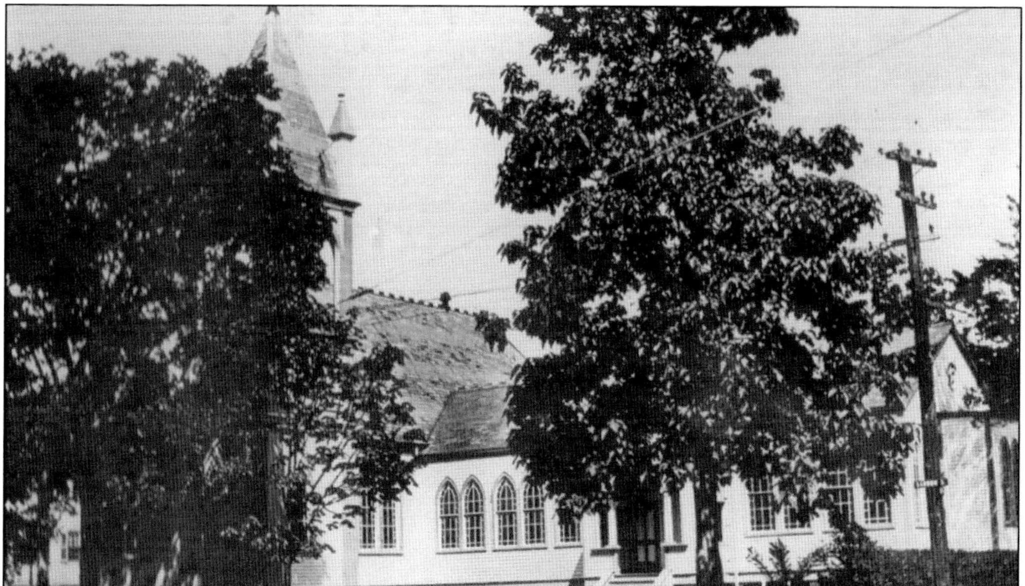

St. Matthew's Episcopal Church was chartered in 1857. The initial land was donated by Robert Ruffin Barrow, and two additional lots were donated by Henry C. Minor of Southdown Plantation. Barrow donated the bell, which he called Susanna Roberta. The bell ceased in 1926 when a hurricane destroyed the bell tower. (THACS.)

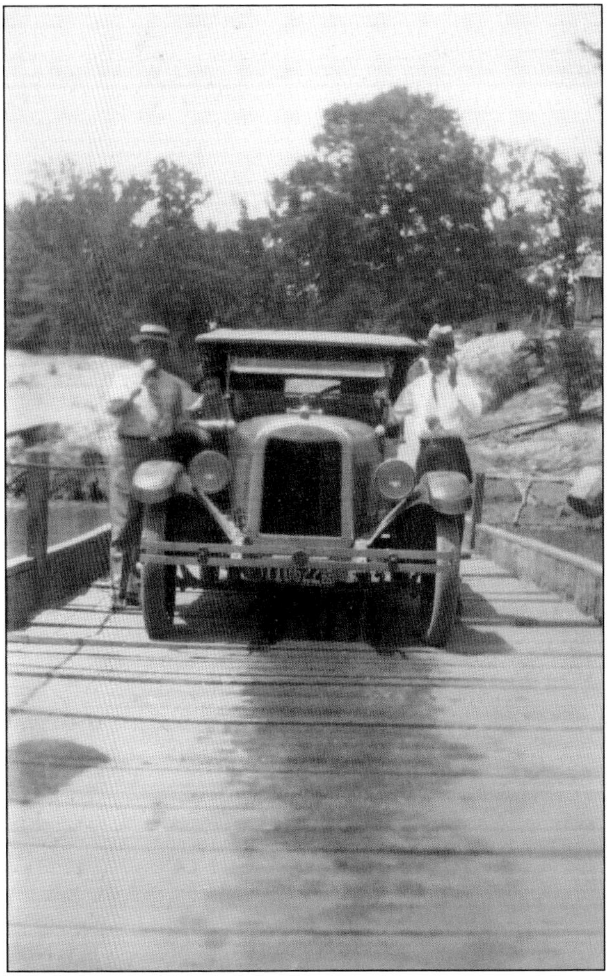

A pontoon bridge is an alternative to a suspension or beam bridge. Several pontoons, like the one seen here, still exist today. Among them are the Bridge at Bayou Blue, just outside of Houma, and the bridge over Crocodile Bayou. These floating spans vary with the width of the waterway. If people are unaccustomed to the pontoon, the sway can make them swoon. (THACS.)

This is a portion of the Gulf Intracoastal Waterway—a navigable inland waterway running approximately 1,050 miles (1,700 kilometers) from Carrabelle, Florida, to Brownsville, Texas—in the 1920s. It was not completed until 1949. When the waterway was finally finished, the tonnage going through the waterway was greater than that of the Panama Canal. (THACS.)

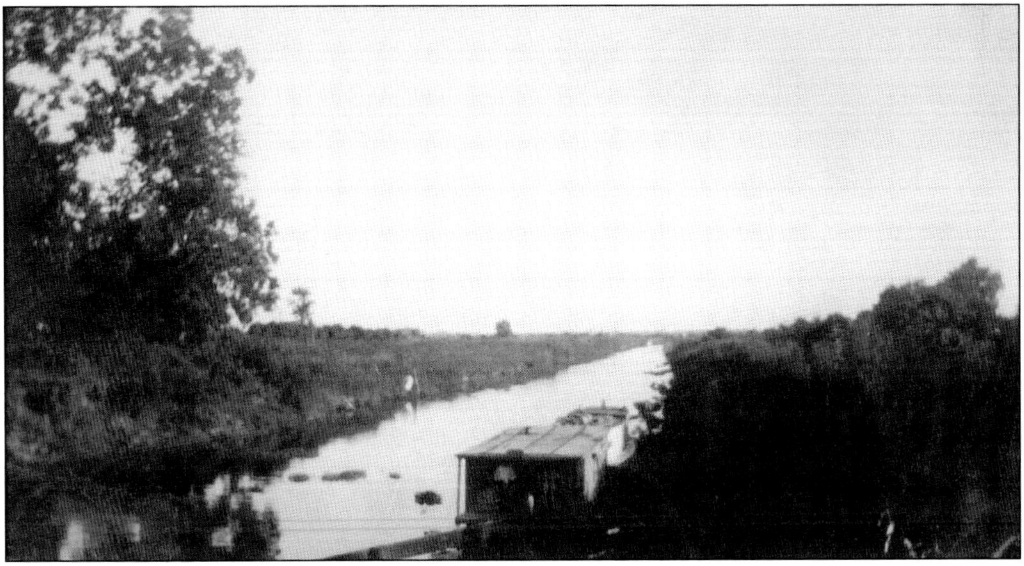

Two

Down the Bayou

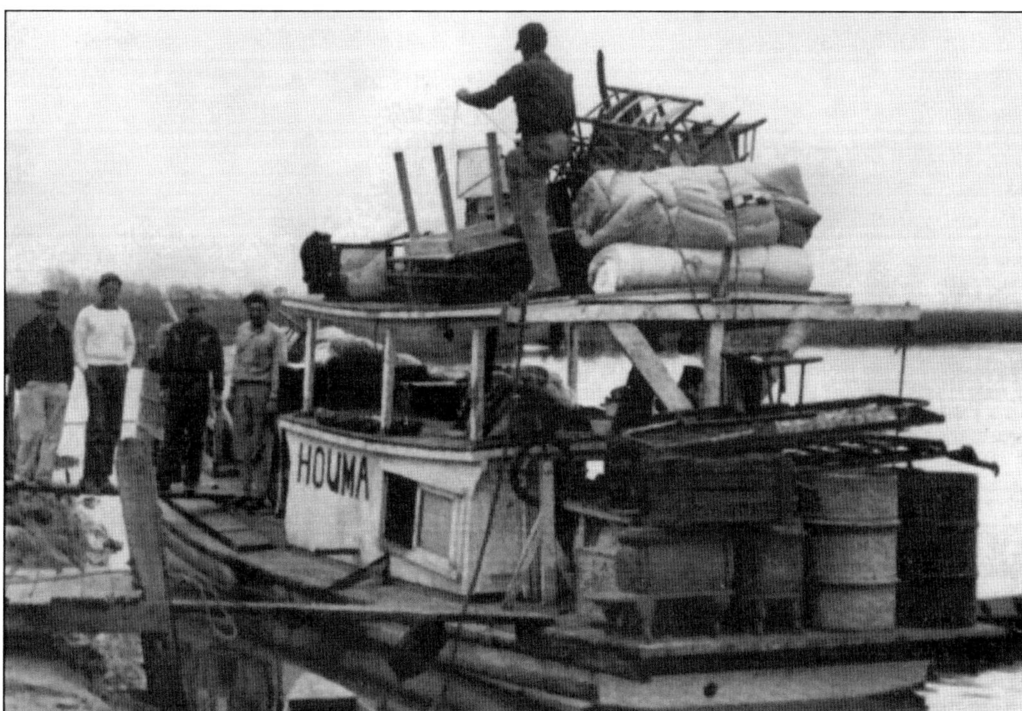

Moving day for many living on or near the abundant waters that make up the finger-lands of Terrebonne Parish (small pieces of land stretching like fingers into the water) could be a challenge with limited roads early in the 1900s. Packing iron stoves, chairs, and mattresses on the vessel called *Houma* would have been an easier alternative to navigating the shell roads. (UHN.)

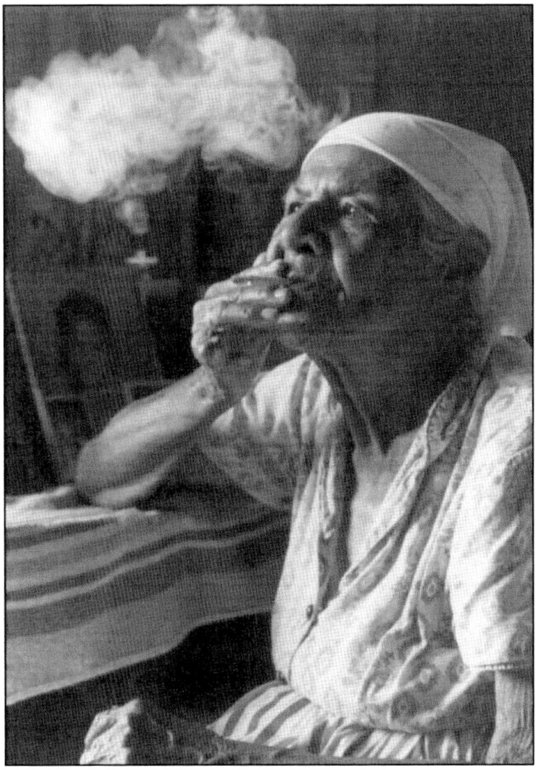

The namesake of Houma comes from the Choctaw word *humma*, meaning "red." The symbol of the native peoples in the area is the crawfish, which is also red. Why Tobias Gibson, sugar planter, named the small French village Houma is not known, but the people around the area known as the Houmas Indians have a rich and long history in the area. The unidentified woman pictured at left is a typical resident of the lands known by the folks who live in the city as "down the bayou." Seen below, the most common mode of transportation from the first settlement in the area was the pirogue, or flat-bottom boat, used to navigate the sometimes treacherous waterways. (Both, UHN.)

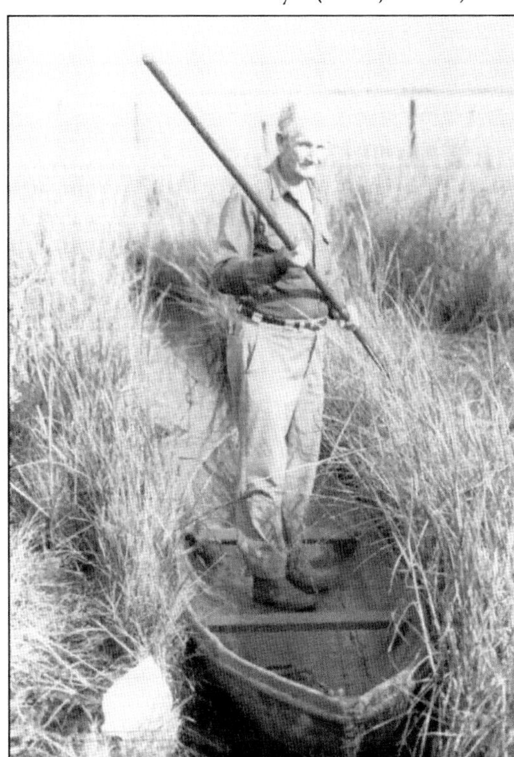

Frank Naquin was the leader of the Houmas at Golden Meadow. The seven principal Houma settlements at the beginning of the 20th century were DuLarge, Dulac, Montegut, Point Barre, Pointe-au-Chien, Isle de Jean Charles, Grand Bois, and Golden Meadow. It was Naquin who first sent Delores Terrebonne to the American Indiana Conference in Chicago in 1963, starting the united movement of the Houmas to become a federally recognized nation. (UHN.)

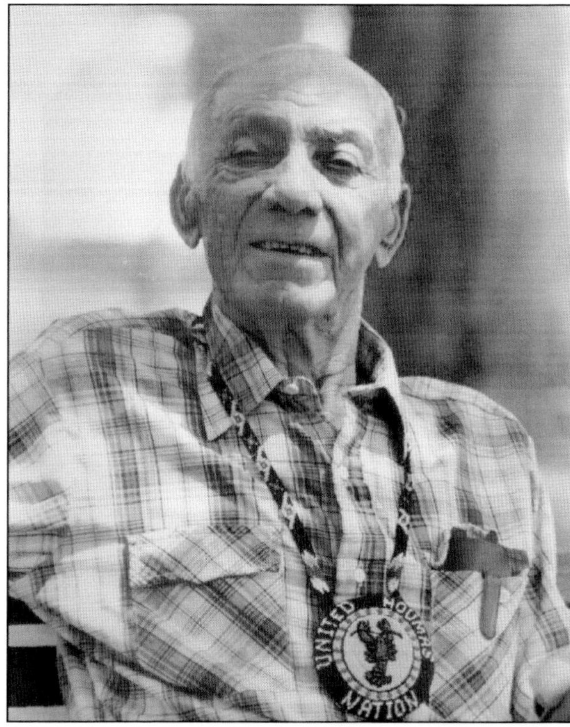

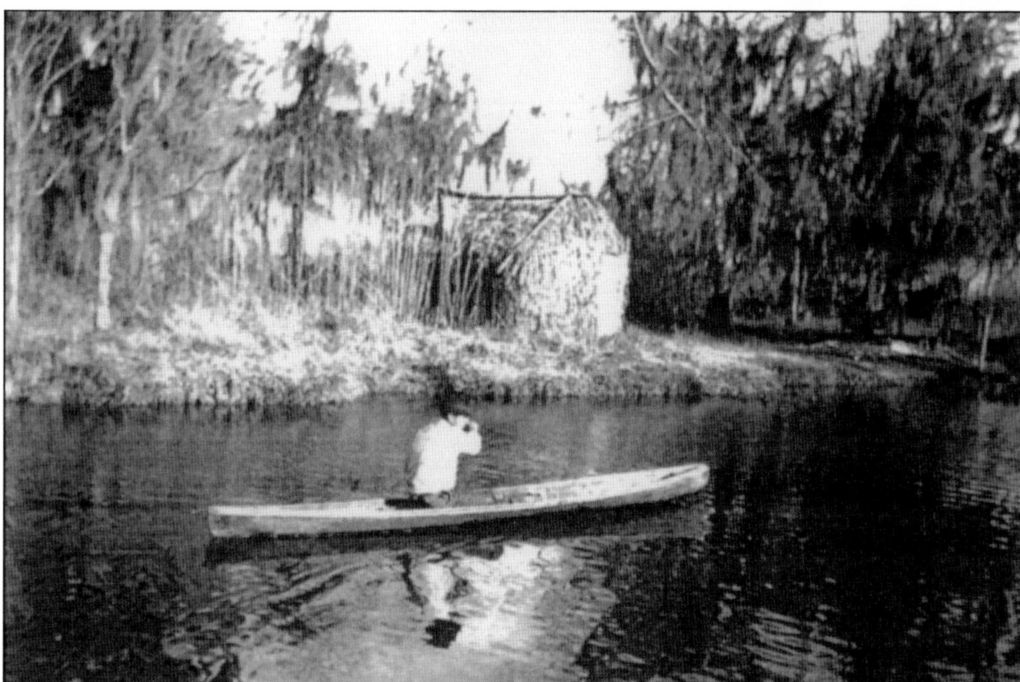

George Billiot is pictured in a pirogue. The Houmas Indians were pushed to the farthest reaches of land that extend into the Gulf of Mexico. Conflicts with the Tunica Indians, in addition to tensions with the early French and English settlers, kept them traveling south into the marshlands, where they established themselves as great hunters and fishermen. (UHN.)

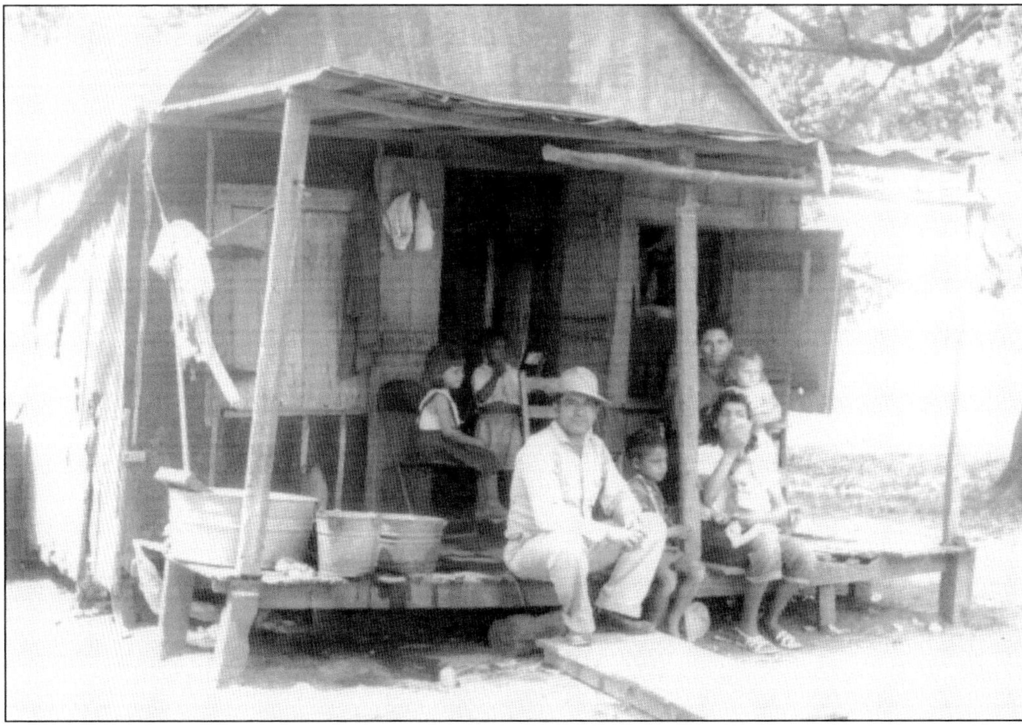

The original language that the Houmas spoke was a Muskhogean dialect, but as marriages with the Cajun French increased, French became the predominate language. George Verdin and family, of Bayou Blue, are pictured. Bayou Blue is one of three bayous that set the eastern boundary of Terrebonne Parish in Houma. (UHN.)

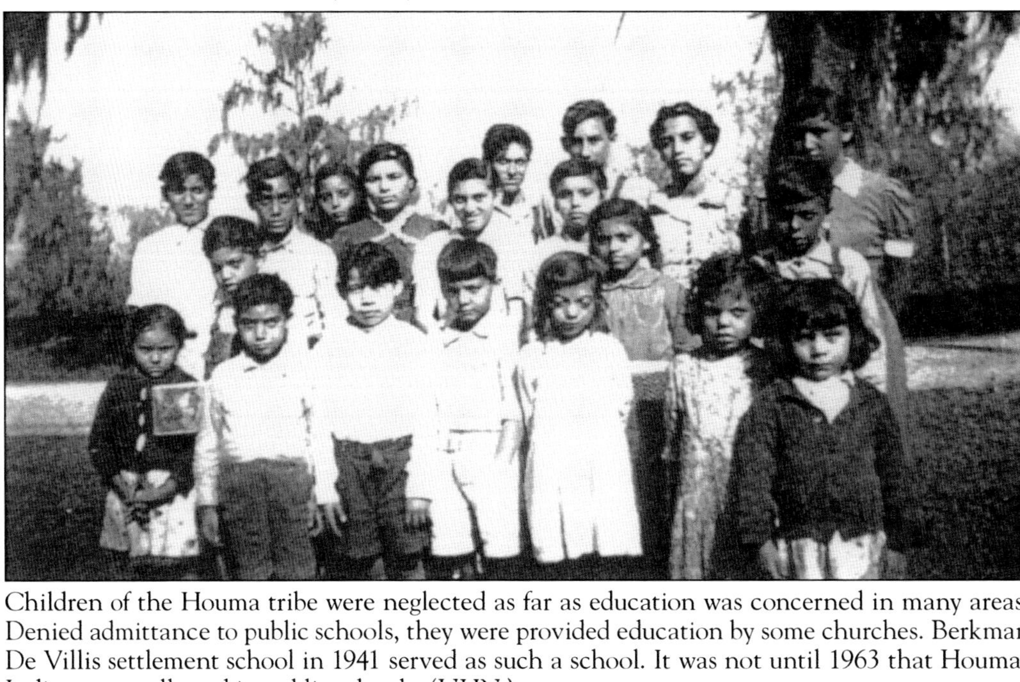

Children of the Houma tribe were neglected as far as education was concerned in many areas. Denied admittance to public schools, they were provided education by some churches. Berkman De Villis settlement school in 1941 served as such a school. It was not until 1963 that Houmas Indians were allowed in public schools. (UHN.)

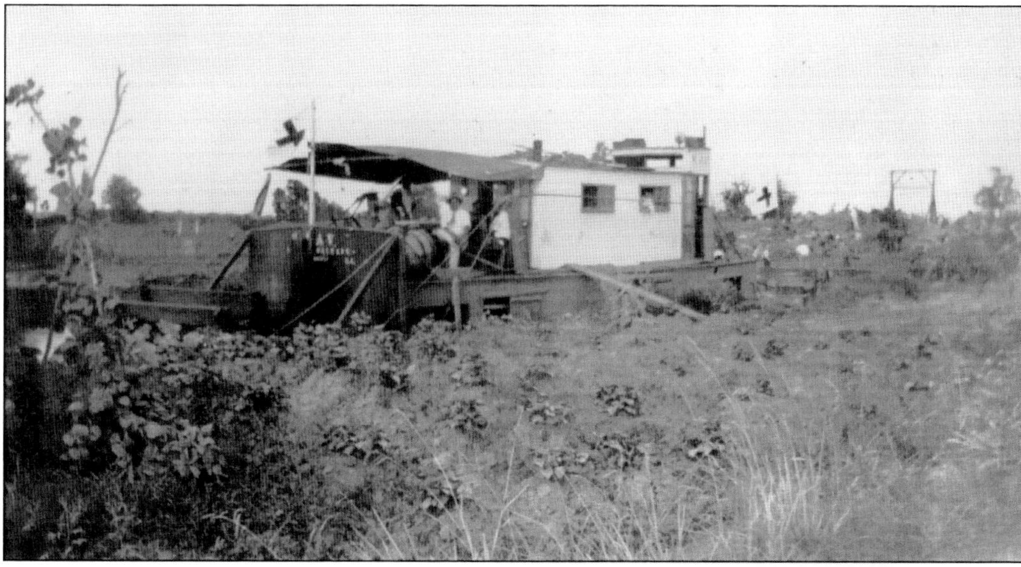

The quiet community of Isle de Jean Charles was beyond the end of the road in the heart of bayou country. The isle had no roads, electricity, or telephones. Bayou Jean Charles flows through the isle, and everyone had to have a pirogue to get to school and church (two of the things Isle de Jean had). The native language of the 165 inhabitants is French, and 22 of the 35 families have the last name of Naquin. Raising geese, fishing, and hunting created self-sufficiency, and the area also came with the blessings of no traffic headaches and lots of socials, like dances and dinners. The palmetto roof on the right is typical of the homemade housing of the isle. (Both, UHN.)

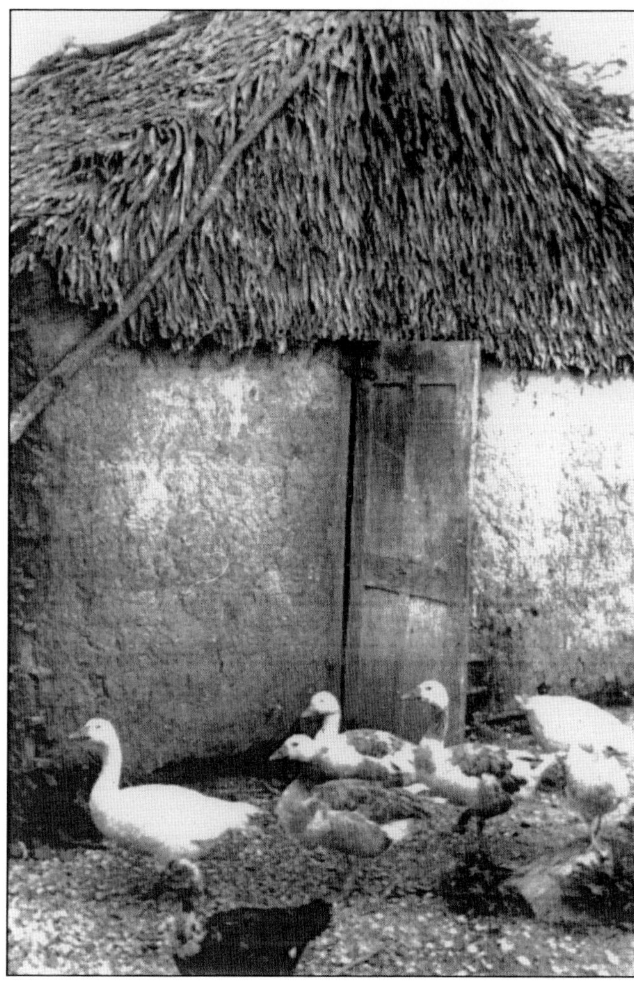

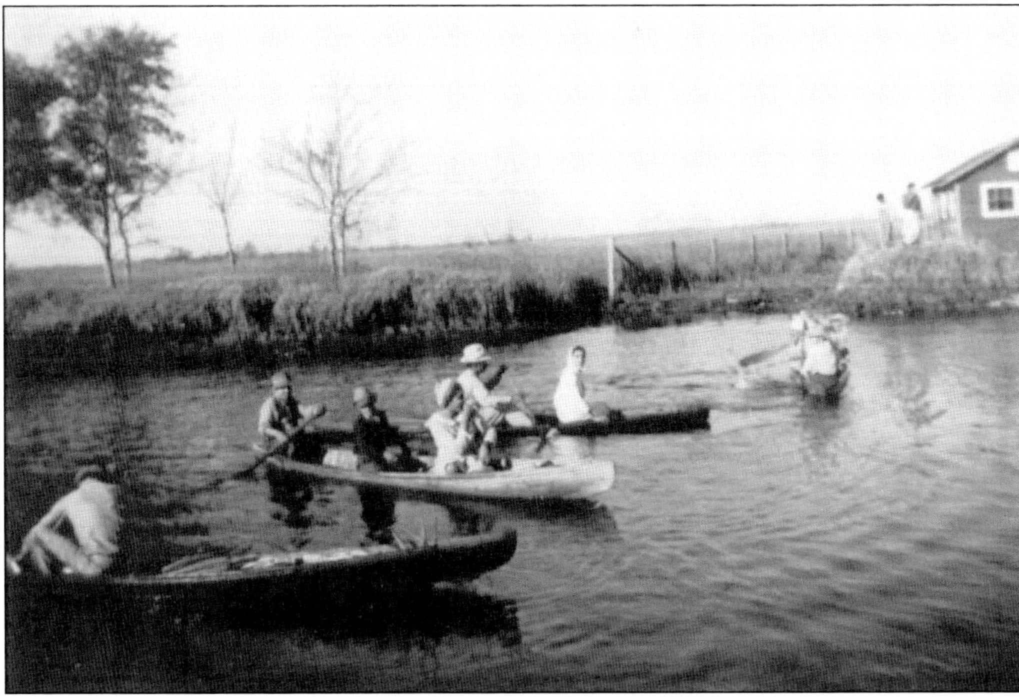

Houma Indians, French and Spanish settlers, and, eventually, the Anglo-Saxon plantation owners utilized the pirogue or canoe to get from place to place, especially during rainy seasons when roads were virtually impassable by horse- or mule-driven wagon. In the early days of Houma history, boats were handmade, and Claudio Belanger was known as the premiere boatbuilder in the area. People commented that he was always making a boat of some sort. Once, he built a boat in a shed and had to tear down the shed to get it out. (Both, THACS.)

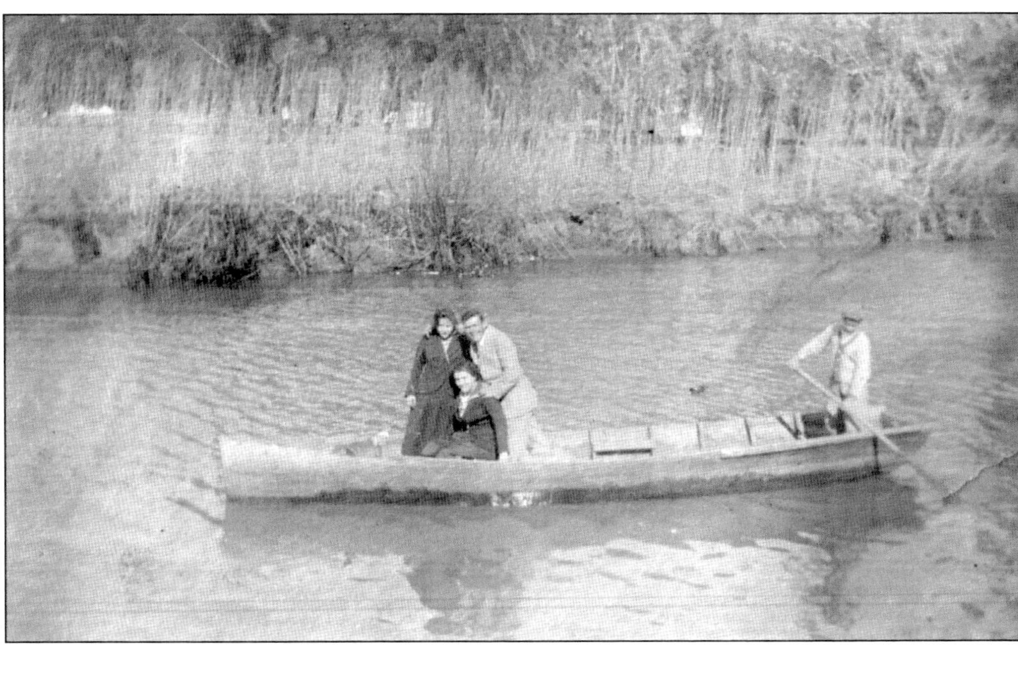

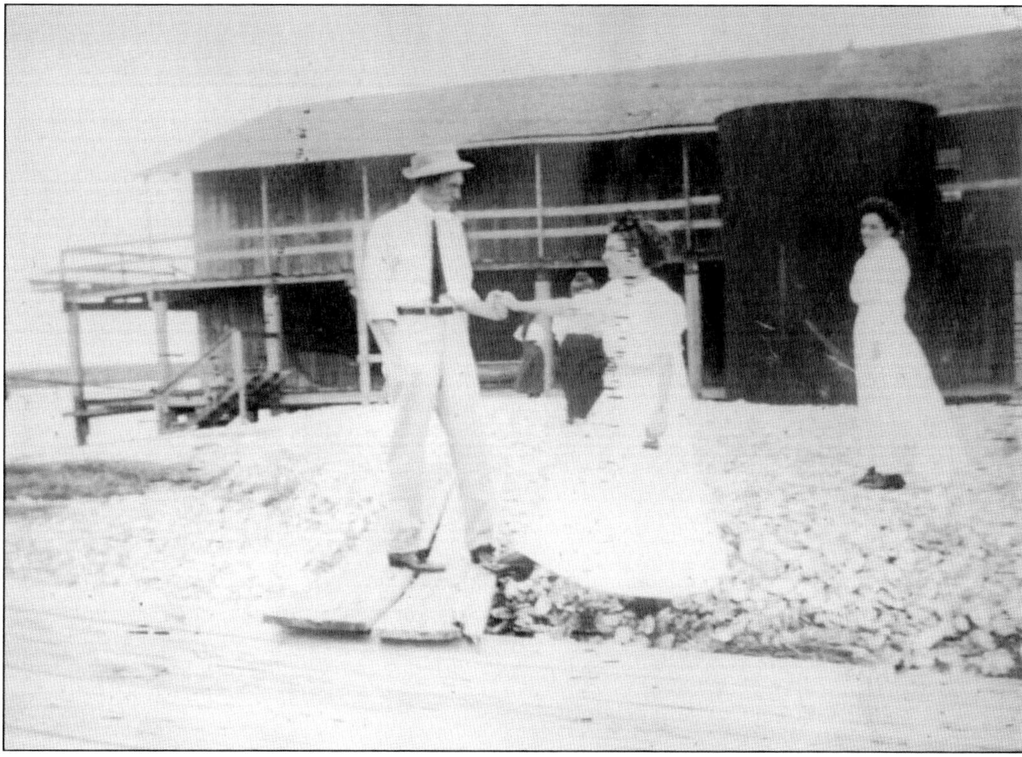

Sea Breeze was located at the mouth of Bayou Terrebonne, where members of the Barrow-Cole family (pictured here) spent many days and nights of fun, sun, and fishing. The entire area was devastated in 1909 when a hurricane ripped through the community, destroying all but the Sea Breeze resort, where 26 people were sheltered during the storm. Other camps were destroyed, and lives were lost. By 9:00 a.m., the camps were under six feet of water. By noon, many of the structures had broken up and floated away. Some people were saved by clutching for dear life onto pieces of rubble as they passed. It was one of the deadliest hurricanes to date in the region. (Both, Robert R. Barrow collection.)

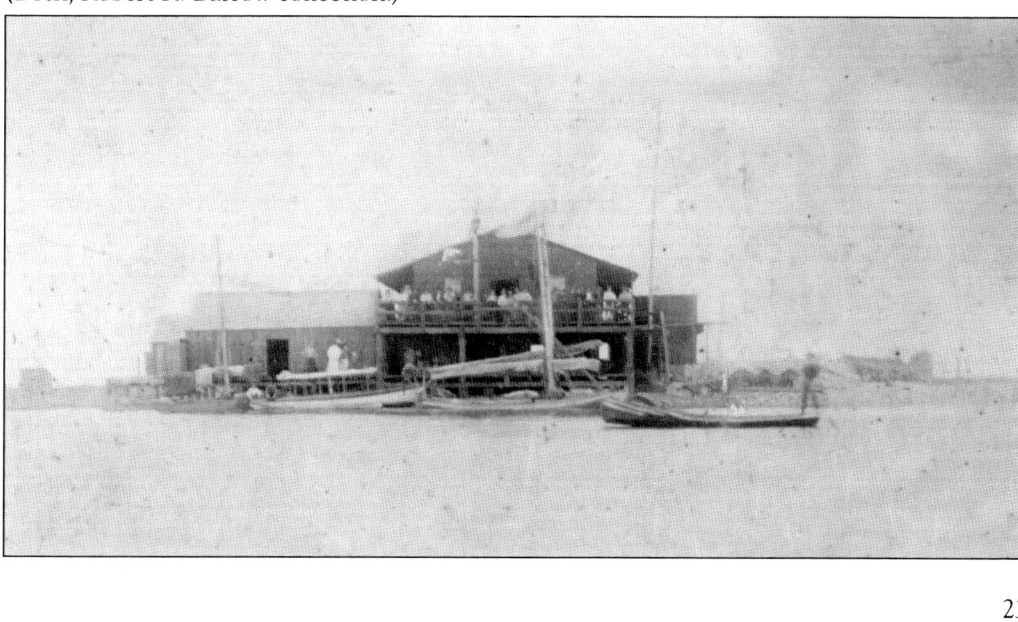

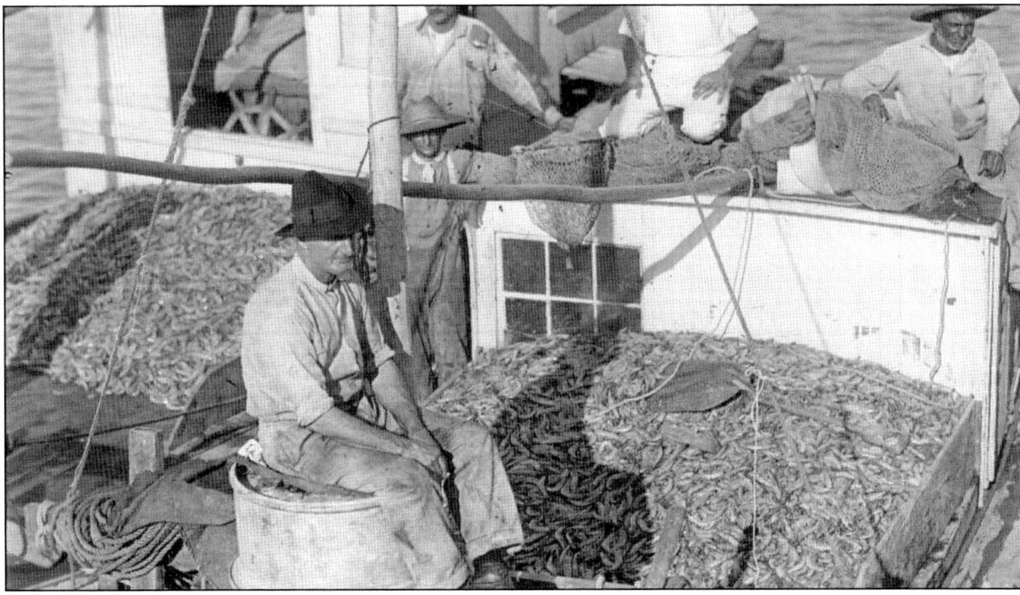

The shrimping industry was only one of many treasures of the sea in the area. Shrimping took hold around 1878, and daily trips were made to catch the shrimp and then to the docks along Bayou Terrebonne. The industry was revolutionized after the invention of refrigerated boats that could keep the catch fresh longer, thus extending the time shrimp boats could stay in the Gulf of Mexico. (THACS.)

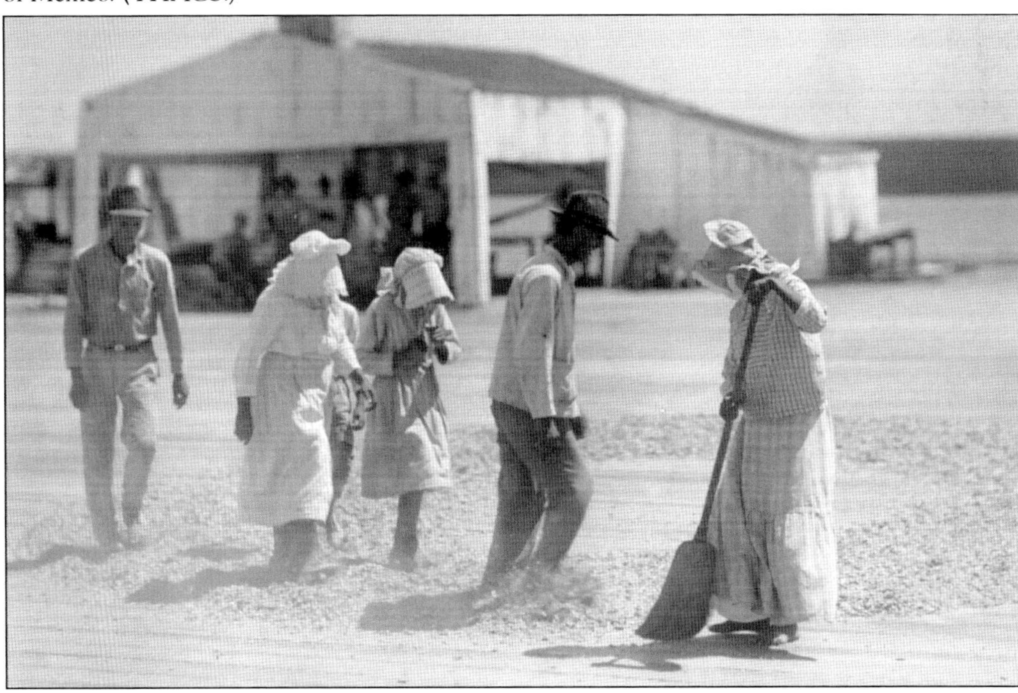

Fresh shrimp was a lucrative business, but there were also platforms built for drying shrimp. Men, women, and children would participate in a practice known as "La Shrimp Danse," shown here, to rid dried shrimp of their shells. The dancers seen here are from the Chauvin Brothers Shrimp Company at Bayou Sevin. (THACS.)

Three

Historic Plantations and Agriculture

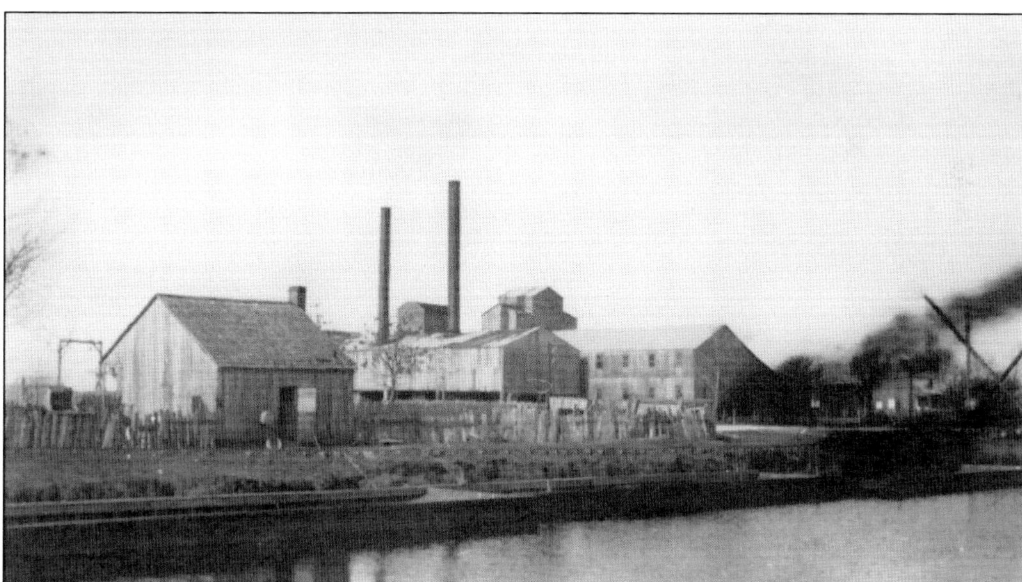

Southdown Plantation Mill and Refinery was built on the banks of Bayou Black in 1846 with alterations and additions made until 1854. The first buildings were made of brick that was fired at the plantation in a kiln. Improvements continued through the years, but the most significant occurred in 1928, when the mill was fully modernized and had the capacity to process 2,000 tons of sugar a day. (THACS.)

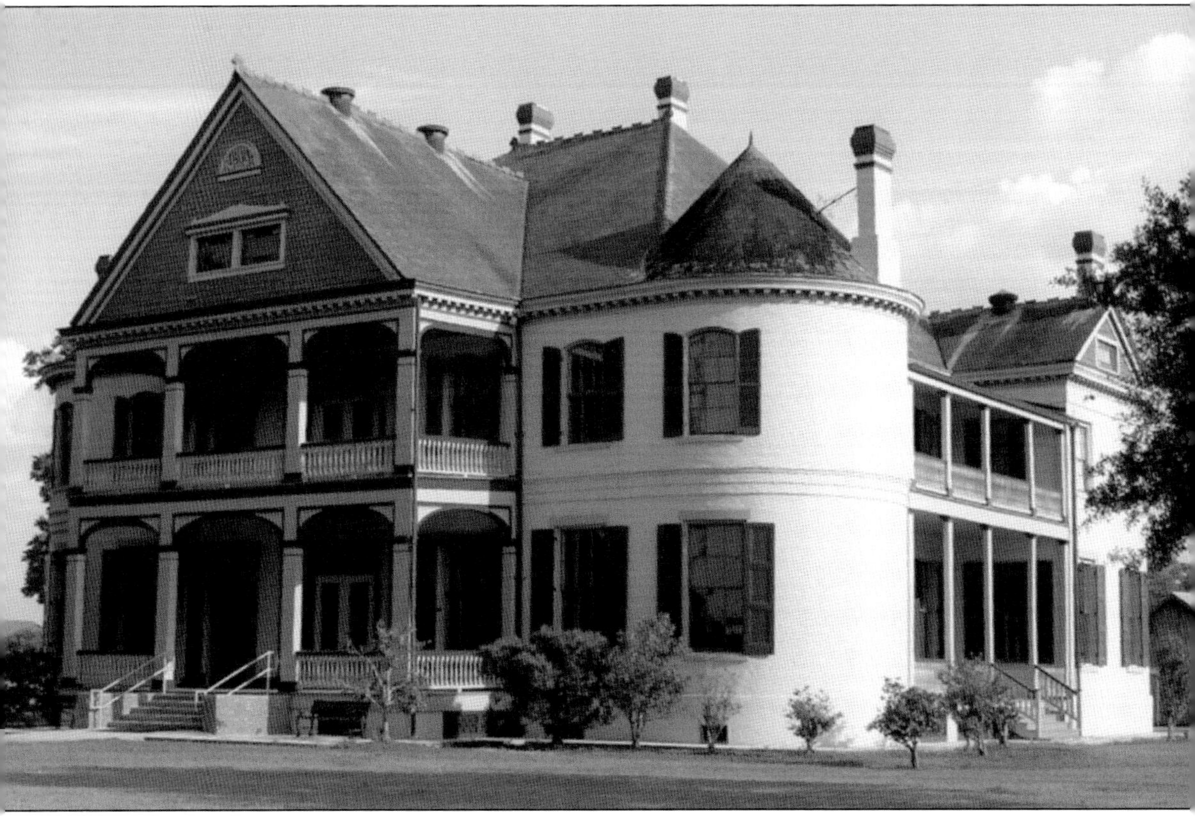

The most famous landmark and tourist destination in Houma is Southdown Plantation House/the Terrebonne Museum. Originally built in 1859 by the William John Minor family, the plantation quickly became an important and successful epicenter for the sugar industry in Houma. Widely known as the "House that Sugar Built," Southdown Plantation serves not only as a testament to itself, but as a historical archive for the parish. The 19th-century plantation houses exhibits from all aspects of local history—including the sugar industry, slavery, Reconstruction, the Civil War, politics, Mardi Gras, industries, and agriculture—all in a 10,000-square-foot pink-and-green brick manor house. Other buildings include an 1885 worker's cabin and the original slave quarters. Fully guided tours are given during the day, and twice a year, Southdown Marketplace Arts and Crafts Festival is held on the grounds. (THACS.)

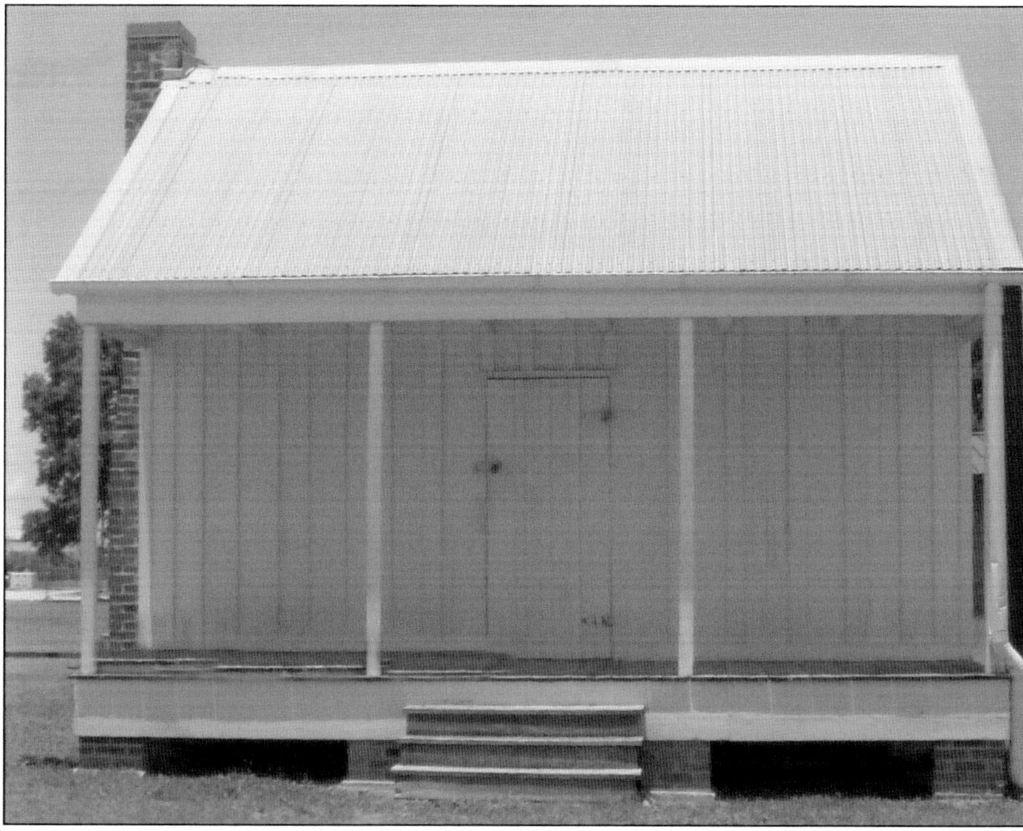

After the Civil War and the end of slavery, many laborers on sugar plantations continued to live in dwellings similar to this cottage built around 1885. It has a fireplace and a typical two-room setup consisting of a kitchen and living/sleeping quarters. Although it was lived in until the 1950s, the house never had electricity, running water, or sewage. The two-storied slave-quarters structure below was built in 1848 out of bricks fired in a kiln on the property. It was the first living quarters built at Southdown Plantation. The cottage is open for exhibit, and the slave quarters houses the gift shop and administrative offices. (Both, THACS.)

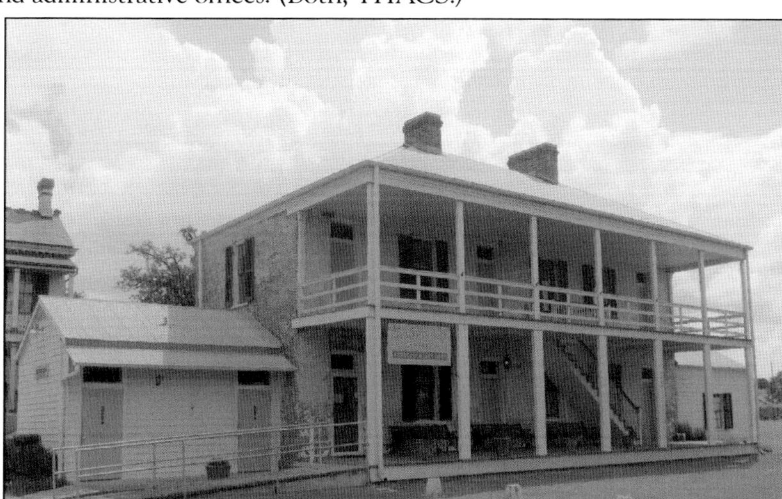

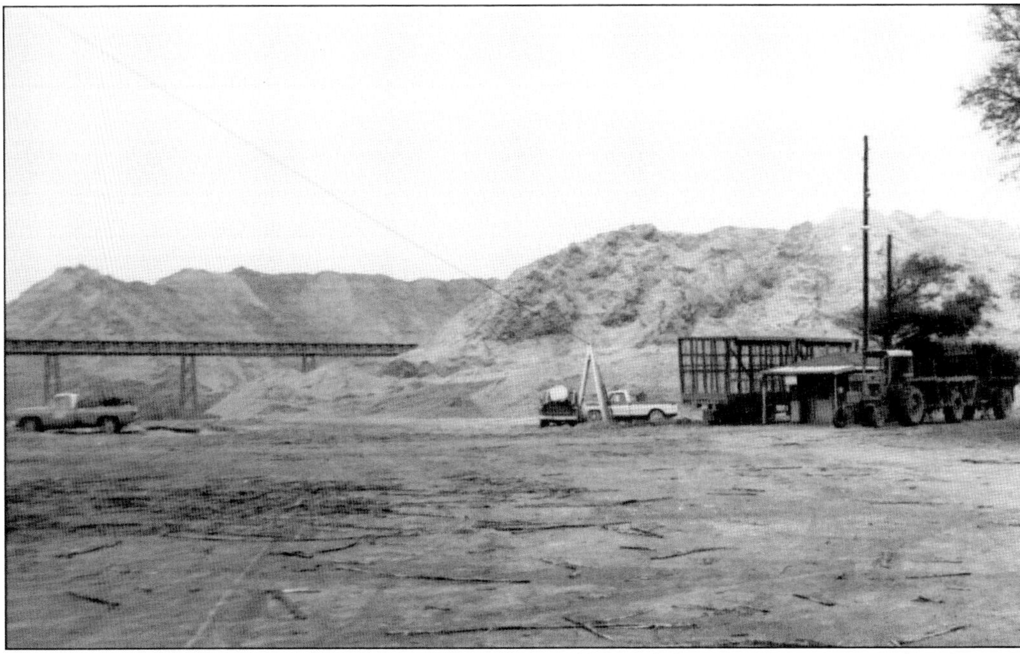

Used as fuel in the mill, bagasse, as seen here, was the fibrous leftovers of sugarcane after the juice had been extracted. With so much bagasse produced in the process of making sugar, alternative uses for the material were created at Southdown Sugar. The factory is credited for the first usage of bagasse in fiberboards sold commercially. (THACS.)

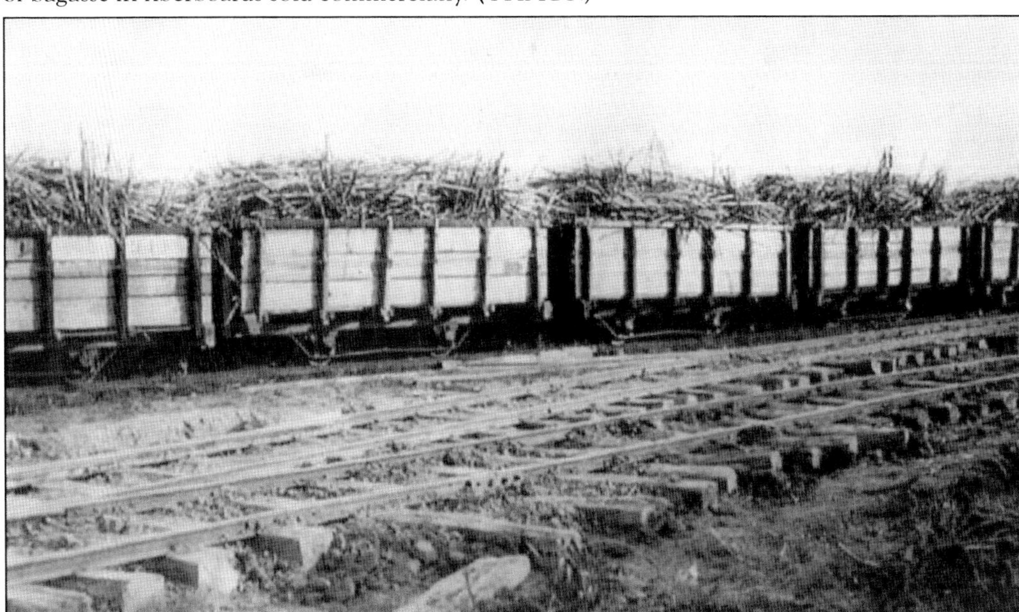

According to the book *Sugar Plantation Railroads in Louisiana* by W.E. Butler, "The Southdown Plantation Railroad was the bonanza of all the tram roads to operate in Louisiana, having accumulated fifteen steam and one gas locomotive." The Southdown 36-inch-gauge railroad, with 26 miles of tracks, resembled a spider web as it threaded its way through some 8,000 acres of cane fields. (THACS.)

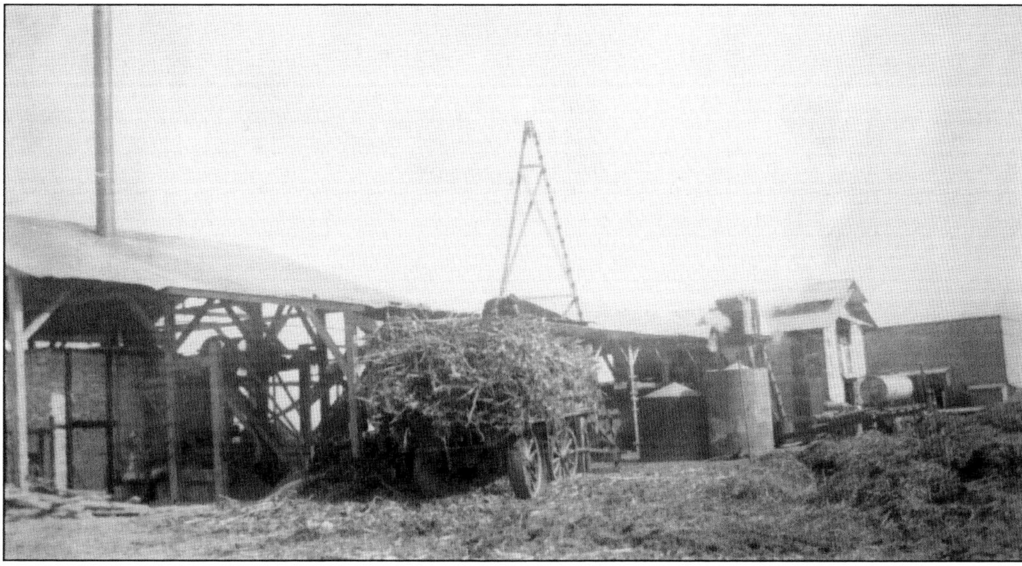

A view outside of the Southdown Sugar mill and refinery shows a loaded cane wagon with boilers in the background. Southdown not only processed cane to raw sugar, it also refined it into white sugar and made molasses and syrups that were sold at the plantation store across the street from the mill. (THACS.)

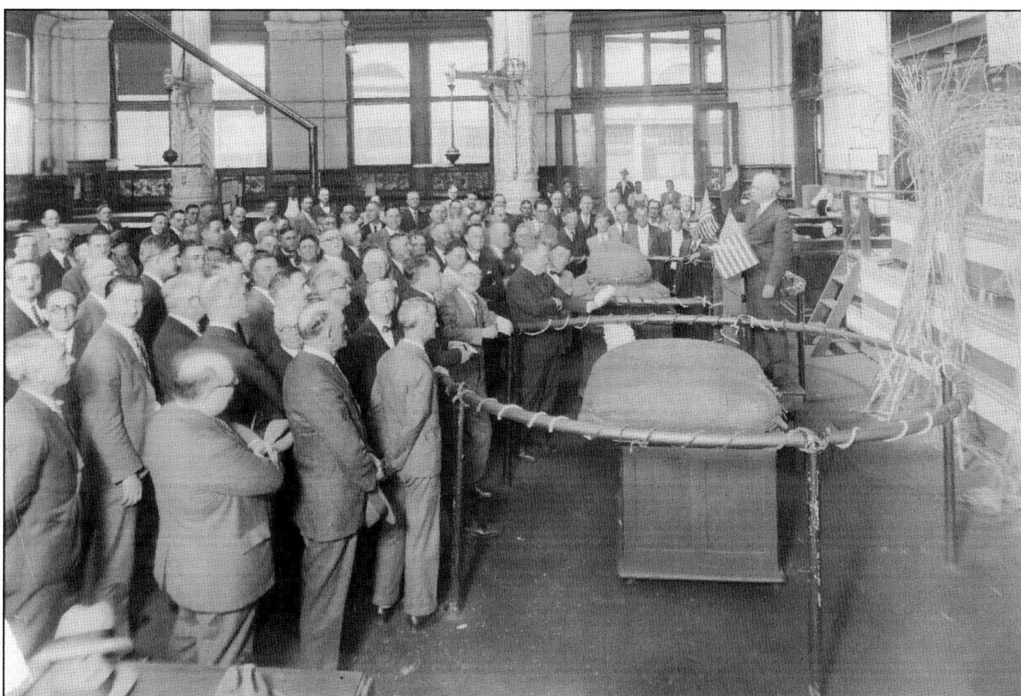

Four generations of the Minor family, along with hundreds of mill workers, field-workers, and their families, lived and labored at Southdown Plantation. Over the years, the plantation owners, managers, and workers helped launch the local sugar industry, sustained it through difficult years, witnessed the cultural enrichment and progress of its boom times, and revitalized the industry from near-fatal crop disease. Pictured is the New Orleans Sugar Exchange. (THACS.)

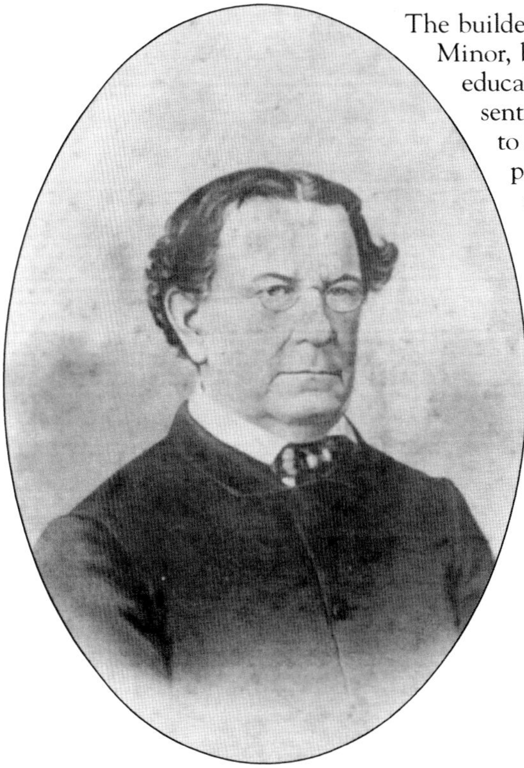

The builder of Southdown Plantation was William John Minor, born in Natchez, Mississippi, in 1808. He was educated at Concord Plantation in Natchez and then sent to university in Philadelphia. In 1828, he sought to diversify his cotton business and purchased the property that would become Southdown. An ambitious man, he was a Whig and opposed secession of the Southern states from the union prior to the Civil War. (THACS.)

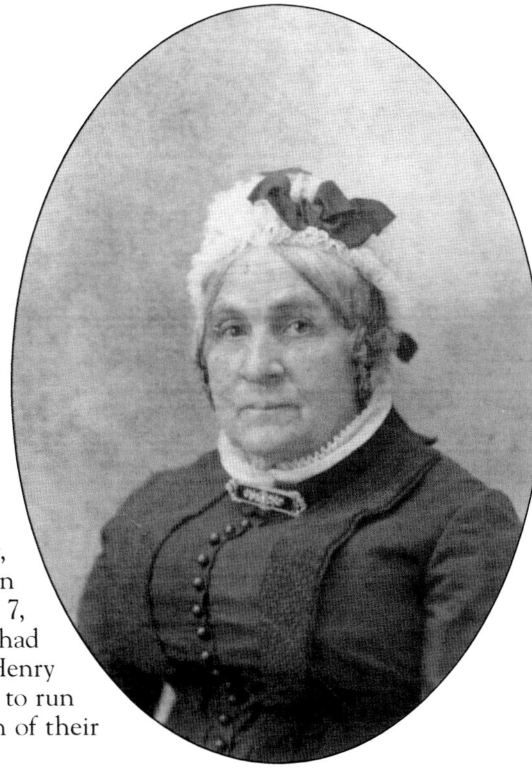

Born to a prominent Pennsylvania family, Rebecca Gustine Minor met William John Minor in Philadelphia. They married July 7, 1829, and resided at Natchez. Together, they had nine children: eight boys and one girl. It was Henry Chotard and Katherine Lintot who went on to run Southdown to much success after the death of their father in 1869. (THACS.)

After Reconstruction, Minor's son Henry ("Hal") rebuilt and made the plantation and mill at Southdown more successful than his father had. He is responsible for the addition of the second story, adding 5,026 square feet to accommodate his growing family. Henry and wife Anna Louise made Southdown their family home. (THACS.)

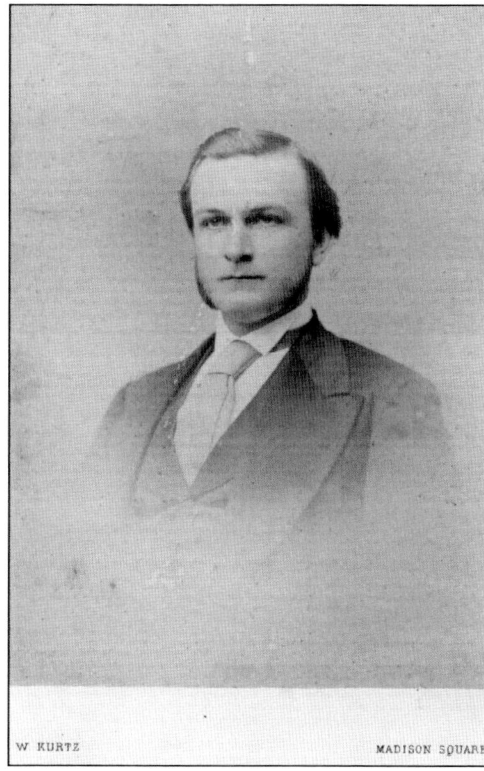

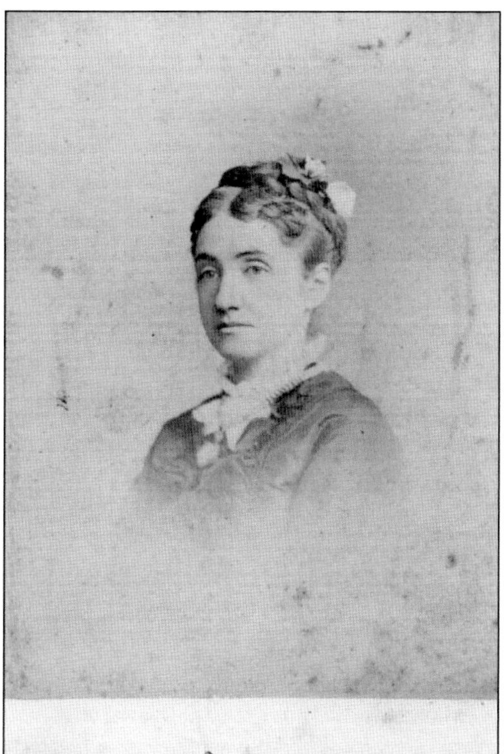

Anna Louise Butler was born and raised in St. Francisville, Louisiana. At Southdown Plantation, she and Hal raised John Duncan (April 26, 1876–August 7, 1937) Anna Ellis (March 11, 1878–May 23, 1893), Mary Louise (Pipes) (August 24, 1886–October 4, 1961), and Margaret Gustine (Krumbhaar) (May 2, 1883–March 13, 1936). (THACS.)

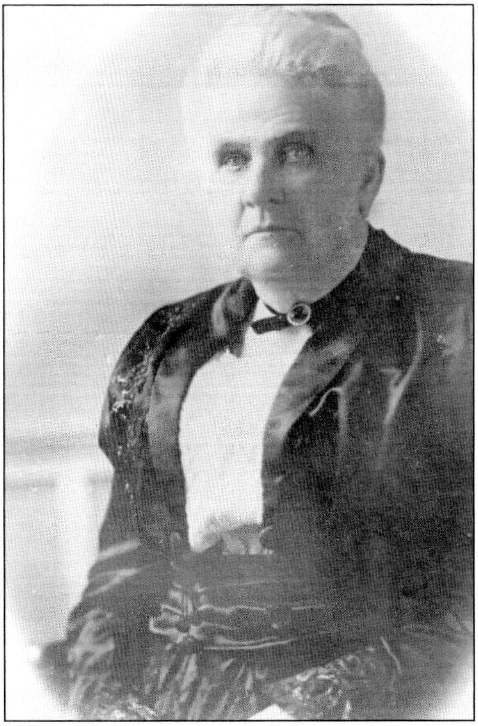

Katherine Lintot Minor, also known as "Aunt Kate," was the youngest child and only daughter of William and Rebecca. She never married. An integral part of Southdown Sugars, she was awarded a certificate for her participation as a successful woman in the sugar industry at the World's Columbian Exposition in Chicago in 1893. (THACS.)

The 10,000-square-foot house at Southdown Plantation boasted porches on all sides upstairs and down. Each porch could be accessed by a minimum of two doors from each room in the house. These access points also made the house cooler with cross-ventilation, but the multiple porches were likely the areas most occupied in the warmer months. (THACS.)

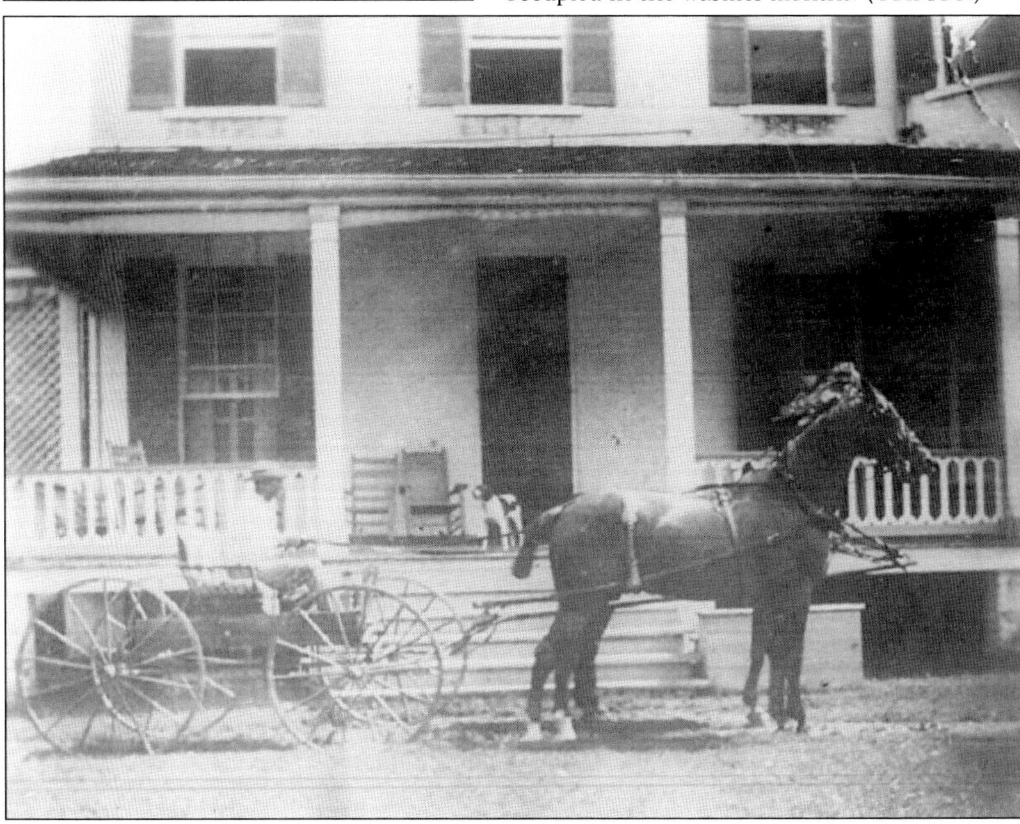

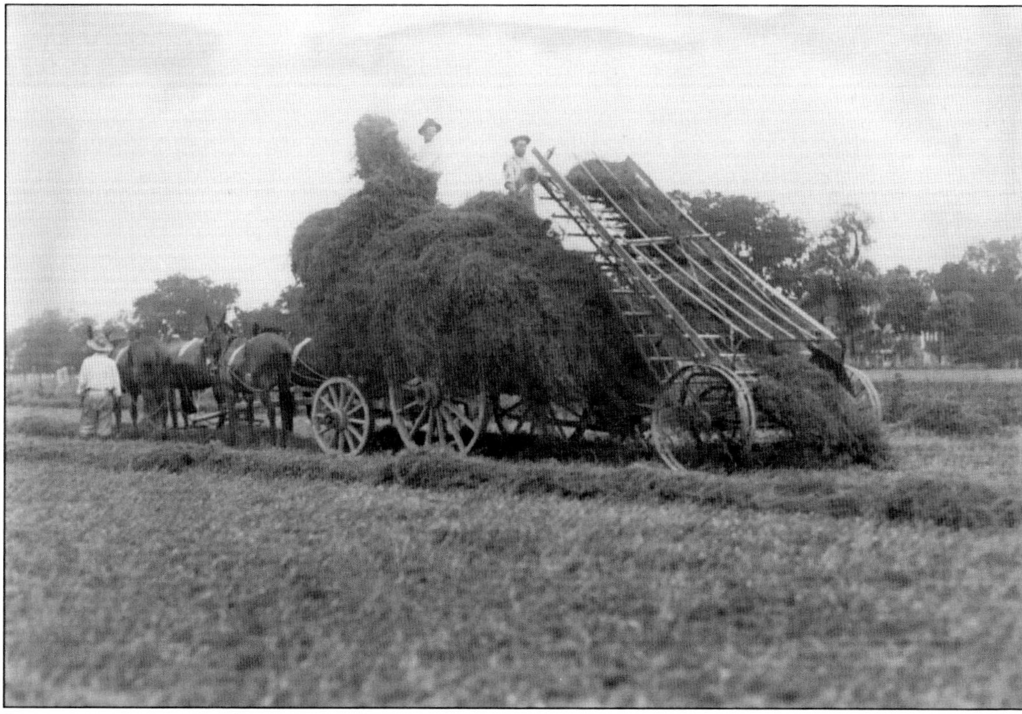

Beginning in 1848, the great industry in Houma and the surrounding parishes was sugarcane production. Many mills dotted the lands and were surrounded by cane fields as far as the eye could see. What started out as an agricultural adventure eventually became king in Terrebonne Parish. (THACS.)

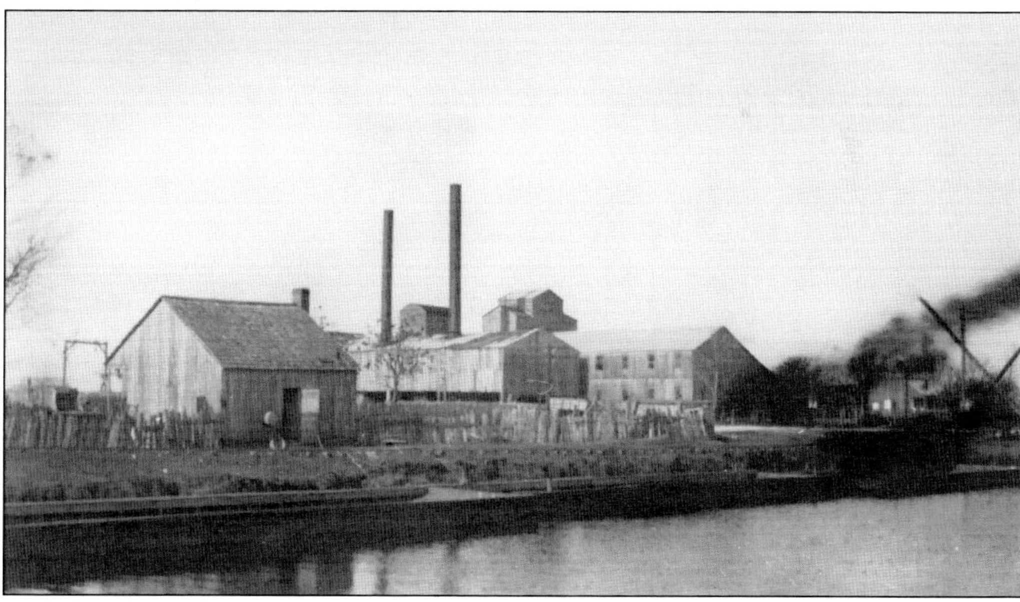

Settled on the banks of Little Bayou Black, Southdown Plantation House is a lasting tribute to the sugar industry, which helped to nurture Terrebonne Parish from its infancy to its present population of over 100,000 residents. Four generations of the Minor family, along with hundreds of mill workers, field-workers, and their families, lived and labored at Southdown Plantation. (THACS.)

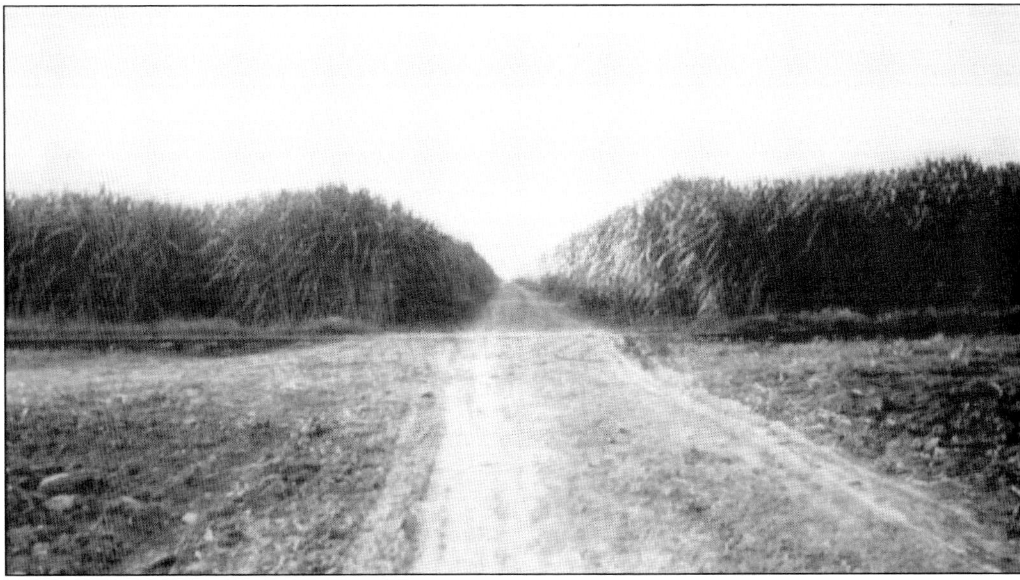

Sugarcane fields reaching up to the horizon and as far as the eye can see was the norm for Houma. Sugarcane first took its roots in Louisiana in 1785 when Étienne de Boré planted the first successful crop in New Orleans where the modern-day Audubon Park exists. Jesuit priests, however, were responsible for bringing the first plants to Louisiana. (THACS.)

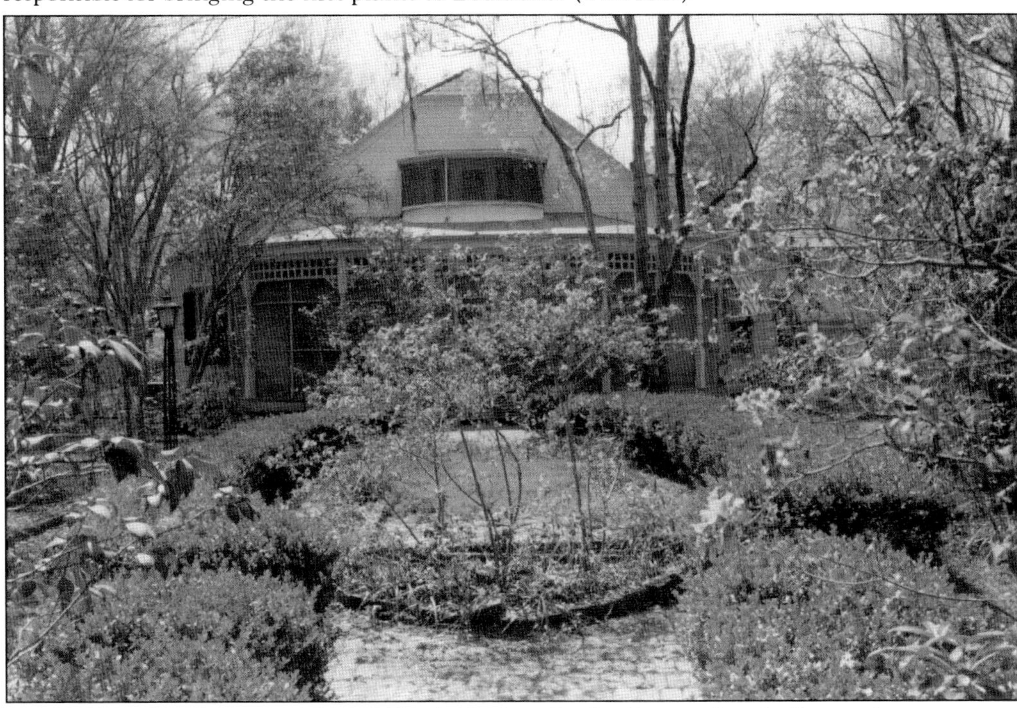

Other sugar plantations were owned by the Robert Ruffin Barrow family. Barrow became one of the largest and most prominent planters, and in 1860, he owned 21,256 acres. The ancestral Barrow family home, Roberta Grove, is pictured. Other prominent planters were of the Pugh, Bisland, McCollum, McBride, Bond, and Schaffer families. Other important farming families included the Ellenders, Thibodaux, Champagnes, Goodes, Krumbhaars, and Vigueries. (THACS.)

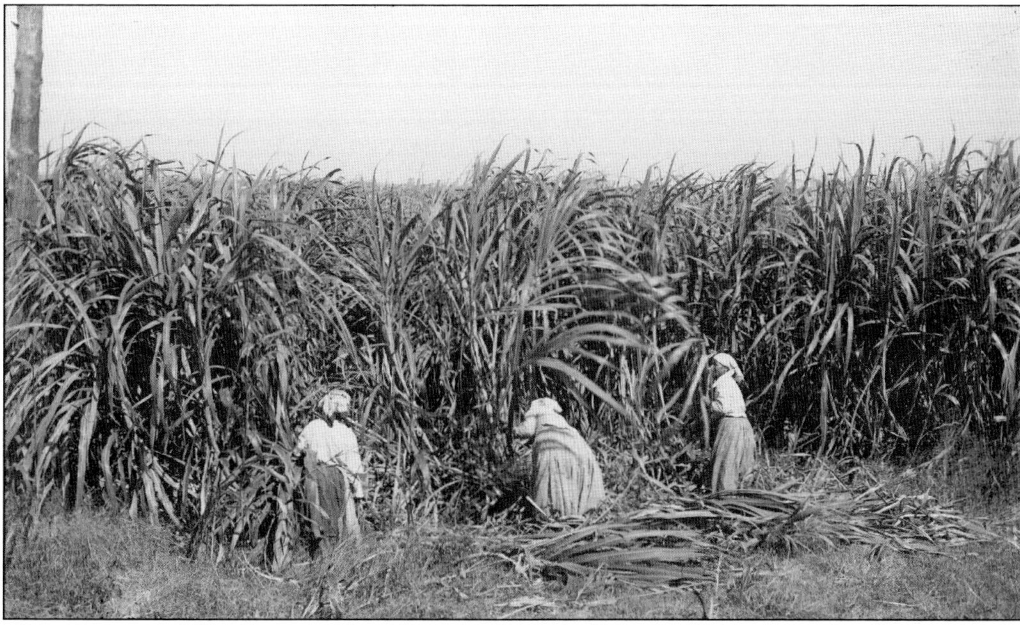

The community of Schriever hosted an experimental government program in the 1935. The US Department of Agriculture Farm Security Administration stressed "rural rehabilitation" to improve the lives of sharecroppers, tenant farmers, and poor landowners. The main idea was to bring workers together in a community to work large government-owned lands using modern techniques. (THACS.)

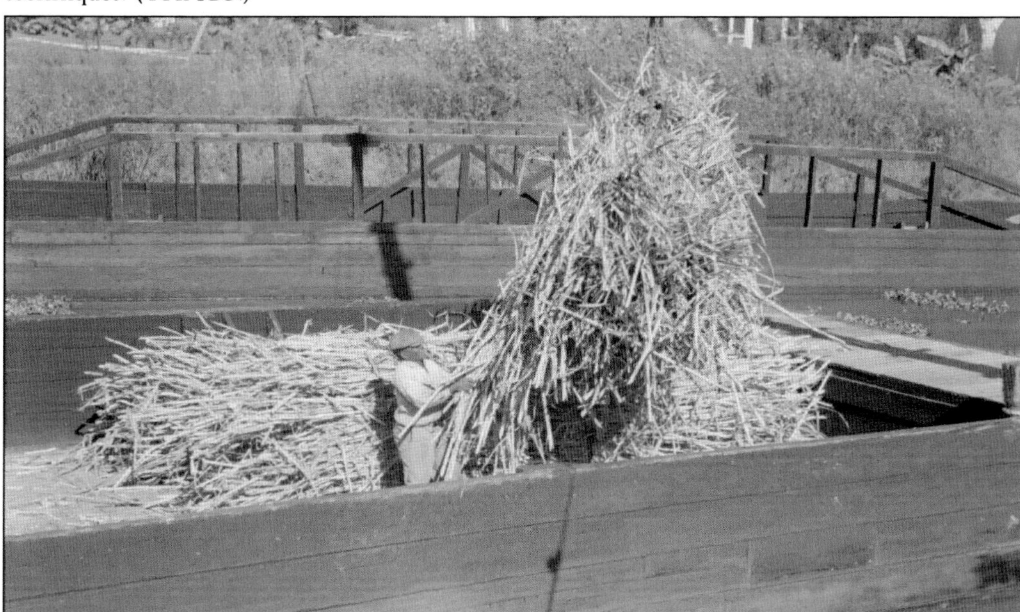

Main Project Road and Back Project Road were established for the Farm Security Administration during the Depression to combat rural poverty. Incorporated as a cooperative, four-acre tracts were leased by the farmers at the cost of $30 per year. There were 71 homes built on the new roads, and a 99-year lease was taken by the government at the surrounding plantations that had available lands. (THACS.)

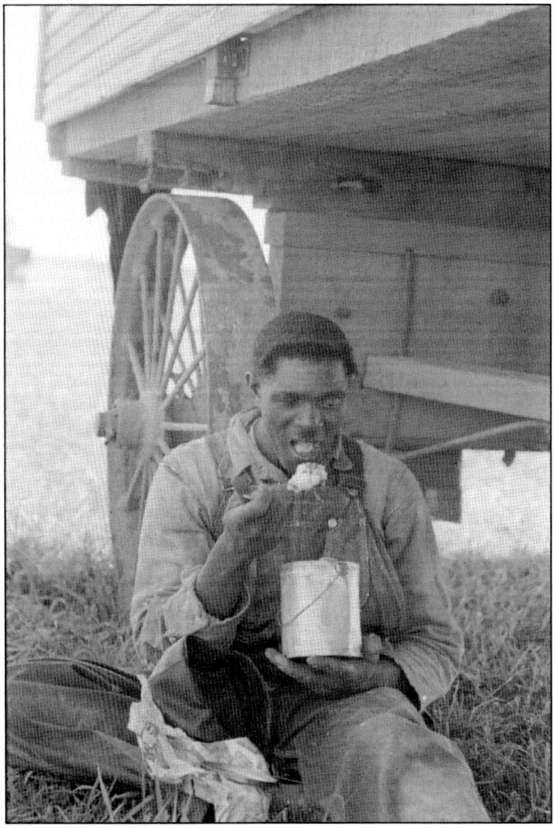

Included in the program were health care, social services, and educational opportunities, but delays and bureaucracy were frustrating for the largely French Catholic inhabitants. In 1943, the Agricultural Appropriation Act essentially shut down the funds for the program. The government cancelled the lease, and properties were put up for sale. (THACS.)

Many plantations had diverse crops such as sugarcane, alfalfa, oats, and hay. Waubun Plantation at Schriever was one held by the John T. Moore Planting Co., Limited's holdings, north of the Southern Pacific Railroad. Like Southdown, Ardoyne, Waterproof, and Hollywood, the company also operated its own railroad of one locomotive and 150 cane cars in its sugar industry. (THACS.)

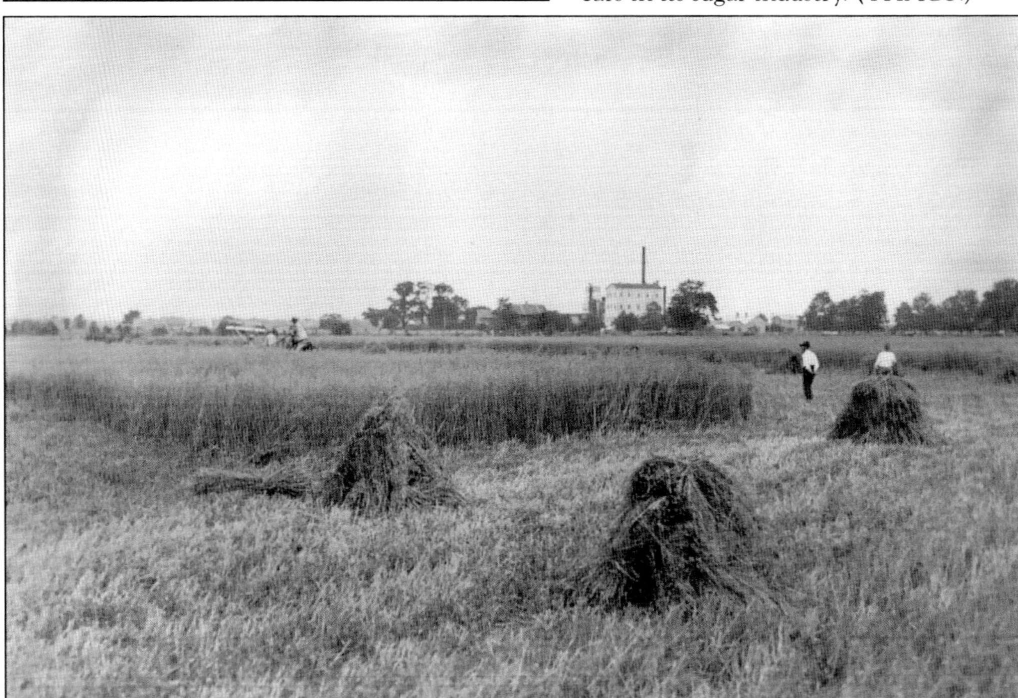

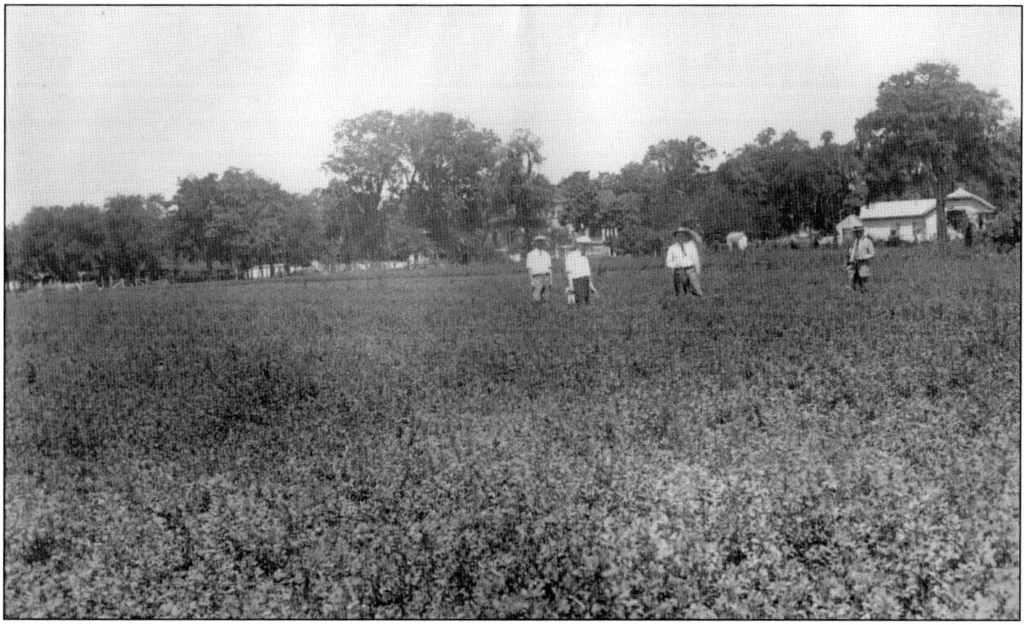

In this image, J.H. Thatcher stands in a field of alfalfa at Waubun. Alfalfa could grow for up to 20 years and was used mainly as a hay substitute for feeding cattle. Thatcher made history with his contributions to sugar plantations when he piped natural gas to six sugarcane factories in Houma. (THACS.)

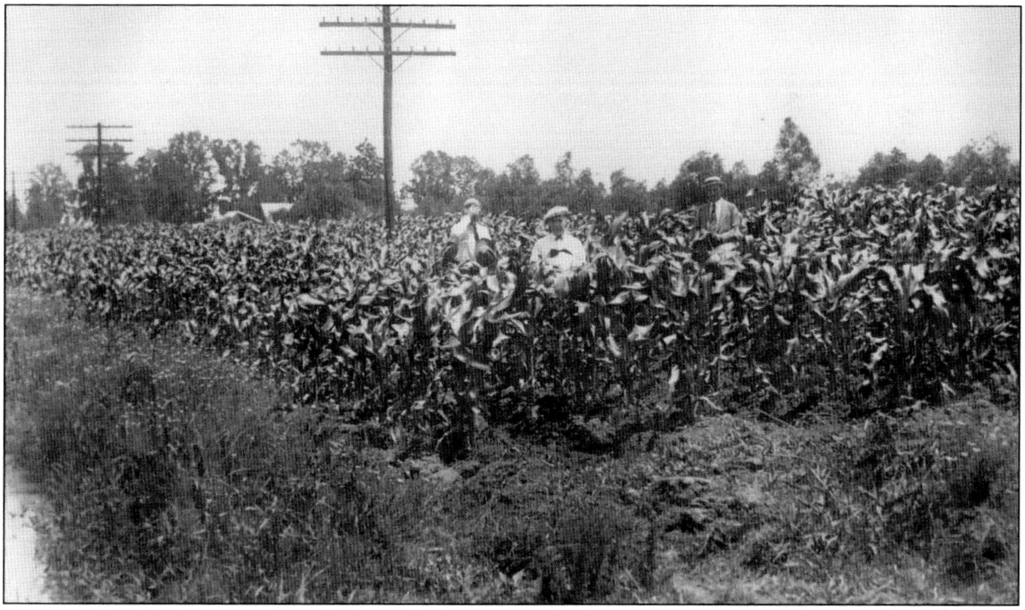

In addition to hay and alfalfa crops, corn was planted for use by both humans and animals. One variety, field corn, would be ground into a meal and added to the cow's diets. The field shown here is sweet corn, which would be harvested and sent to the farmer's market in Houma. (THACS.)

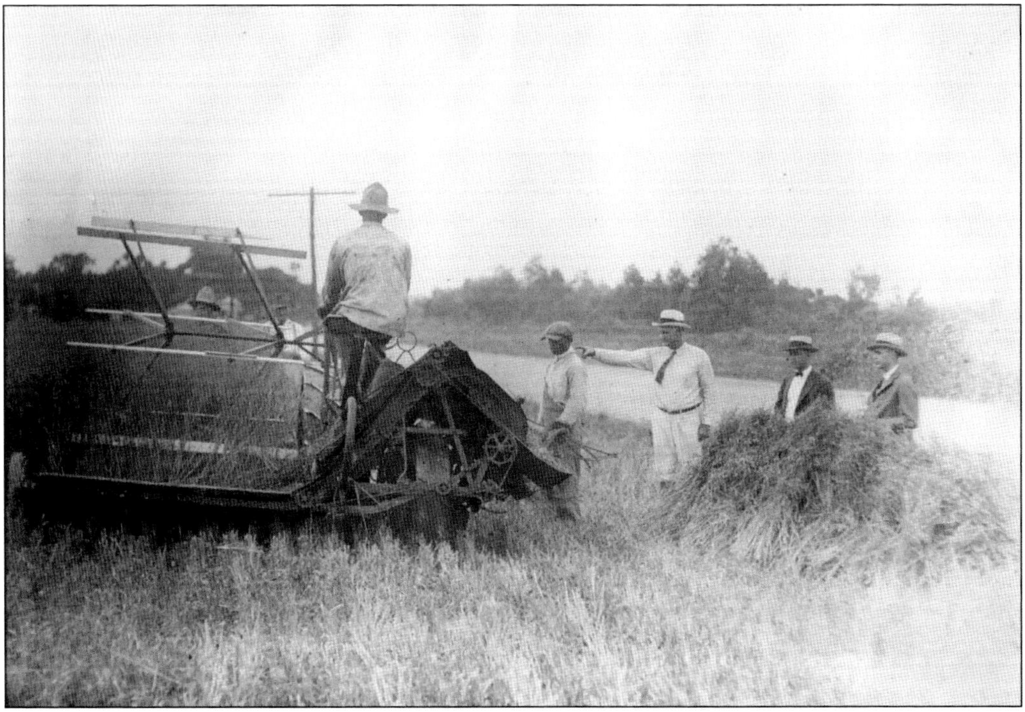

The overseer of a plantation would direct the field-workers in their duties. Here, the overseer at Waubun plantation in 1917 is instructing the field hands and the harvester as they cut the oats. Each plantation had an overseer, which was considered to be a prestigious position of experience and knowledge. (THACS.)

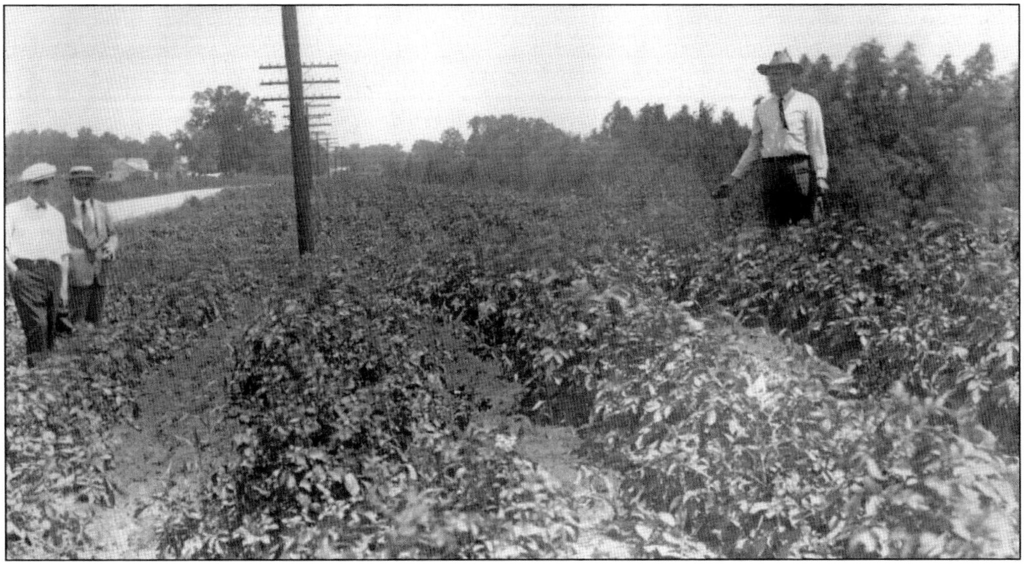

Sen. Allen J. Ellender revolutionized the truck farm in Houma. He imported a heartier crop of potatoes, called "Nebraska," and planted more than 900 seed potatoes. He had three-day potato tours sponsored by the railroads to bring in people eager learn about the "good earth." This venture allowed Ellender to raise enough money to campaign for the Louisiana State Legislature. (THACS.)

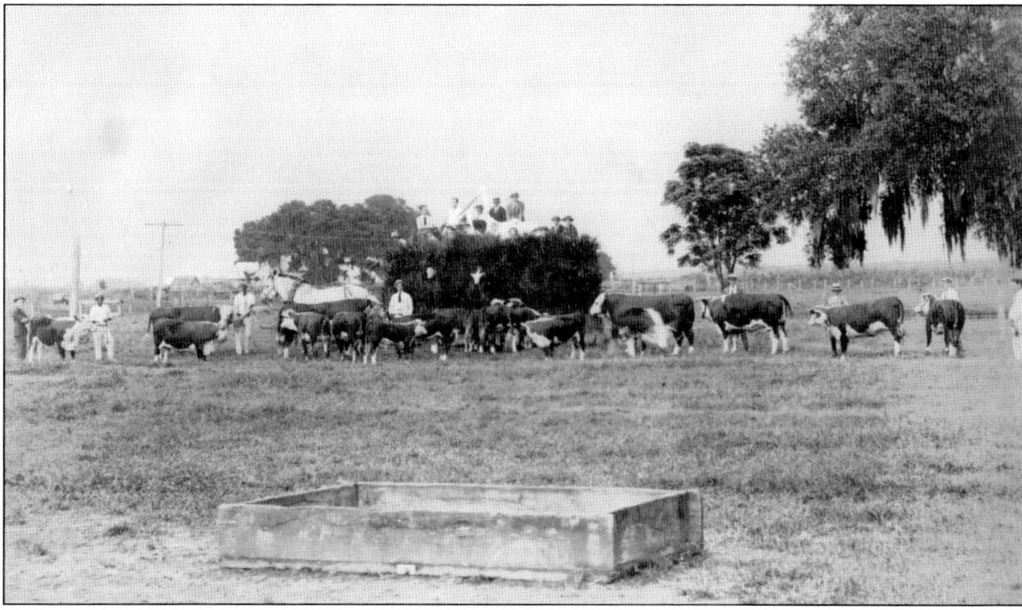

In the *Jersey Bulletin* out of Indianapolis in May 1919, an article written about the quality of stock held by the Minors at Southdown calls it "a model dairy farm in the South." Certified milk of the highest quality was produced for the approximately 5,000 inhabitants of Houma. At this time, Southdown Dairy Farm has a 50-cow steel-and-concrete barn. There were about 250 Jersey cows on the farm. With a large number of Register of Merit cows in this herd with yearly records of 400 to 650 pounds of butterfat, and with three of the best-bred bulls in the country, this herd started at a point that few ever reach in a lifetime. The proprietors were Kate Minor, C.C. Krumbhaar, and D.W. Pipes. (Both, THACS.)

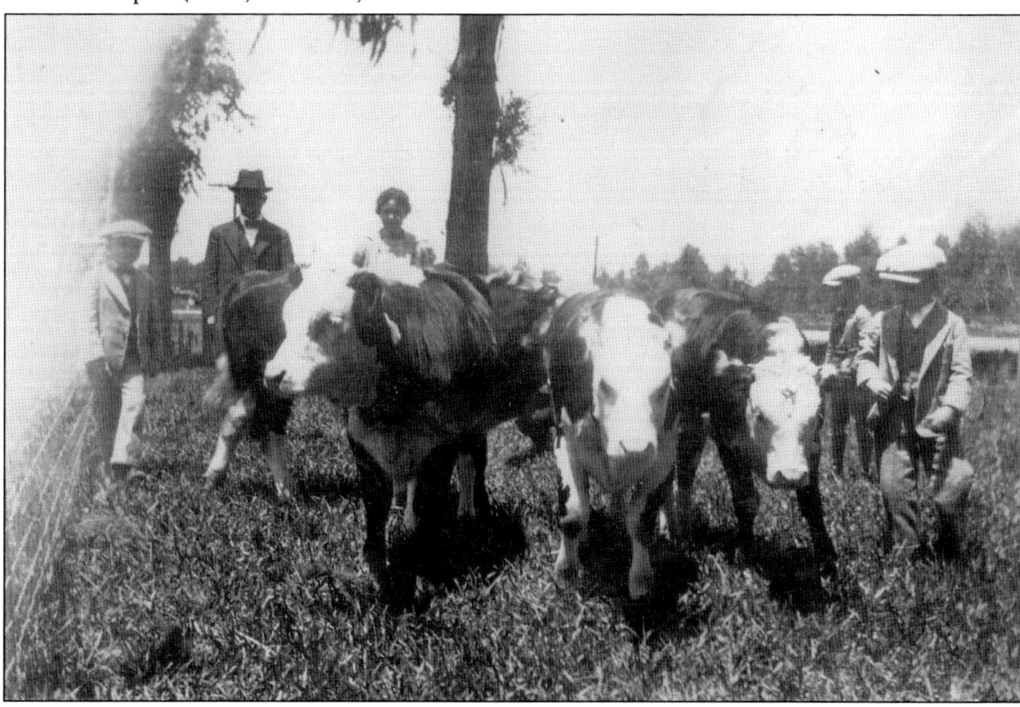

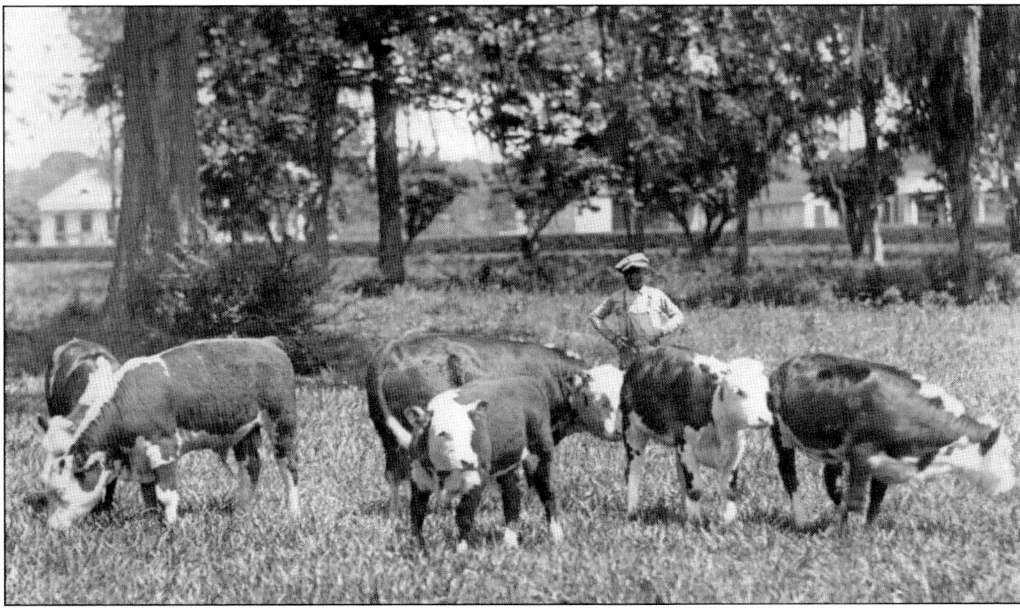

It was required that each plantation owner have his own brand, and over 1,140 brands were registered with the parish at the height of the cattle industry in the bayou country. Hot iron was used to brand the animals by burning away the hair and permanently scaring the flesh. This was the method used for identification of the owner. Annual branding events became a reason for a family outing or picnic. Livestock inspectors under the Louisiana Livestock Brand Commission not only investigated instances of theft but also inspected shipments of cattle to the area. (Both, THACS.)

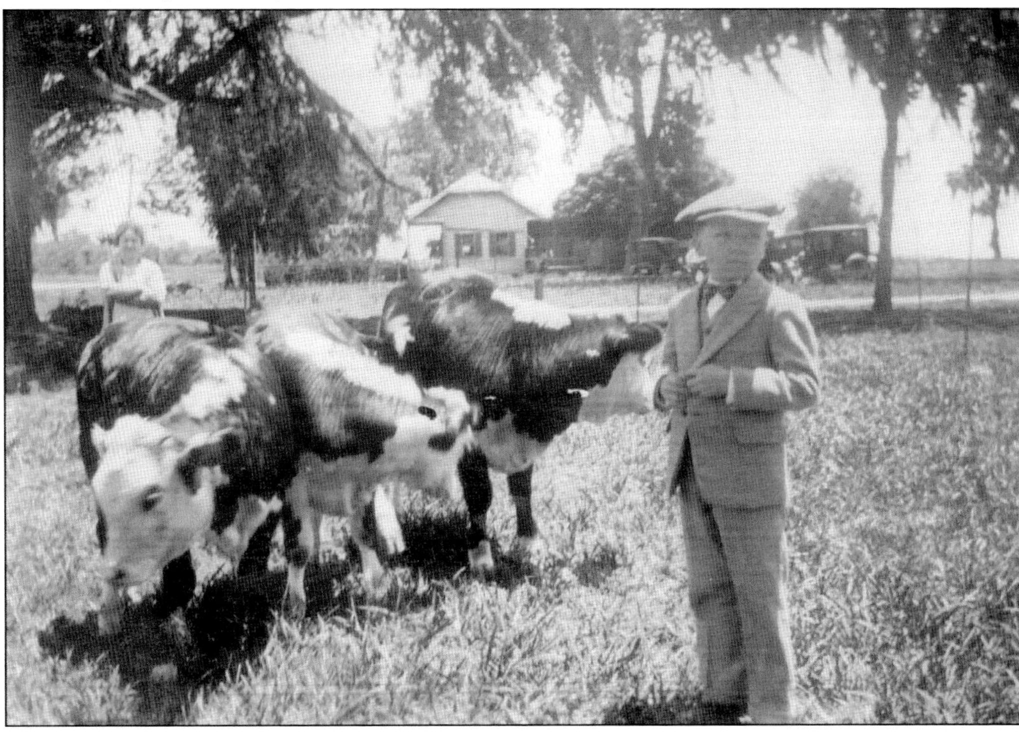

The food (for humans) and feedstuff (for livestock) dryer is pictured here in May 1910. Crops from local farms were trucked in and prepared by drying. The dryer consisted of a motor and fan set up on the outside, with a series of ducts for distributing forced air through the pipes. These crops were then ready to use. (THACS.)

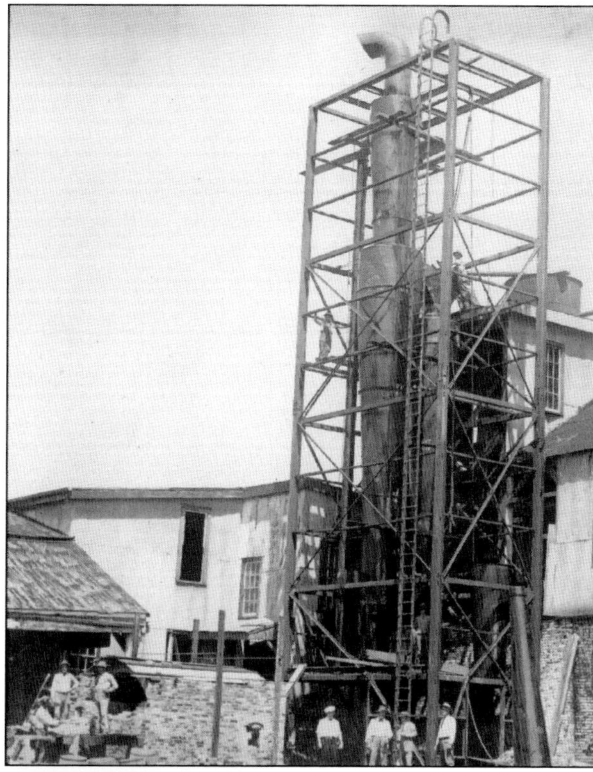

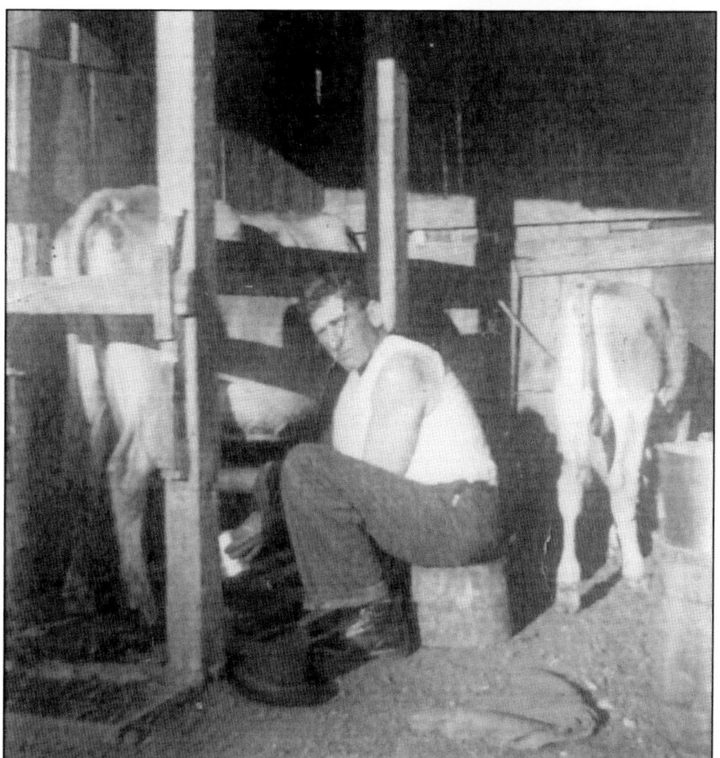

Eugene Bonvillain, father of Ivy Bonvillain of Southdown Plantation mill, milks a cow as a calf feeds nearby. Ivy was a longtime employee at the mill and factory. The Bonvillain family can be traced back to early days of Houma. (THACS.)

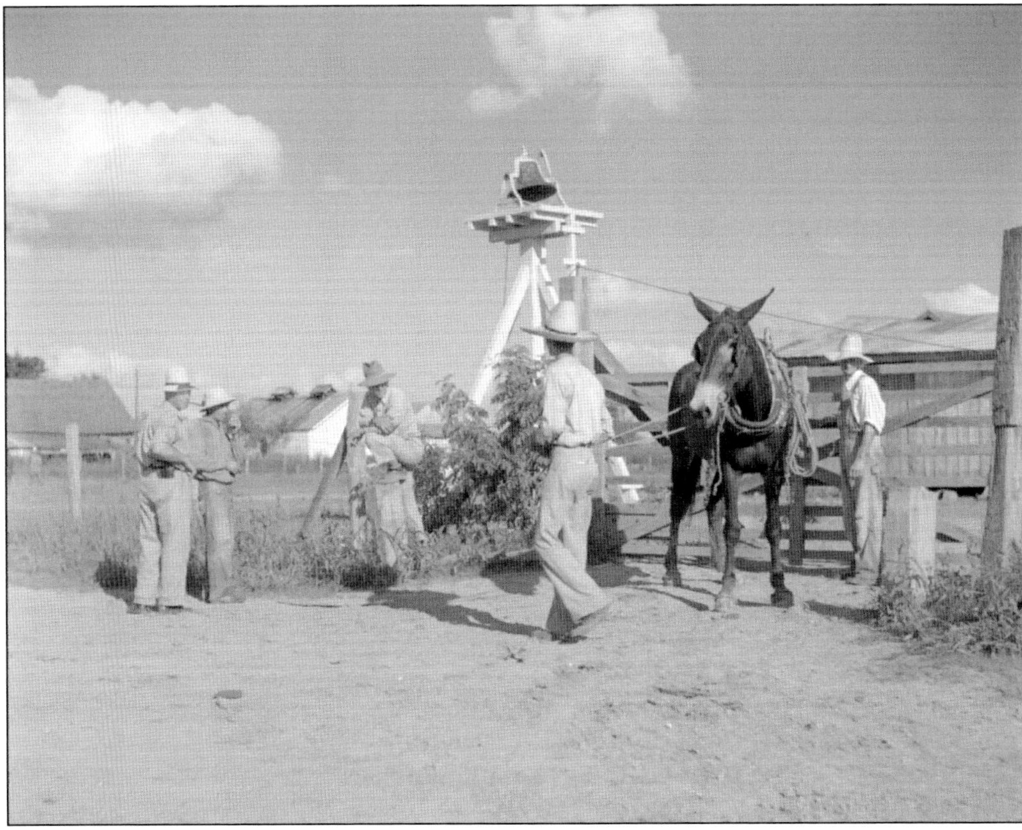

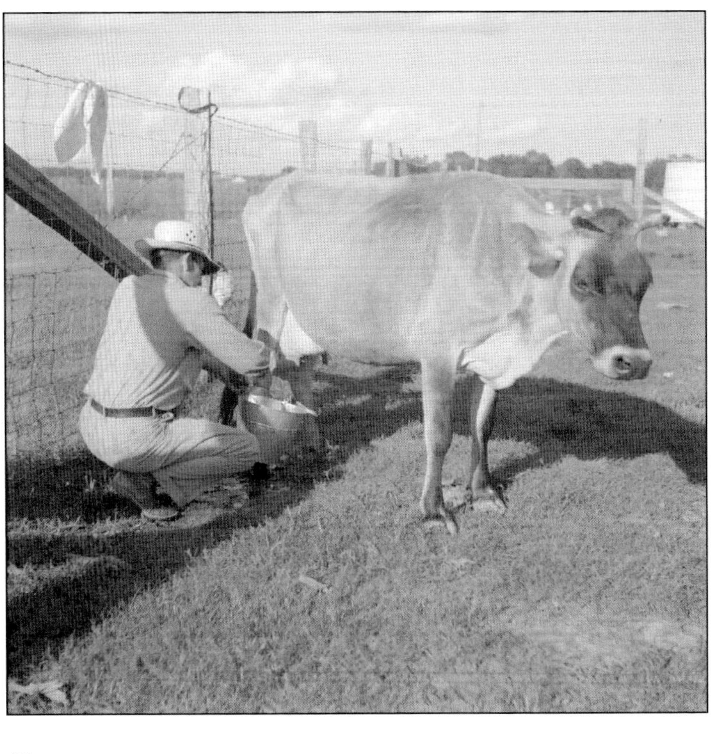

Although there were many commercial cattle producers in Houma, a dairy cow, like this one on Back Project Road, was an important element to any family farm. In addition to cows, farms often also had chickens, rabbits, pigs, horses, and mules. The horses and mules were particularly useful to the farmer who had not yet acquired machinery like tractors, as the larger plantations had. In this co-op system at Schriever, farmers would share the use of service animals to plow and reap the fields. (Both, THACS.)

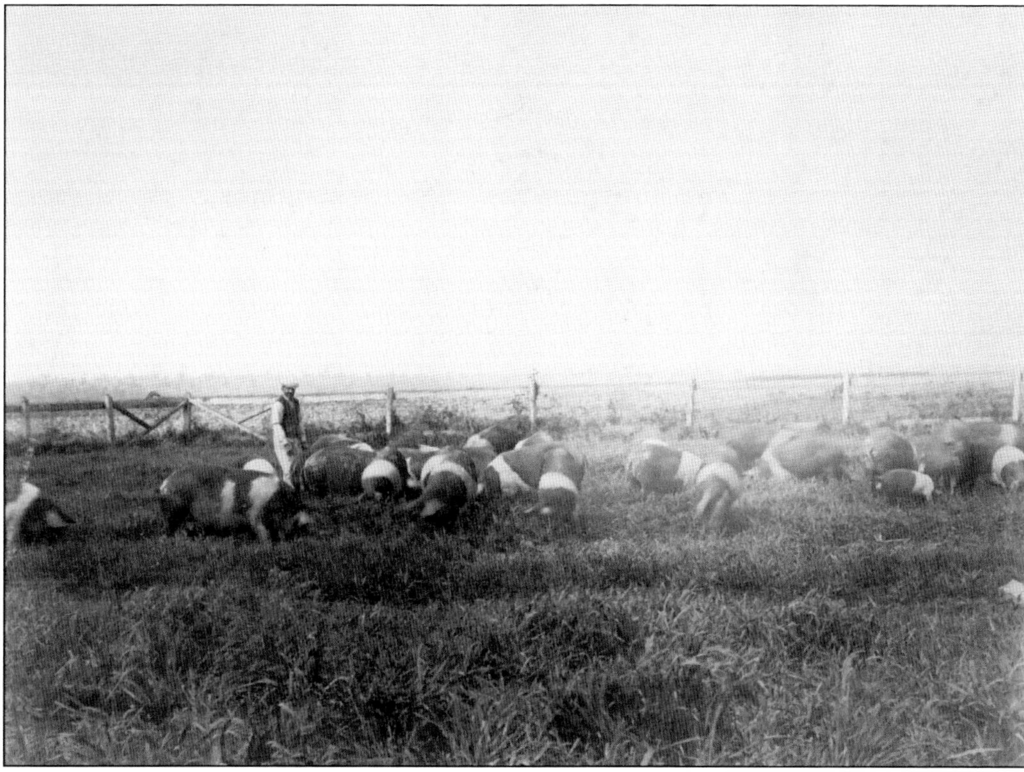

Southdown and surrounding plantations raised pigs on their ample acreage for many years. In 1861, the population of pigs was decimated after the announcement that the slaves would be made free. Soon, there was a decided laxity in obeying plantation orders and regulations, and slaves took to stealing pigs for themselves or to sell in the city. Eventually, sharecroppers, tenant farmers, and men who purchased small pieces of land replenished the former quantities and fine quality of swine. (Both, THACS.)

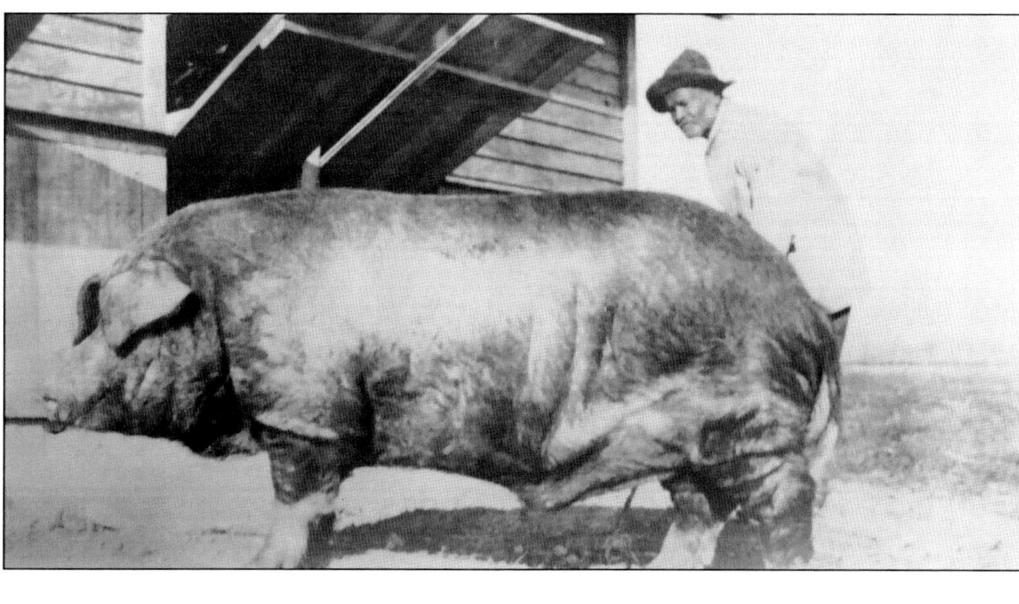

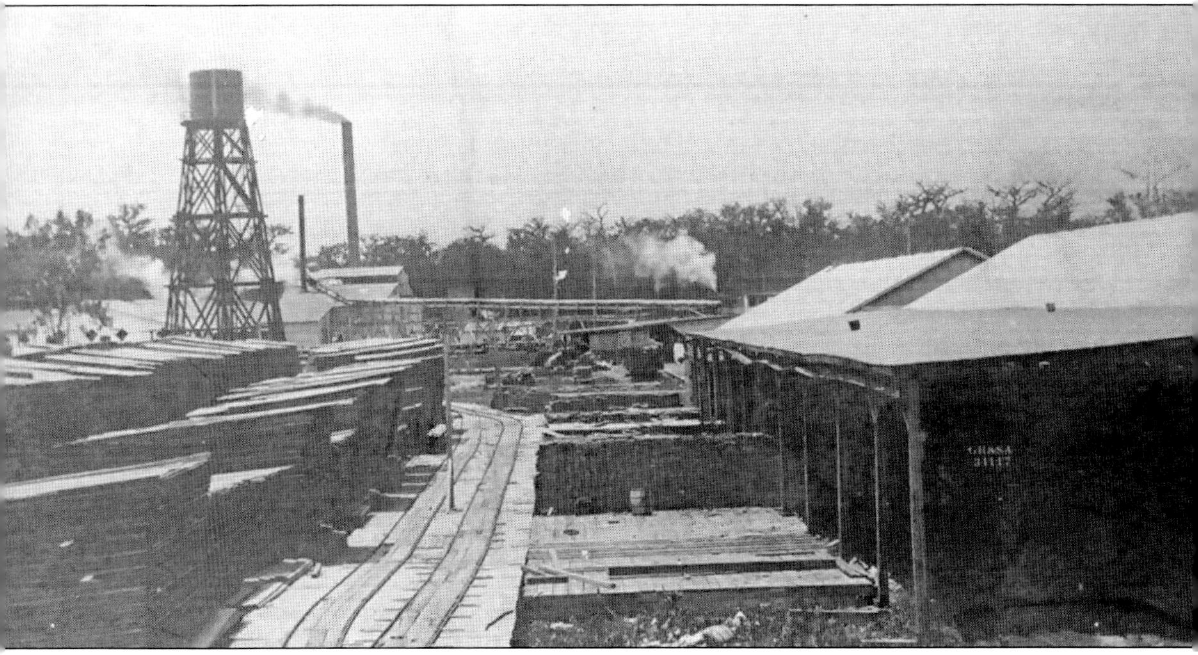

While agriculture was a mainstay in the area, other service industries, such as logging, were active. People had been felling trees since the 1700s, but logging came into its day from 1880 to the 1930s with the advancement of machinery. Sawmills, such as this one at Donner, were able to mass-produce needed wood. The cartwheel pattern of the pull boat trails or runs that can still be seen from the air are the only traces left of the large town of old Donner, Louisiana, where the mill's big saws once hummed day and night. Today, all is quiet and desolate where once was heard the ceaseless hum of the saws and the crash of falling trees in the disappearing cypress forest. Workers at the mill had to be at least 16 years old, and they made $1.10 per week. The mill specialized in building cisterns and coffins. (THACS.)

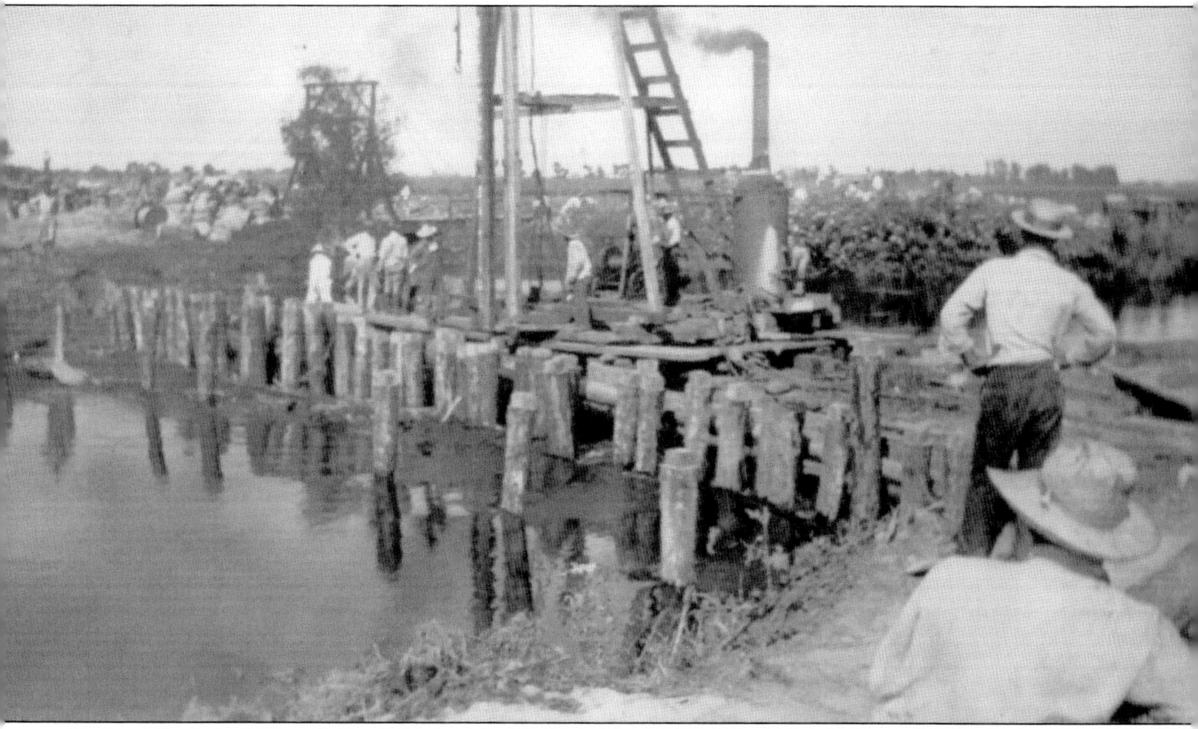

Prior to about 1880, timber production in Louisiana was fairly small, meeting local needs. Mills and logging were confined largely to areas along waterways. By contrast, the so-called second phase of lumbering, the industrial phase, was huge in its output. "These were the days of giant trees, giant mills, and giant lumbermen," notes Louisiana lumber historian Anna C. Burns. In 1880, Louisiana ranked 30th in the United States for the dollar value of its timber product. By 1900, it ranked tenth in the nation, and by 1920, second. In some years in the 1910s, the state led the country in timber production. After the mill closed at Donner, the company sold its timberland between Bayou Black and Morgan City to the Norman Breaux Cypress Company of Morgan City. (THACS.)

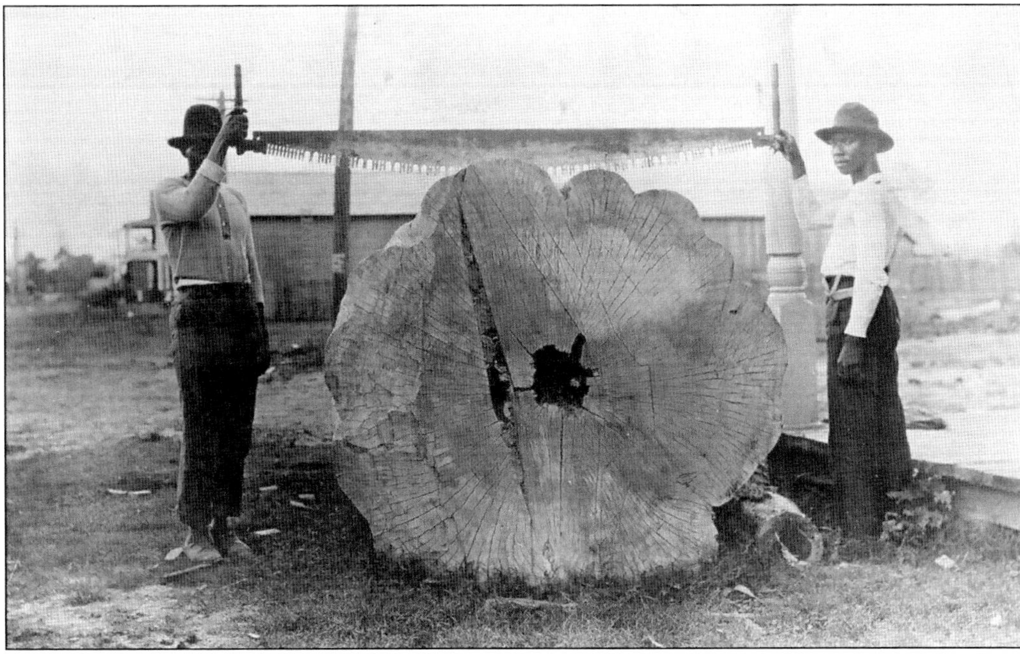

Massive cypress trees that were described as stretching as "far as the eye could see into the sky" and being "as big around as three men are tall" came down in the swamps around Houma. Louisiana originally had 1.6 million acres of cypress forests. These trees were believed to be at least 1,000 years old. (THACS.)

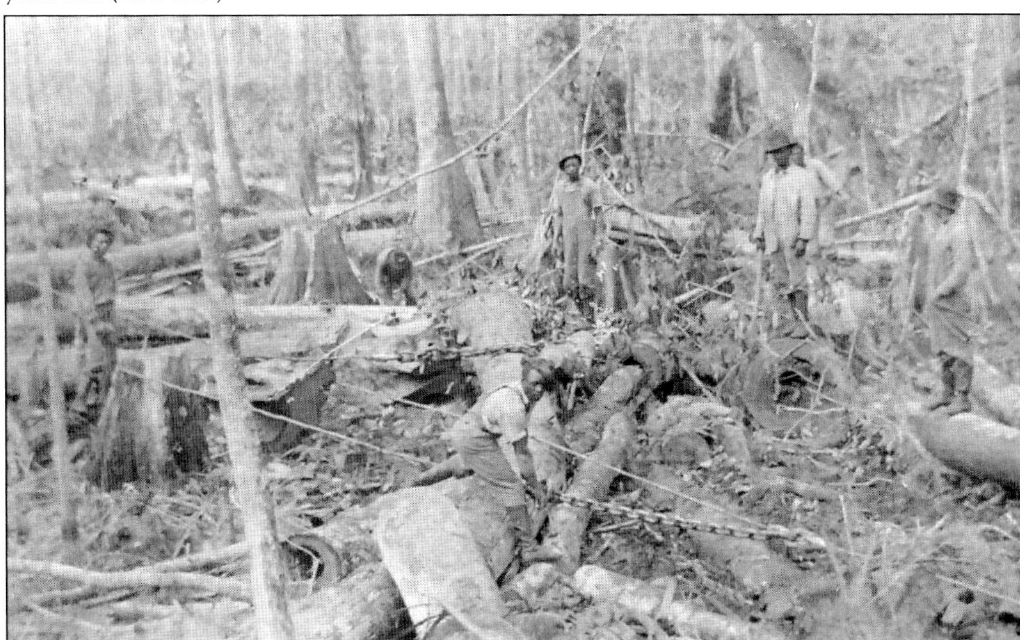

One method used after 1890 to move logs was pull boating. The loggers would visit the swamps in the winter when the water was lower to conduct girdling—the process of essentially pulling back the bark, eventually killing the trees. In the spring, when the water was high, they would cut the trees and float them on the water, pulling them with boats, chains, and ropes. (THACS.)

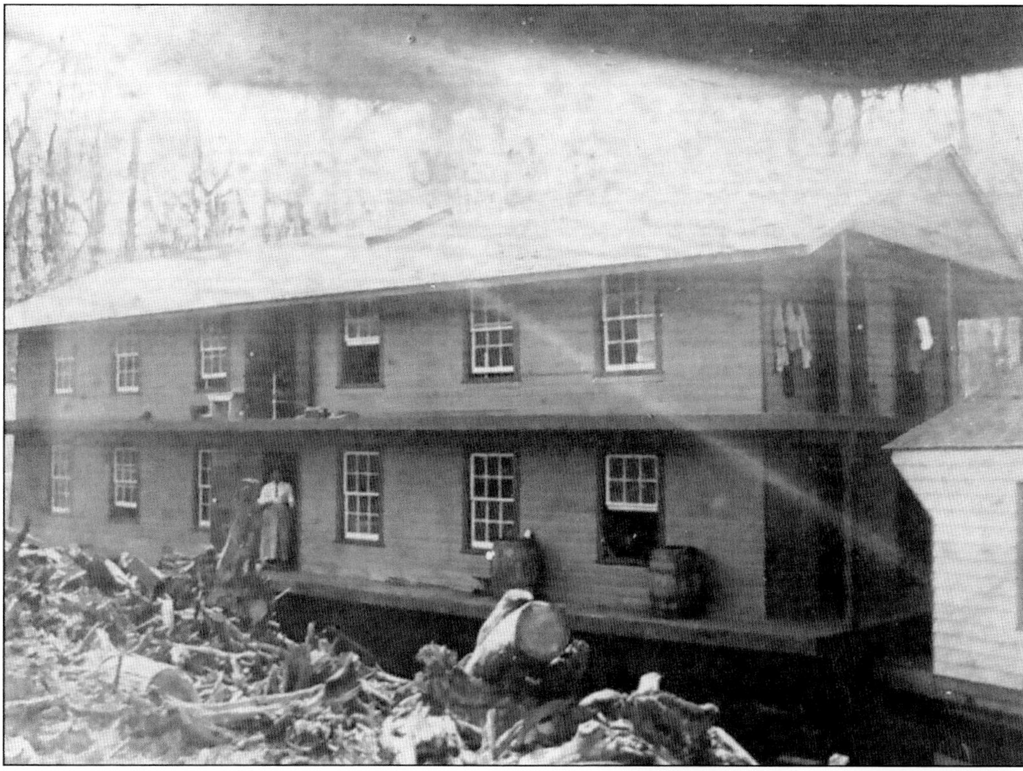

Large houseboats could be used in the swamps to house the loggers. With the invention and application of the steam engine, trees were coming down in record numbers. Canals were formed from pulling the large logs out of the swamps, thus altering the landscape of Southern Louisiana forever. (THACS.)

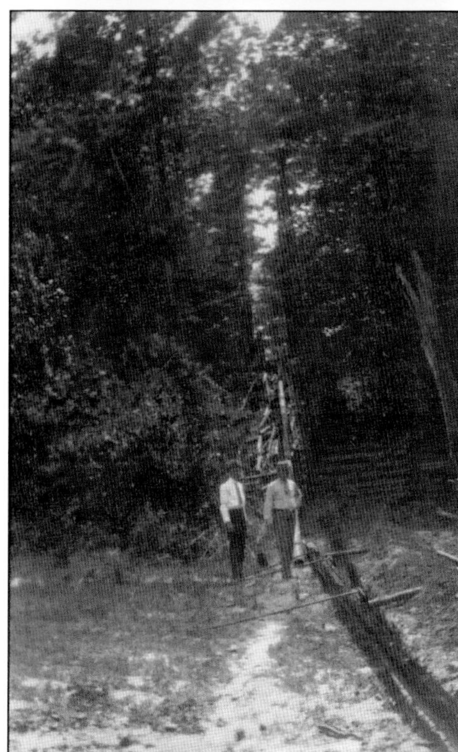

The Timber Act of 1876 made large tracts of swampland available for 25¢–50¢ per acre, a fraction of their commercial value. In some areas, commercial rail lines were laid temporarily to transport the timber from the swamps; they were removed when all the raw material in the area had been taken. (THACS.)

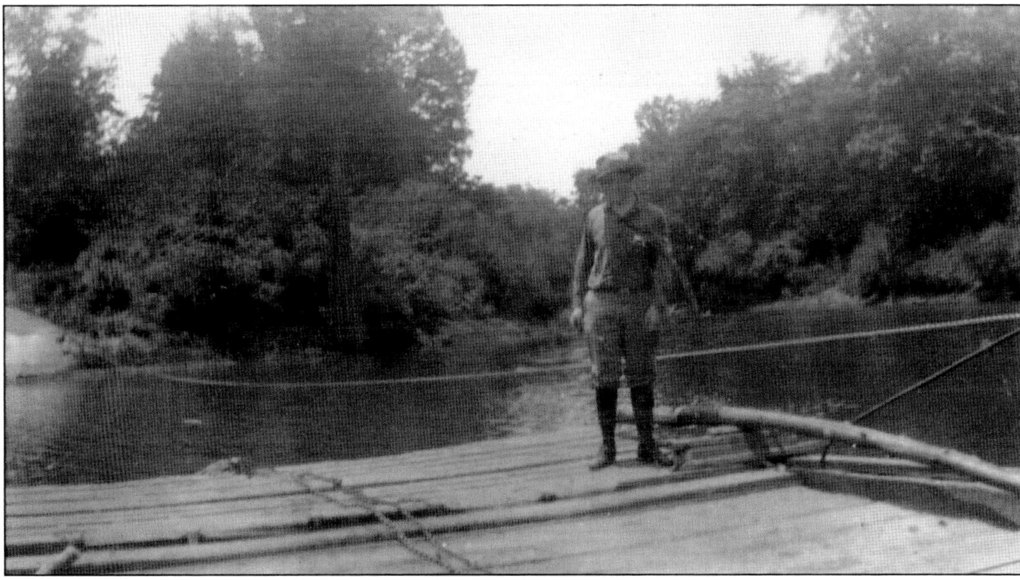

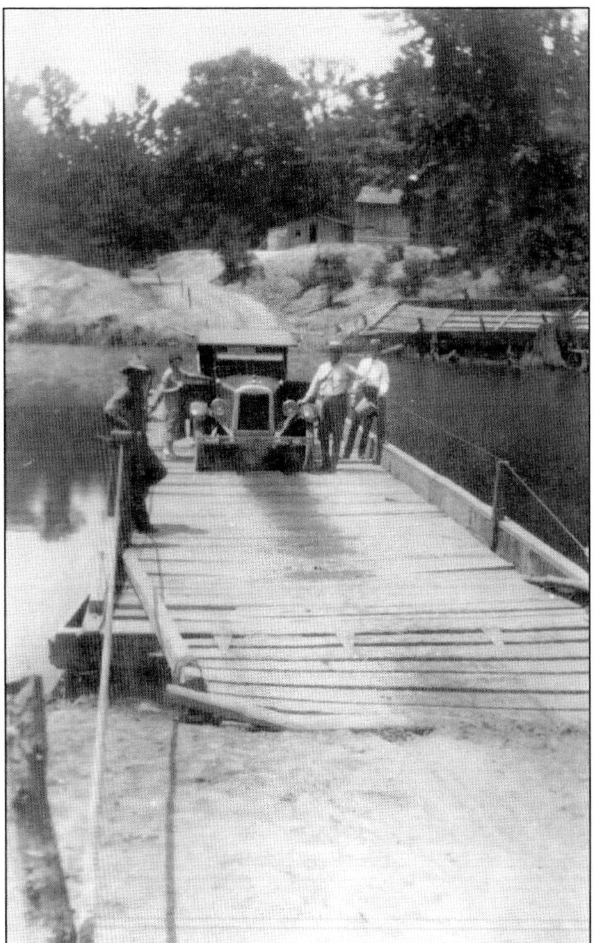

Smaller mills would take advantage of the higher water levels in spring, making rafts by tying the trees together to get them to the sawmills. As the companies were not required to pay taxes, the average citizen gained little or nothing from the extraction of the trees. It was only the small amounts spent by the workers at local businesses that had any benefit. (THACS.)

Senator Hartner stated, "No man has a right to use his property or waste or destroy it to the injury of his neighbor. The owner of a large tract of timber has no moral right nor should he have a legal right to waste or extravagantly utilize the forest for his own enrichment by destroying the seeds of a commodity which could serve the future generations of the race." (THACS.)

Four

Oil and Industry

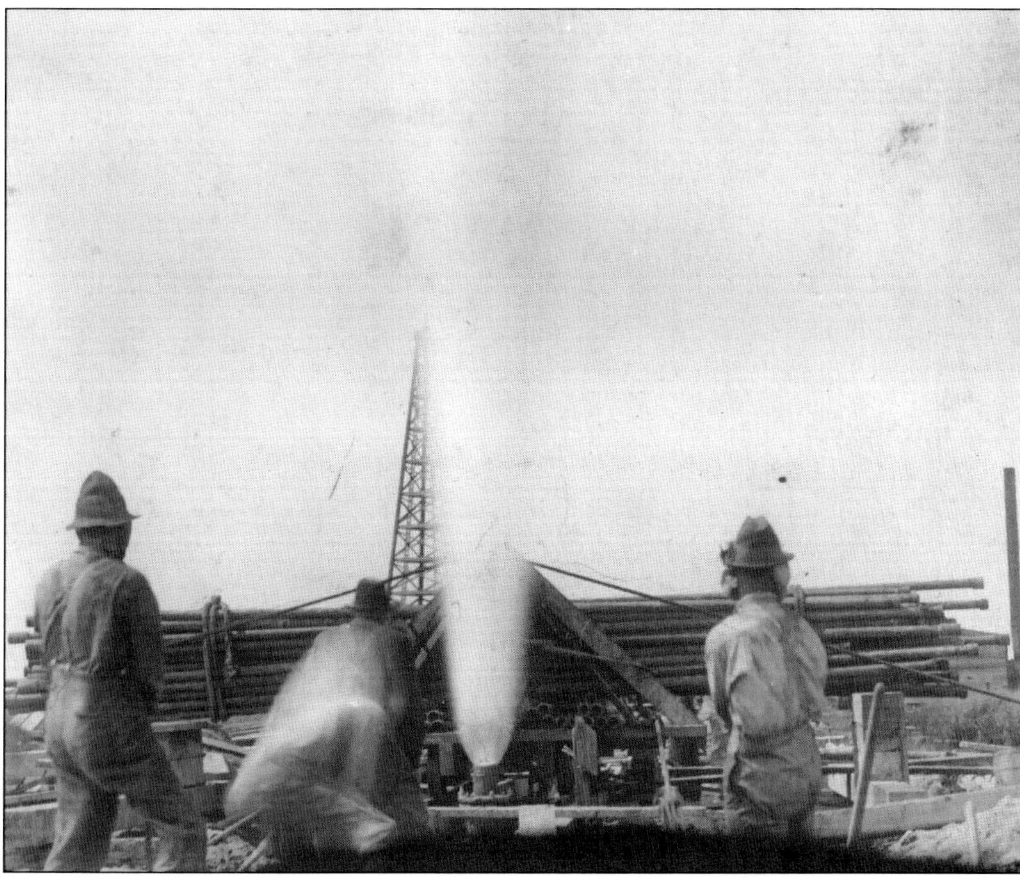

The oil and gas industry took a foothold in Houma in the early 1900s. Both oil wells and gas wells were present in the area. Pictured here is the Lirette Well No. 4 as it blows wild. Owned by the Terrebonne Gas Company of Houma, in 1917, it was the largest six-inch gas well in the world. (THACS.)

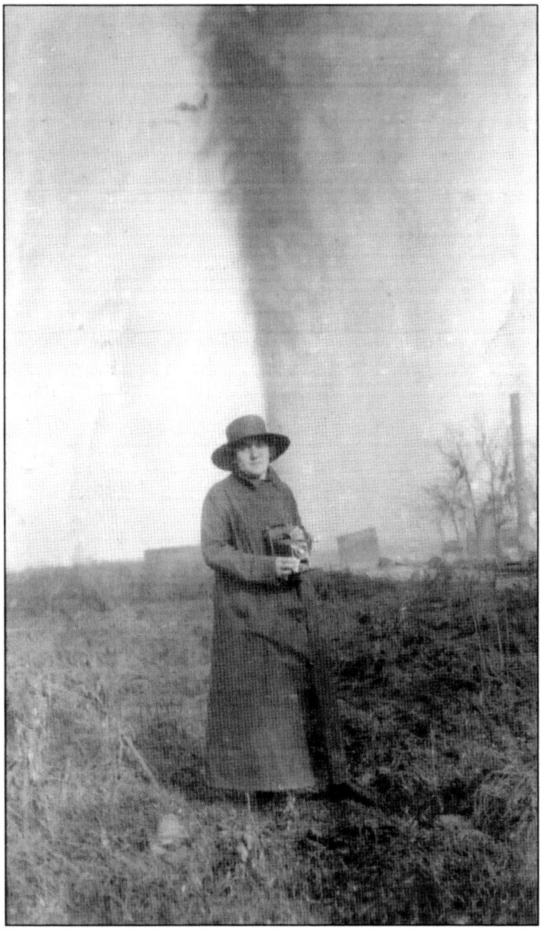

Of course, the novelty of a blowout created opportunities for people to have their pictures taken with the exciting act of power. The blowout was caused when the drilling hit high-pressure reservoirs, thus releasing gas or oil into the air. The woman shown is at the Atlas Blowout in 1919 at a site owned by the Atlas Oil Company, which a June 11, 1919, article in the *National Petroleum News* notes was part of the Potter Palmer estate. (THACS.)

Some referred to the wells on the horizons as "Christmas trees." Some Houmas Indians, according to Emile Billiot, called an oil well *la fountaine,* or "the fountain," but were known to stay clear of them while in their fishing boats or pirogues so as not to be sunk in the event of a blowout. (THACS.)

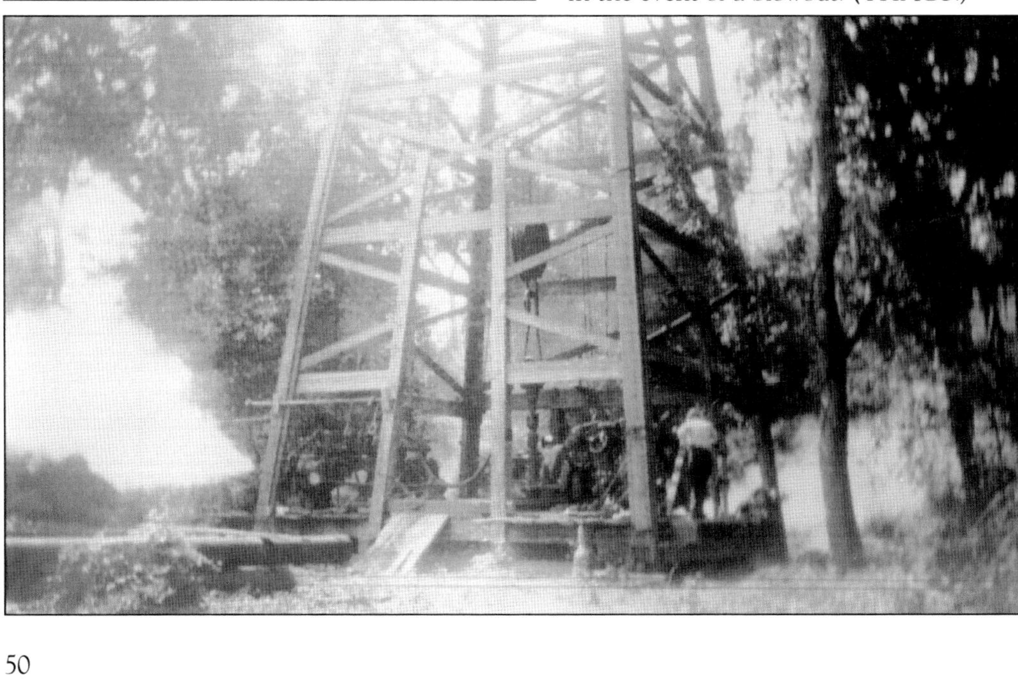

Shown here is the inventor of one of the devices that would revolutionize drilling. Developed by J.P. Miller for the Terrebonne Gas Company, the Miller bit was one of the first drill bits that could be opened or closed. (THACS.)

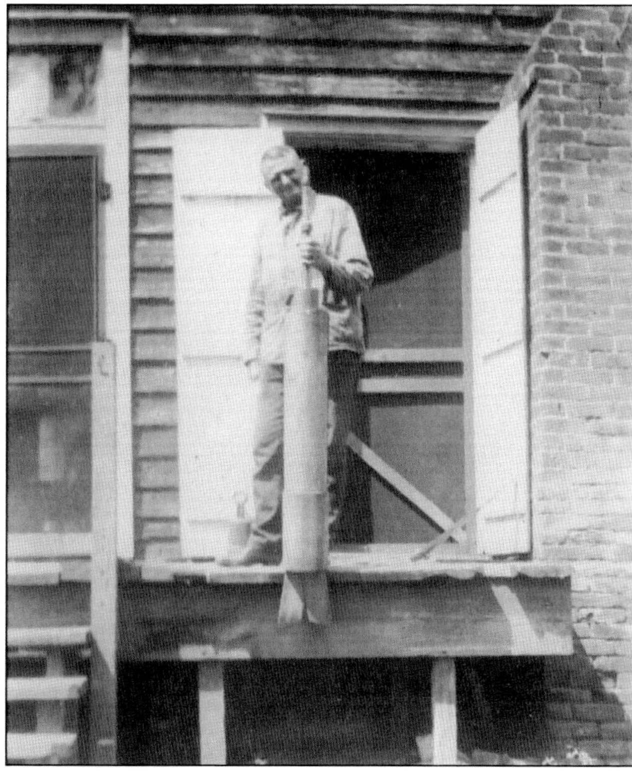

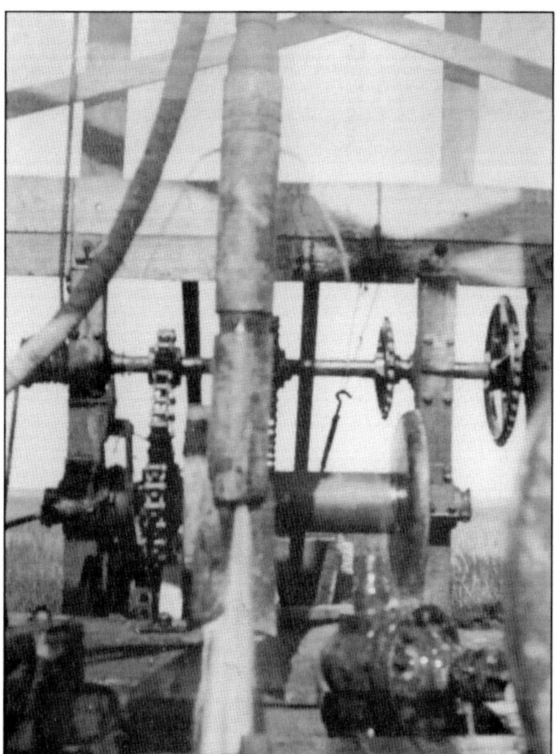

Although oil was first discovered in south Louisiana in 1902, it would not go into full production for the next 15 to 20 years in Terrebonne Parish. A wave of investing brought many businesspeople to Houma as well as a new position of lease broker. One of the first was Frank Wurslow Sr. (THACS.)

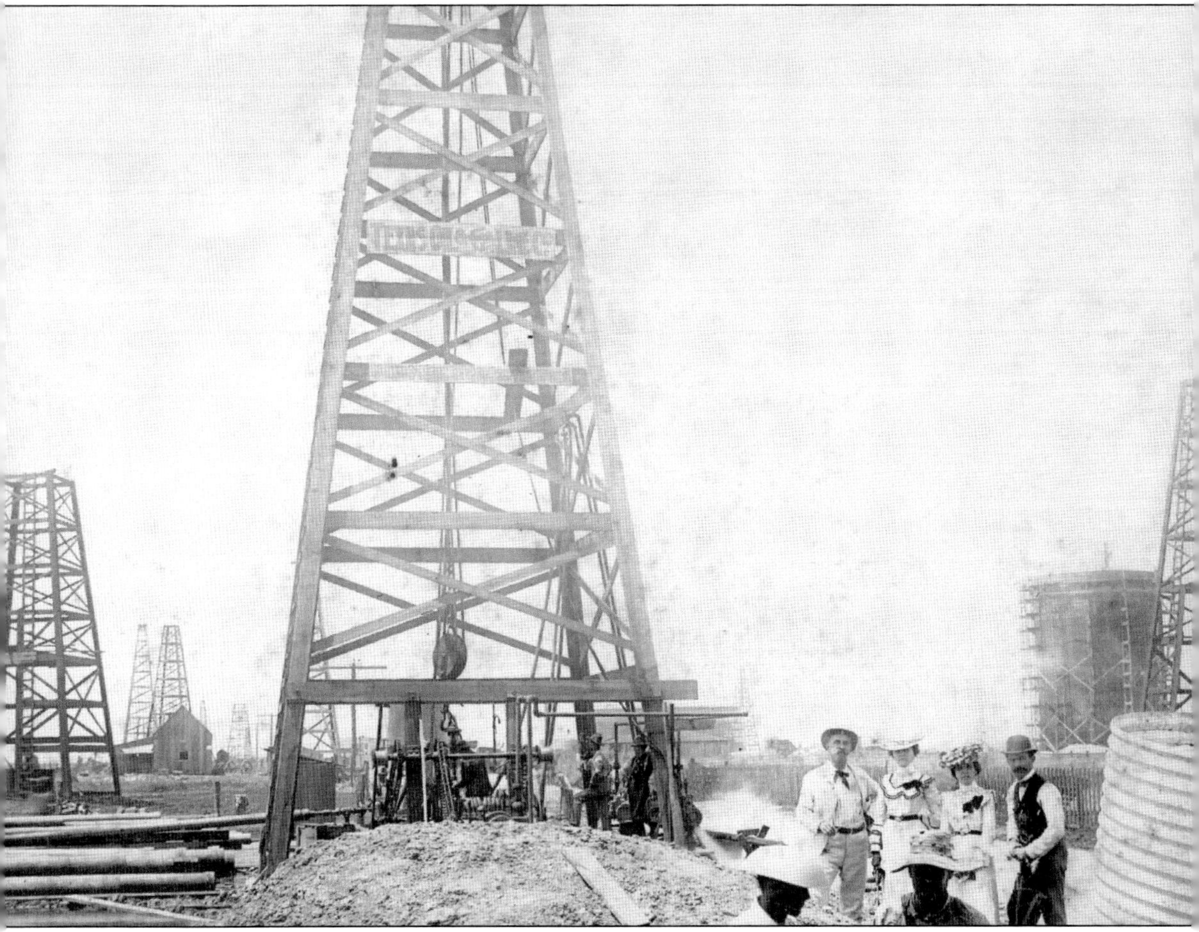

A great deal of wealth was gained with the discovery of oil and gas, but it came at a high price to some who worked in the oil fields and on the wells themselves. The highly flammable substances were very dangerous, and sudden gushers of oil or gas had the potential to ignite, causing serious destruction and even death. The owners of the wells, however, were happy to dress in their Sunday best and take a stroll or even a picnic at the sites to show off their newfound wealth (as pictured). The signs on the oil well read, "Texas Oil and Pipe Line Co., John O'Neal and Company Contractors." The Texas Company (Texaco) was one of the first to establish itself in Houma. (THACS.)

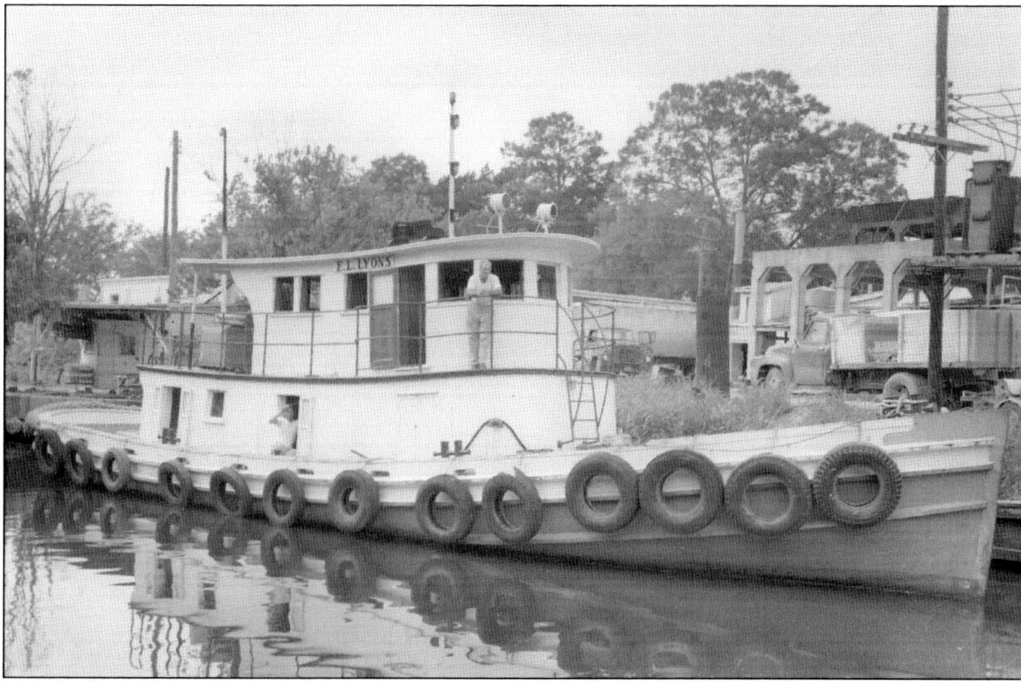

Texaco brought in so many people to work in the oil fields in Houma that services for the employees became a burgeoning business in the 1920s. Edward Lyons owned boats in which he delivered groceries to the various "little cities" in the oil field at each rig. Above, he is shown on the deck of the *E.L. Lyons*, one of his grocery boats. The Houma Ice Company can be seen in the background of this c. 1956 image. The *Lillie Marie*, another of Edward Lyons's boats, is pictured below. There were three grocery boats that supplied Texaco. (Both, THACS.)

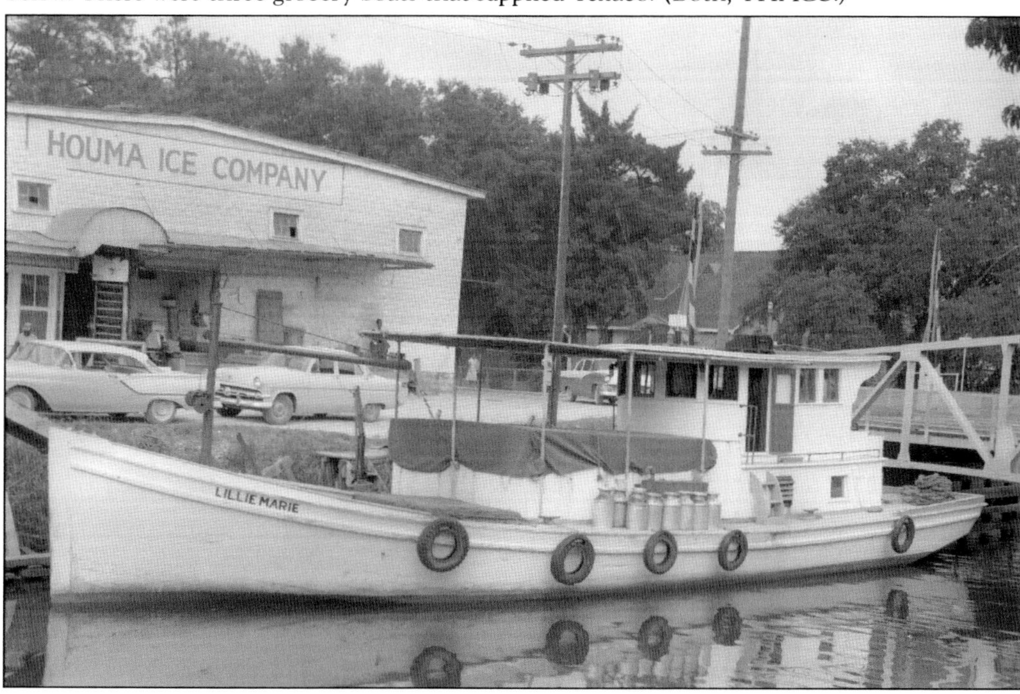

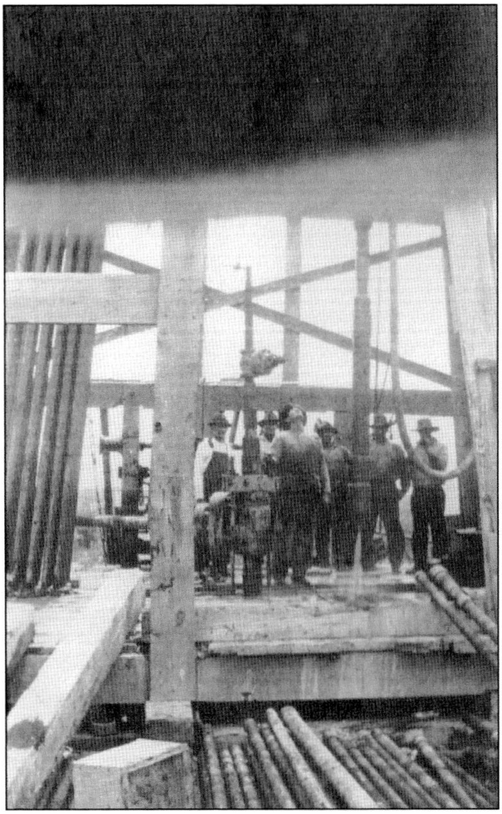

Prior to the opening of the oil fields, inhabitants of the isolated communities hunted and fished, planted and harvested oysters for the markets in New Orleans, trapped fur-bearing mammals and alligators in the swamps, tended gardens and livestock (largely for household and neighborhood consumption), and grew sugarcane.
Some of the skills and know-how of the inhabitants were of immediate use to the oil companies, such as how to navigate the bewildering mazes of bayous and waterways in the marsh. Beginning in the late 1920s on vast parcels of land leased from the Louisiana Land & Exploration Company and the State of Louisiana, the oil giant floated and hauled rigs into the swamps, bayous, backlands, and lakes and built production platforms, living quarters, and tank batteries to store crude oil awaiting transport to refineries. (Both, THACS.)

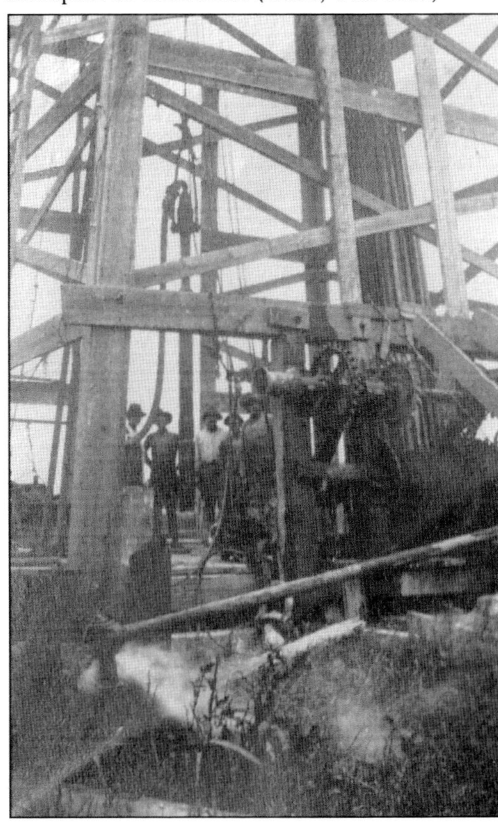

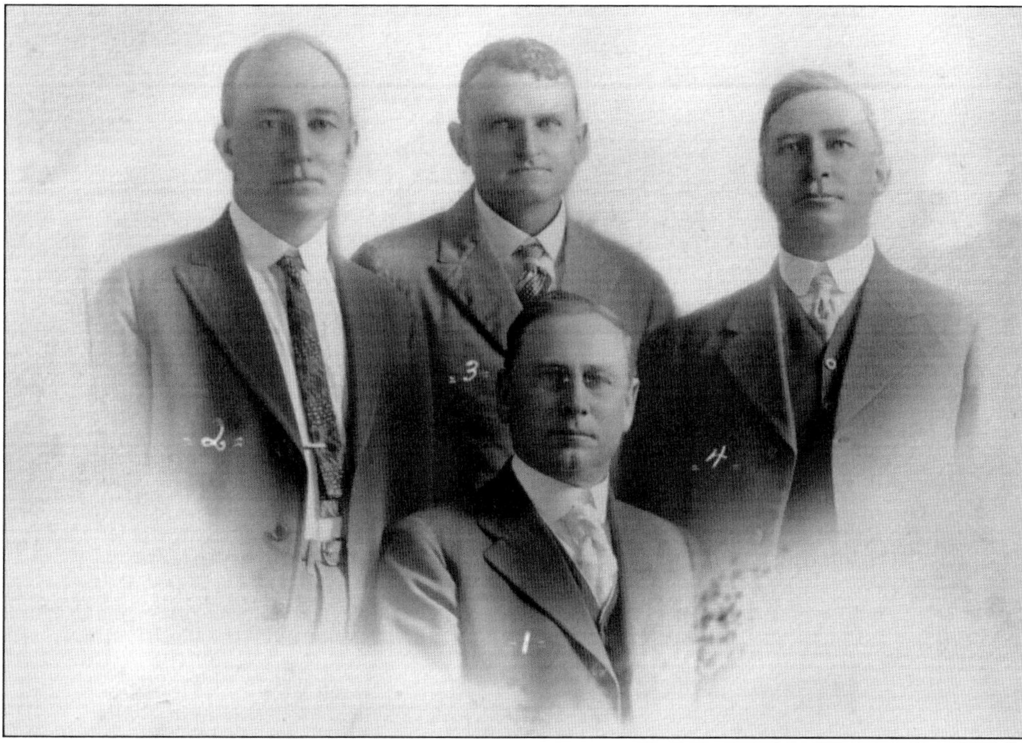

When J.H. Thatcher brought in two large wells at Lirette Field and gained the title of "Mr. Natural Gas," he began an industrial boom. Thatcher is pictured at the bottom center of the photograph and is labeled with the number *1*. Behind him, from left to right, are ? Leach, J.P. Miller (driller), and W.H. Sedbory. (THACS.)

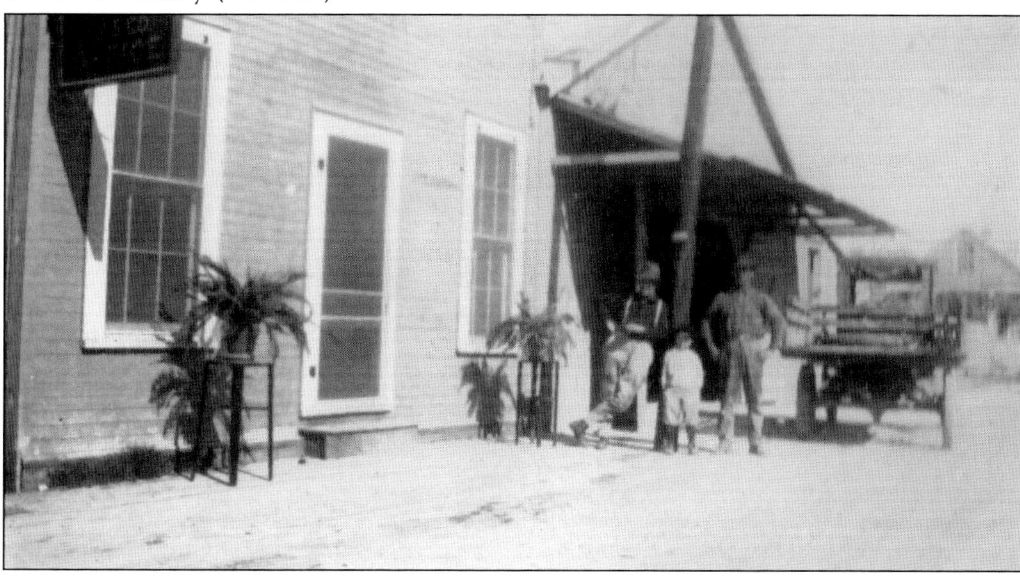

Houma was supplied with natural gas from the Terrebonne gas fields. Factories and homes were powered by the gas, found in abundance under the ground. Several families with the means drilled small wells in their yards and were provided with natural gas for many years. Pictured is the office building of the Terrebonne Gas Company on Court Street in downtown Houma. (THACS.)

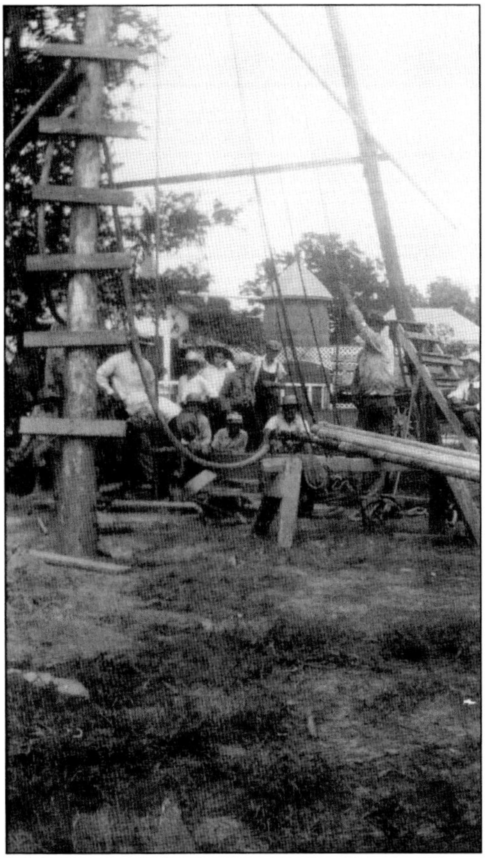

The well pictured at left is on the personal property of J.H. Thatcher. The image below shows the well at Verret Field before it was producing. According to Dora Thatcher, the year 1917 will go down in history as "The Year of Natural Gas." It was this year that the Terrebonne Gas Company was formed with W.B. McCormick as president and with stockholders as J.B. Hutchinson, J.Y. Snyder, and J.H. Thatcher. The company headquarters first stood on Belanger Street across from the Thatcher Hotel. This started Thatcher's 12-year reign as "Mr. Natural Gas." (Both, THACS.)

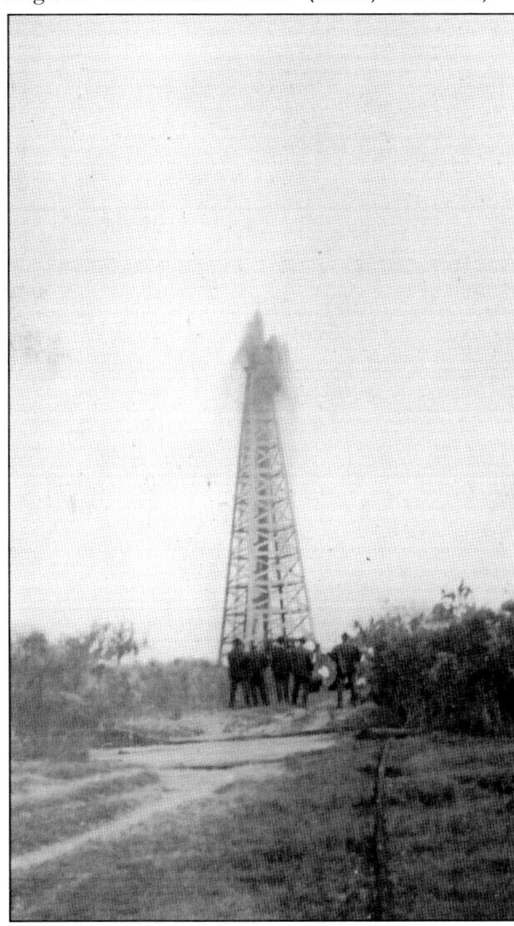

Important discoveries of oil and gas wells all over the Houma area led to major innovations in other industries, such as the sugarcane business. It was J.H. Thatcher who was responsible for piping more than 20 sites during the years he served with the Terrebonne Gas Company. (THACS.)

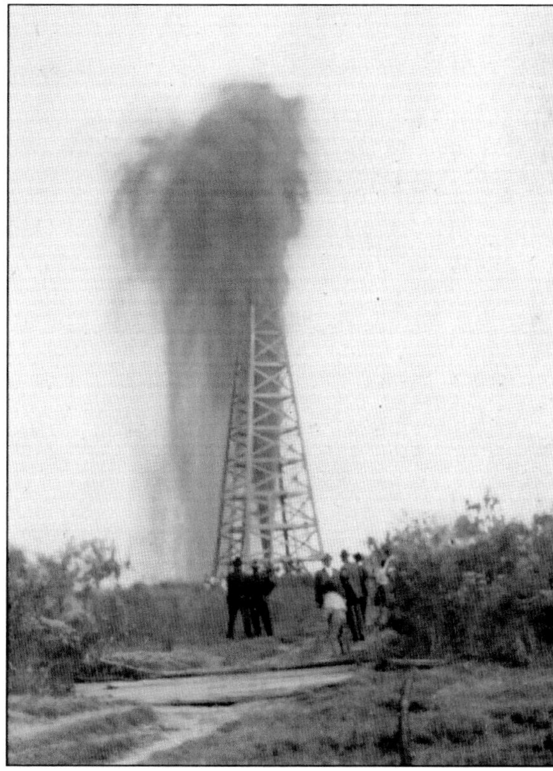

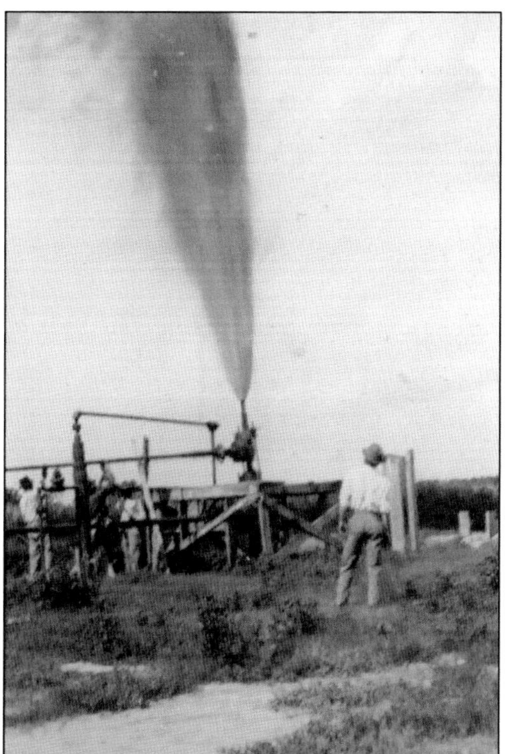

The industry was fledgling in these days, and numerous inventors and scientists devised plans, invented mechanical devices, and set out to best harness the power of oil and gas. The first blowout containment arrived on the scene in 1924. This was the first in a long list of innovations that would secure the safety of workers on the wells. (THACS.)

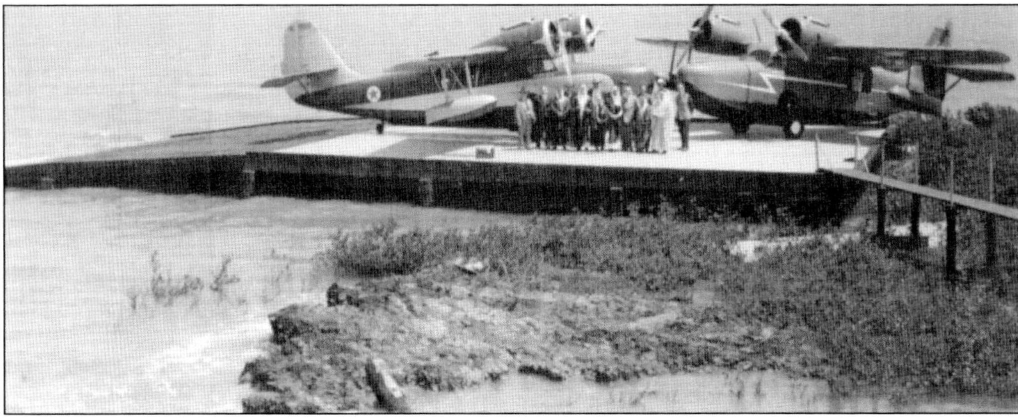

After the oil industry was established in Louisiana, major oil companies reached out to the other areas of the world that were potentially rich in oil. It was with Texaco that the uses, production, and drilling of oil were shared with countries like Saudi Arabia. The princes of Saudi Arabia were brought in to see the production facilities of Louisiana in an effort to promote global partnerships and insight on oil drilling. (Both, Dr. Chris Cenac Sr. collection.)

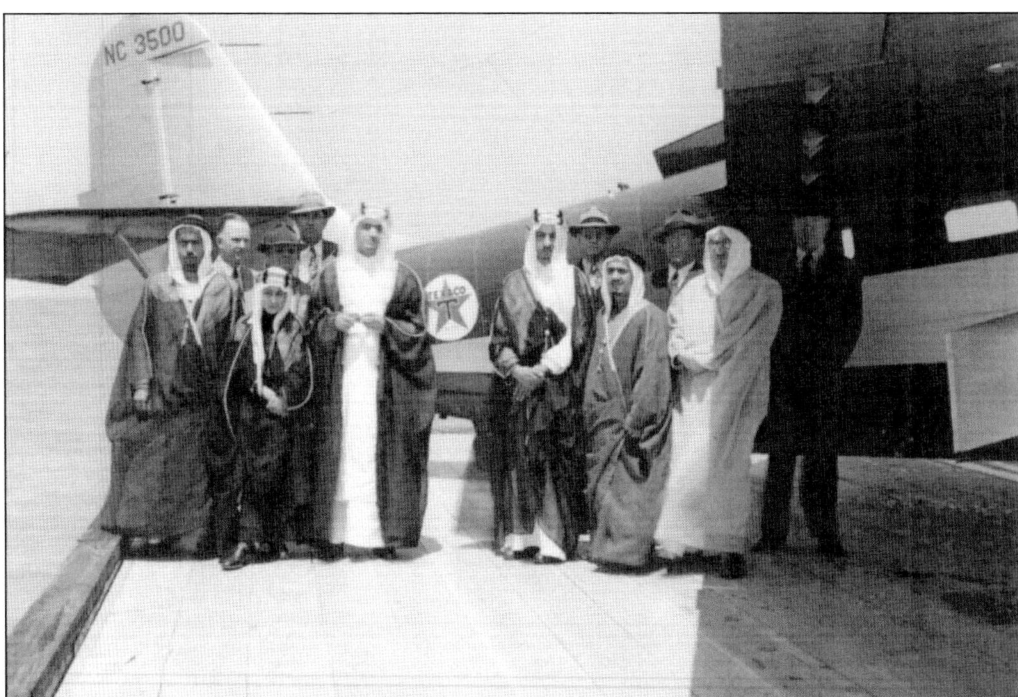

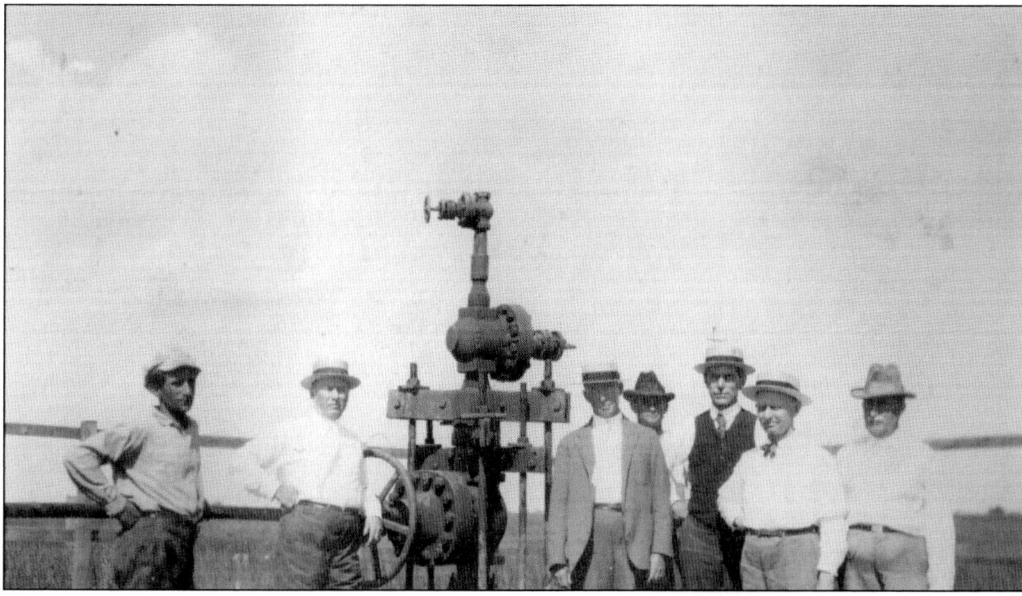

As with every big business that had nosed its way into Houma and the lands beyond, the men who established the oil and gas fields were to be the patriarchs of a burgeoning economy; these forefathers would forge a lasting testament of ingenuity and perseverance to last through the next century. (THACS.)

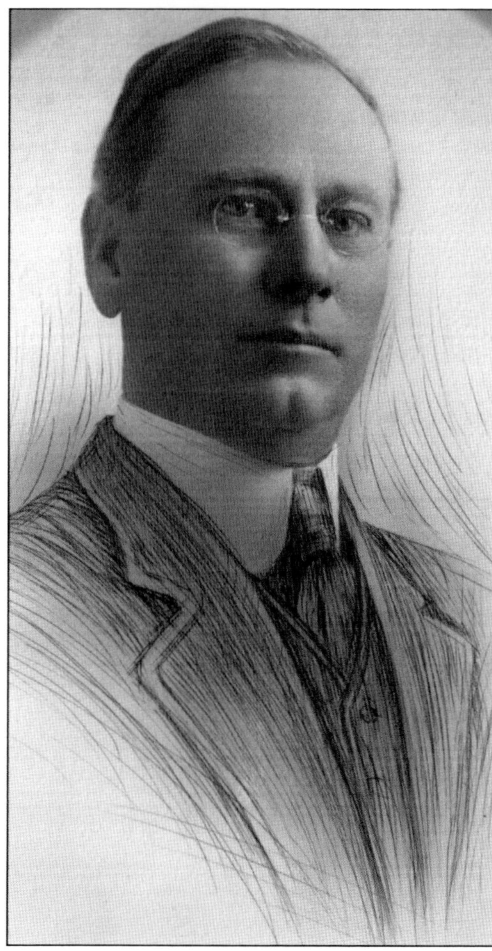

The onset of big oil and gas companies in Houma was not solely the act of one man. J.H. Thatcher was certainly a catalyst to better innovations, lifestyles, and improvements in daily life, but he just scratched the surface of how life would be in Houma for the generations to come. (THACS.)

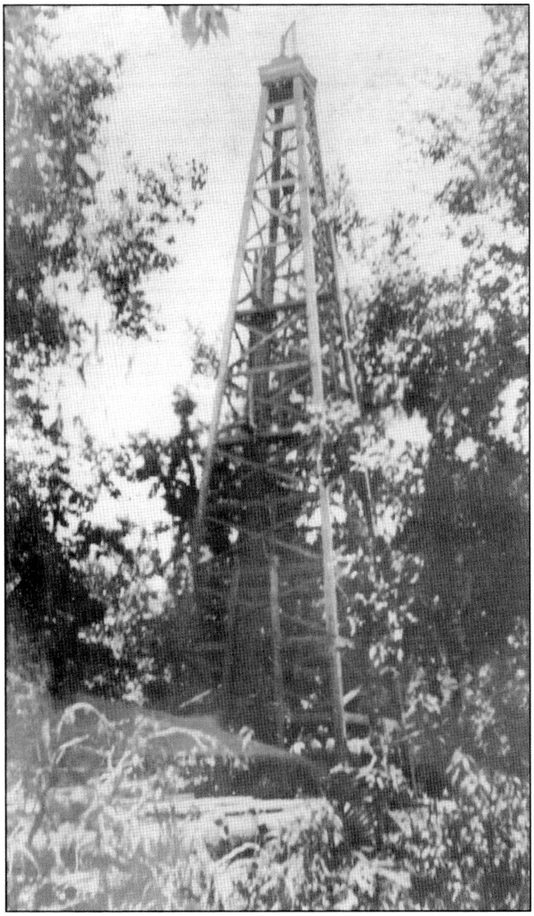

With humble beginnings on a plantation called Hardscrabble, Wallace and Victoria Ellender had a son born September 24, 1890, in a little Acadian-style cottage. This child, Allen Joseph Ellender, would go on to be a well-known US senator and Terrebonne's most famous son. His father and uncle, along with Allen Sanders, owned the Lower Terrebonne Refining and Manufacturing Company. Later, Allen Ellender himself would own lands used for truck farming and eventually would produce oil. These wells—such as Ellender Well No. 2, shown here—would help secure the futures of his 13 grandchildren born to his only son, Dr. Allen J. Ellender in Houma. (Both, THACS.)

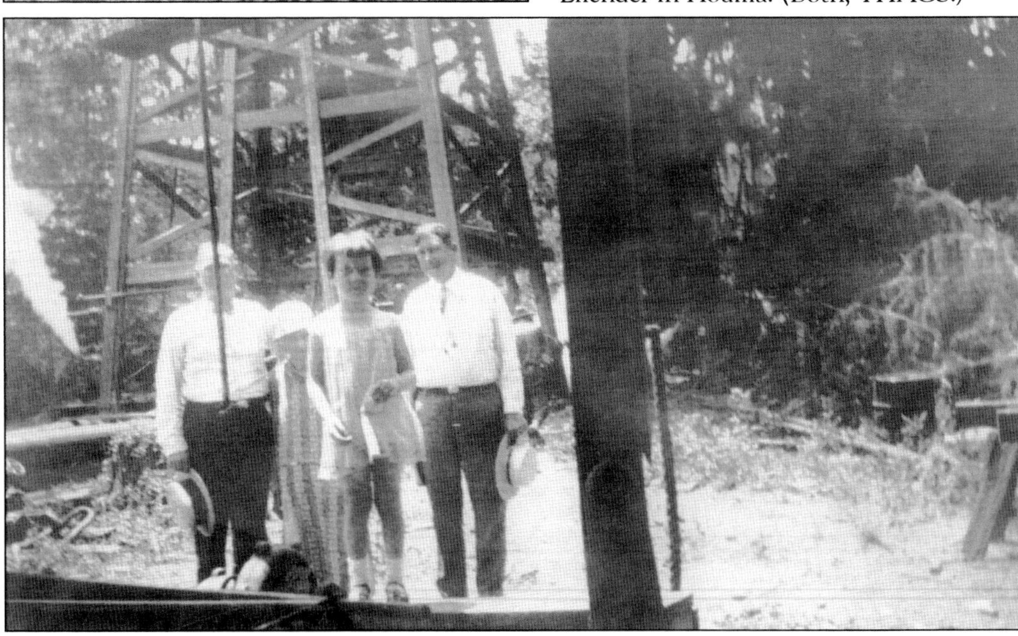

Five

Industrial Modernization

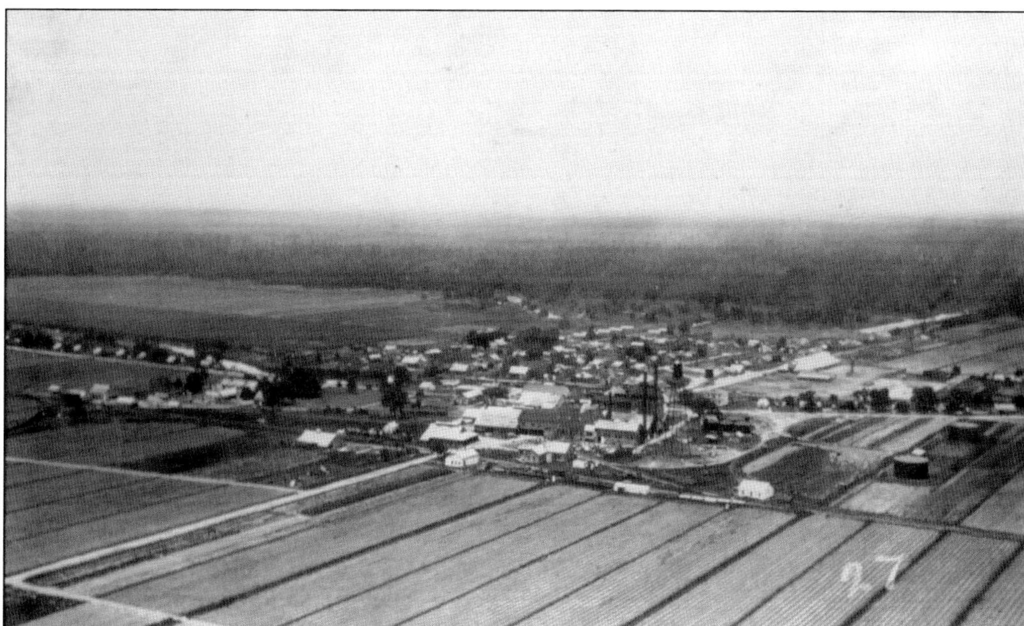

With the discovery of natural gas in the parish, the major industrial giants were able to add improvements to their industries. Six major sugar factories took advantage of this opportunity, and it was these innovations that secured a previously nonsecurable market from the 1930s to the 1970s for Houma industries, such as the refurbished refinery at Southdown Plantation, which would eventually be called Southdown Sugar. (THACS.)

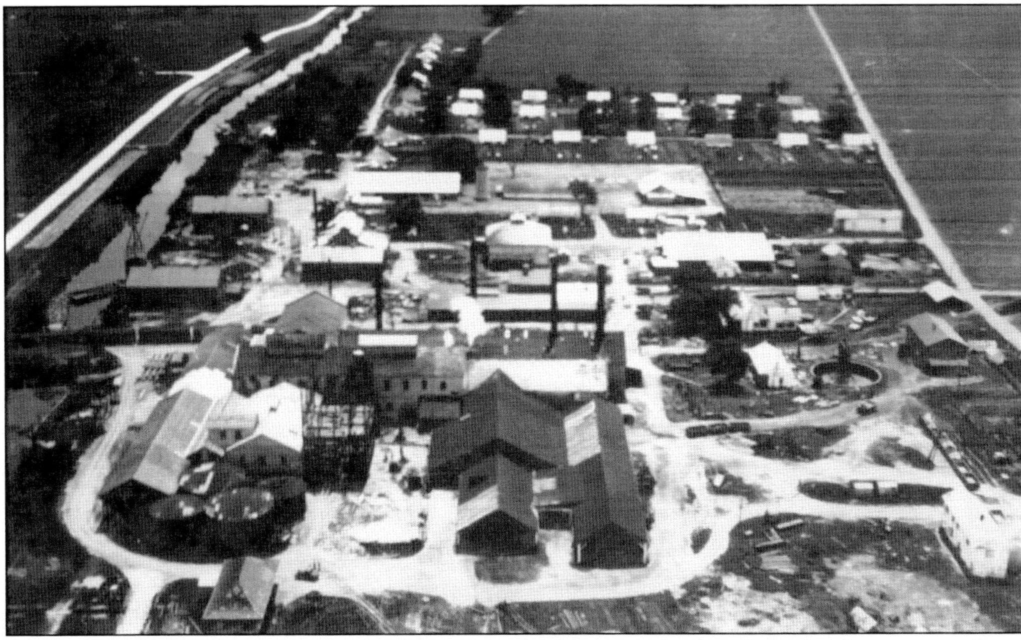

These images of Southdown were taken in 1920 (above) and 1970 (below). The sugar mill ran continuously for 130 years from 1848 until 1978, employing the people of Houma. Three major fires over the years required portions of the mill to be rebuilt, but each time it was made better and more efficient than the last version of itself. The first structure, in 1848, was made of bricks that were fired on a kiln on the property like the existing Southdown manor house and original slave quarters had been. Subsequent builds included steel and other metals as they became available. (Both, THACS.)

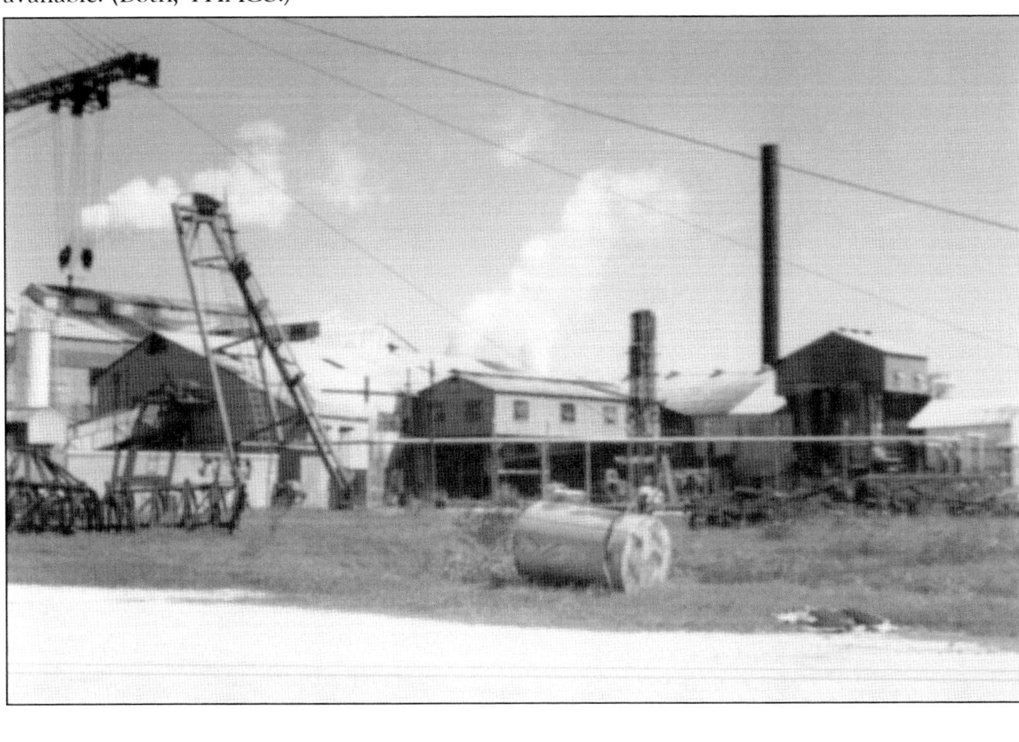

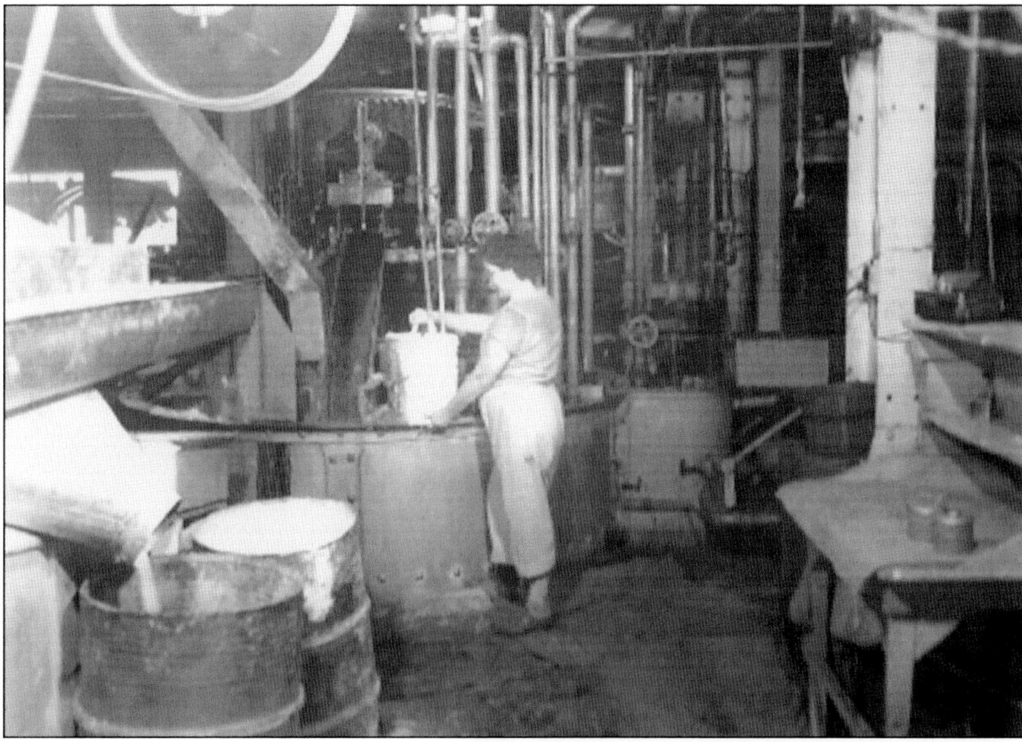

During times of war, the plantation saw hardships but kept the mill running. The Civil War most affected the mill because of the uprisings of the slaves at Southdown. In World War I, the high school boys were pulled in to do the work of the leaving soldiers, and in World War II, women became a primary source of workers. The photograph above shows Dora Hernandez working the blow-up tanks used for clarification of liquid sugar. The photograph at right shows a sugarcane washer. (Both, THACS.)

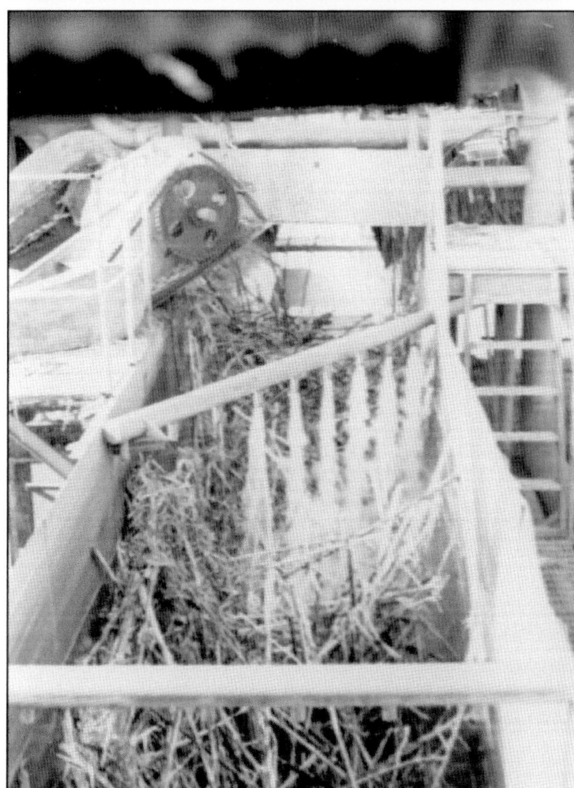

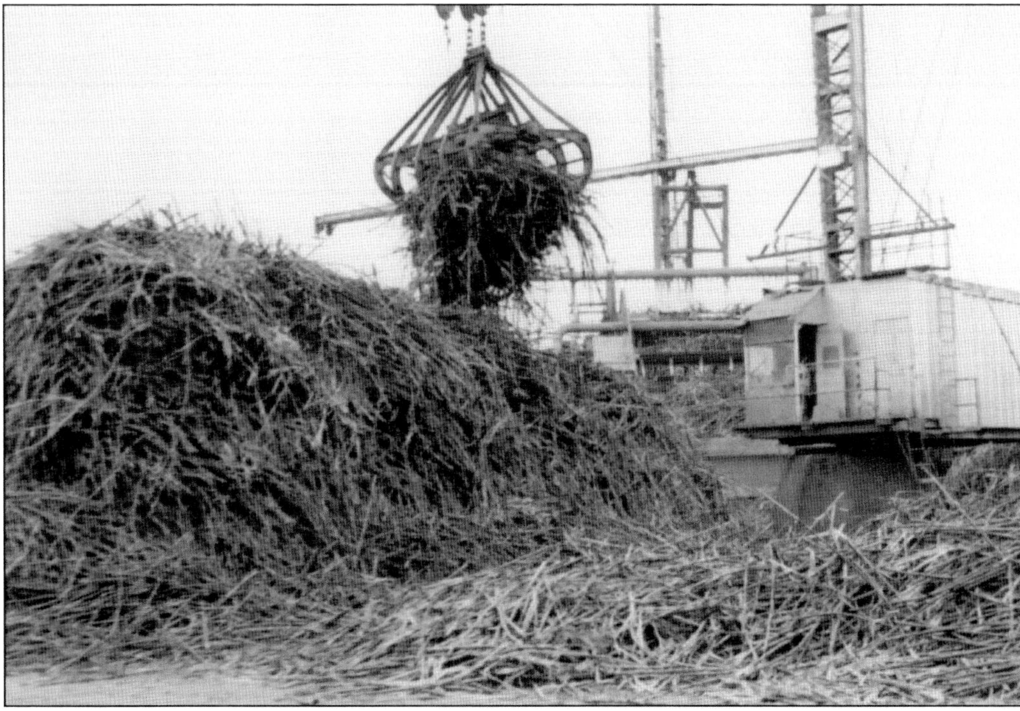

The days of mules and wagons were no longer, although the mill did still use this method up through the 1950s for hauling. The automated cranes enabled several thousand more pounds of cane to go through the process. From 1974 through 1977, according to Francis Mattingly, the capacity of the Houma Division of Southdown Sugars, Inc., was 3,800 tons of cane processed every 24 hours. In 1928, the Fulton Iron Works Company of St. Louis, Missouri, installed a modern sugar mill with the capacity of 2,000 tons of sugar per day. Besides the Houma Division, Southdown had a Vacherie Division, a Thibodaux Division, and a White Castle Division. (Both, THACS.)

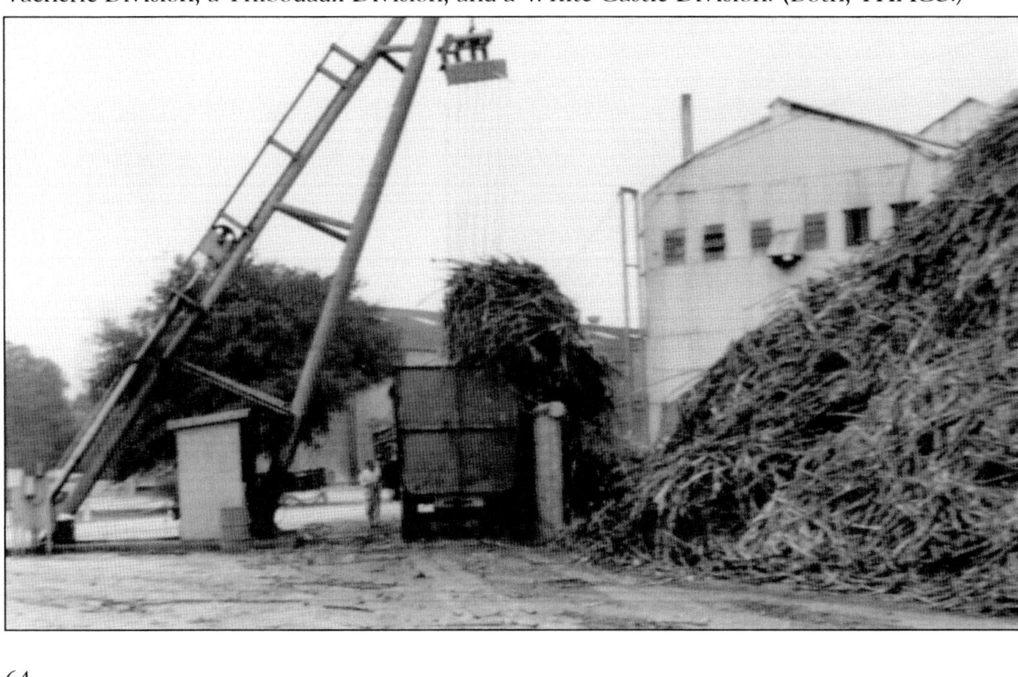

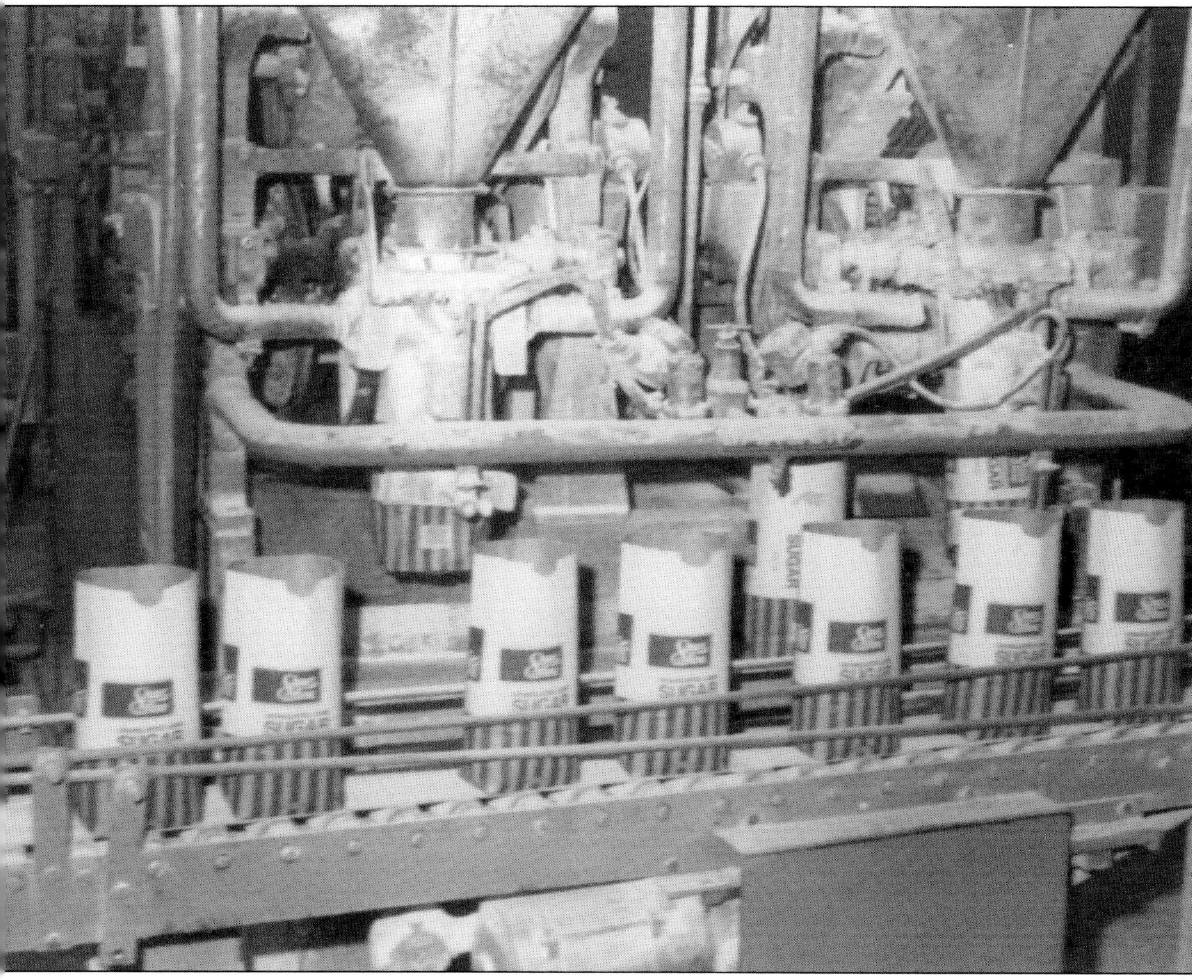

Five-pound bags of sugar make their way around the assembly line at Southdown Sugars, Inc. The process was manual and automated at this point in the history of the mill; in earlier times (before the time pictured), cloth sacks were used and each bag was filled by hand or, for larger bags, by shovel. Workers on this type of machine did not have to place the bags but were in control of the flow and were responsible for checking periodically for misses by the machines. (THACS.)

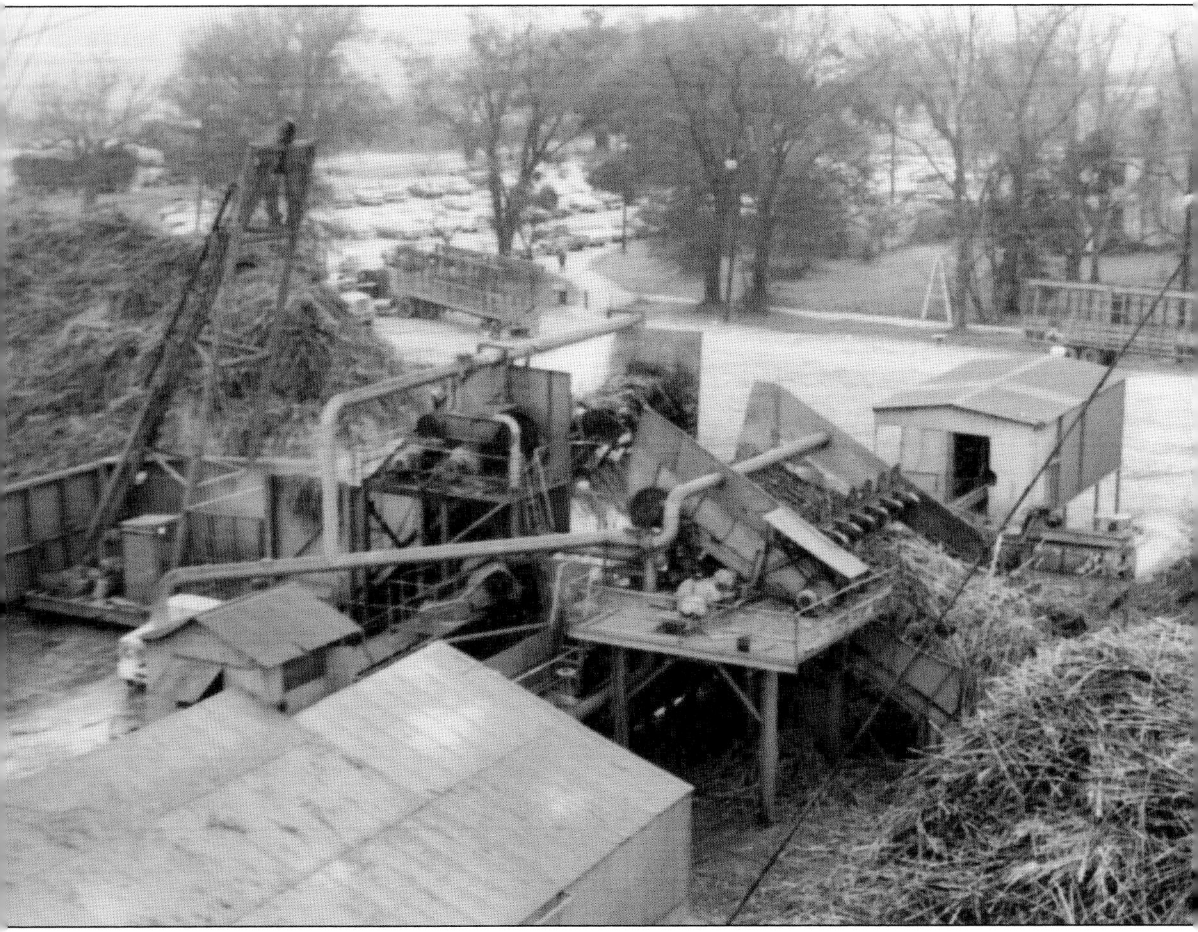

In the 1970s, after all the production improvements, Southdown Sugars was producing 25–40 tons per acre and 160 pounds of sugar per ton. Raw cane was crushed by rollers that weighed 12 tons and could apply up to 350 tons of pressure. More juice was crushed from the cane each time it passed through the rollers. The vital stage in the transformation of cane to sugar was the grinding of the stalks. This process of crushing and squeezing pushed the juices out to flow to filter tanks. This image is of the chopping machines used to get the cane down to a smaller size than the tall stalks. Eventually, the cane would be cut smaller in the field by tractors and combines, enabling the production process to be quicker. Southdown Factory not only ground cane and produced raw sugar; it refined it. The grinding capacity of the mill was 4,000 tons of cane per 24 hours, and the refining capacity was 1.25 million pounds per 24-hour period. (THACS.)

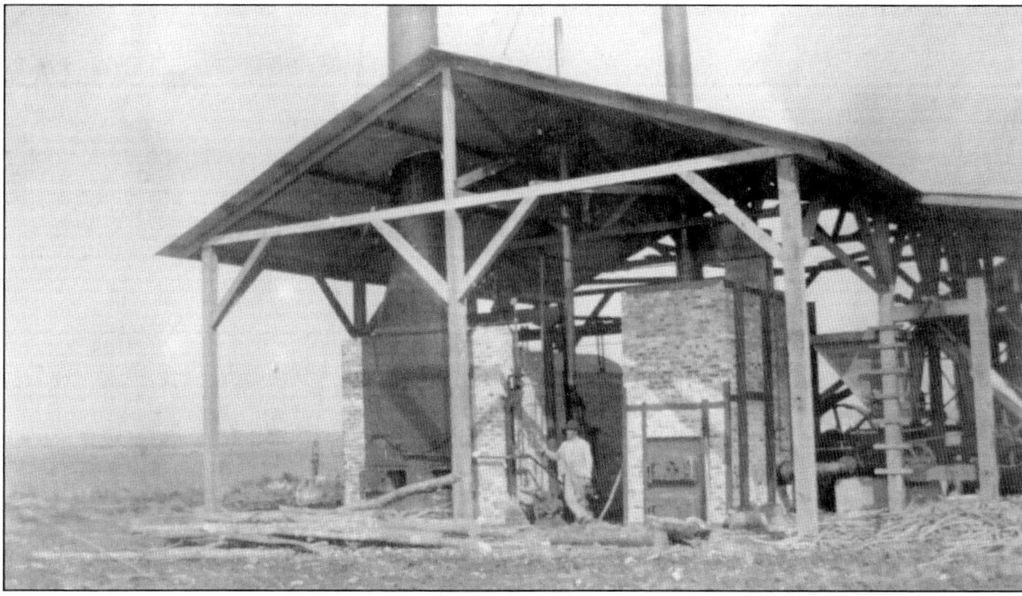

On December 10, 1937, the mill at Southdown Plantation went up in flames. The only things saved were the boilers and the milling section of the factory. The factory was rebuilt in time to grind the next crop, and the destruction enabled Southdown to get better equipment to increase efficiency and productivity. This was not the first or the last fire at the mill. William John Minor saw the destruction of the mill in the 1850s, and it was lost again under the H.C. Minor Company in the 1890s, but it was always rebuilt. The images shown are of two different furnace and boiler operations at Southdown, built about 100 years apart. (Both, THACS.)

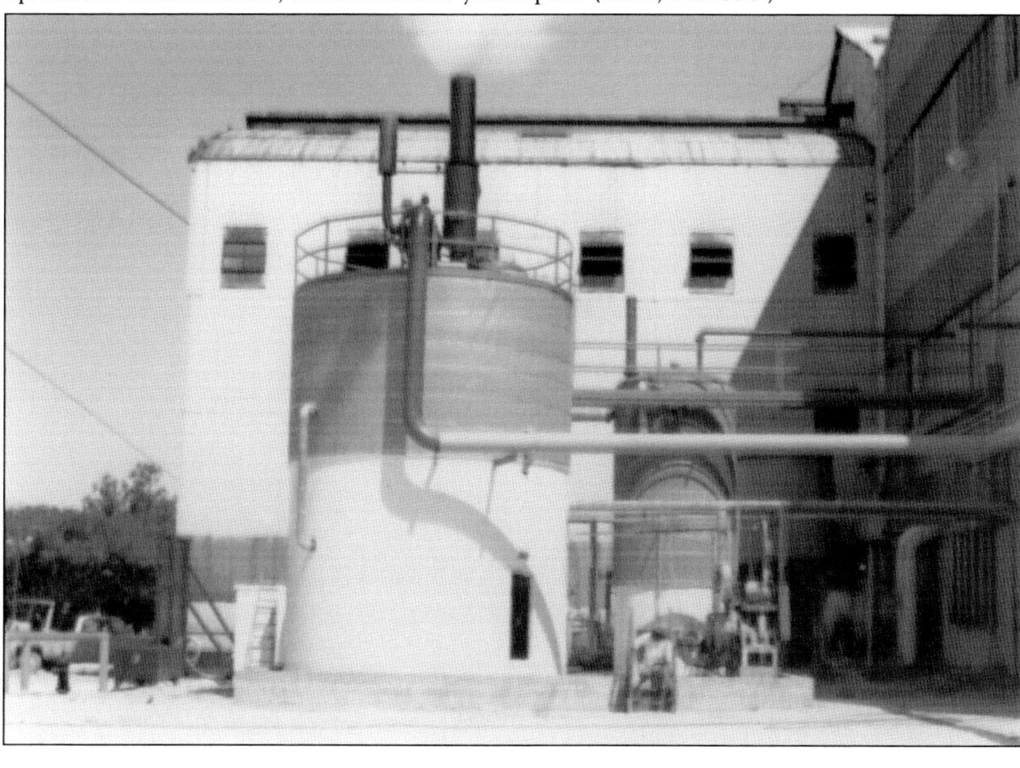

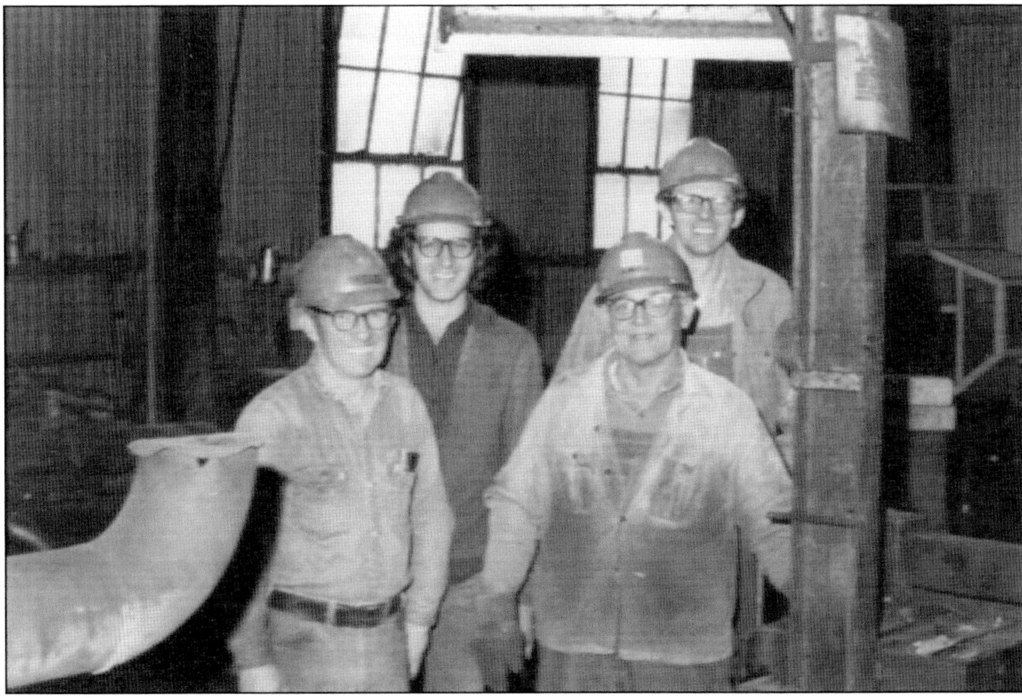

A mill and factory is only as good as the workers within. Southdown Sugars was a tight-knit group—almost a family—during the 1970s. There were workers in the warehouse, machine shop, laboratory, maintenance, and purchasing department, and there were multiple positions within each of these, such as superintendents, directors, manager, and hourly wage earners. The machine shop was just one of the many areas that was pivotal to make up the whole of processing and refining. Unidentified maintenance department workers are pictured above. Pictured below, from left to right, are Olden Freeman, Mary Boudreaux, E.J. Bonvillain, and John Campbell near the front office. (Both, THACS.)

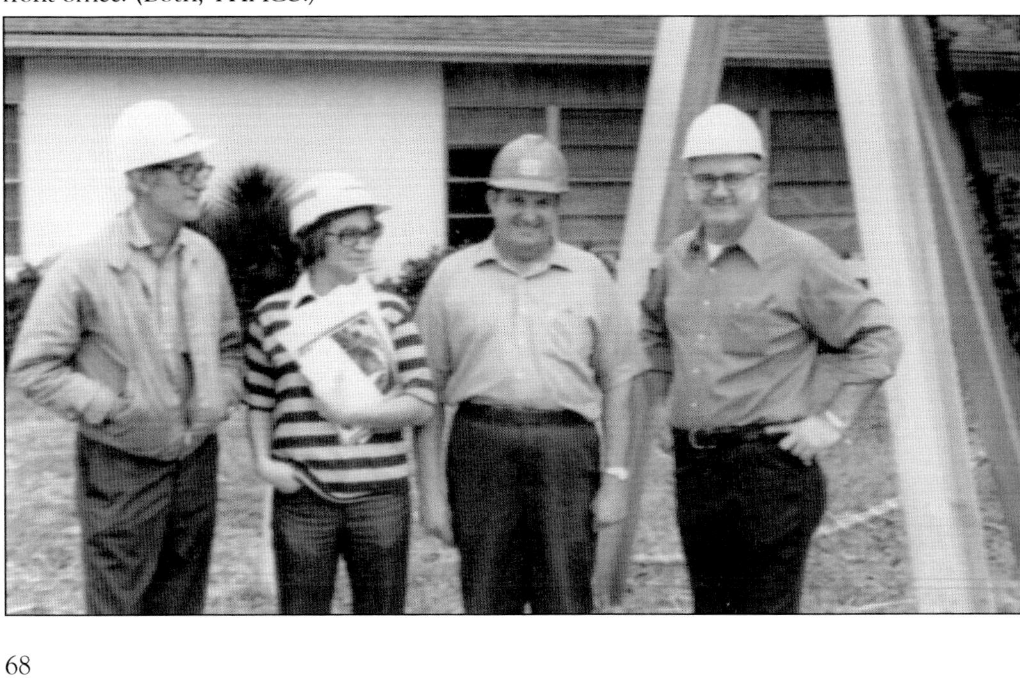

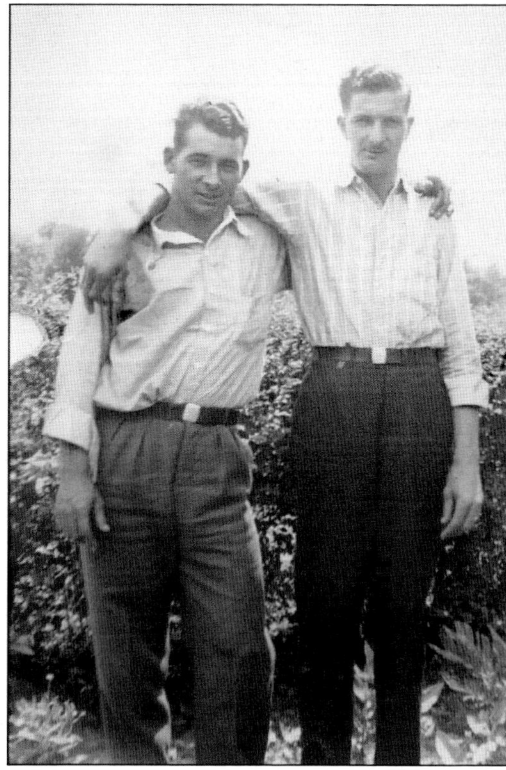

Ivy Bonvillain (right) worked for Southdown for most of his career, until the mill closed in at the end of 1977. His friend (on the left) is unidentified. Ivy is pictured below with his whole family: his wife, Velma; their 10 children; and son-in-law Speedy Collins (back row, far left). Velma worked in the mill as a small package operator. In the history of the Bonvillain family, there was also the Wilfred Bonvillain family. Wilfred was born on Southdown and worked for over 50 years for the plantation. He and his wife, Hazel, had six children who were also raised at Southdown—Leroy, Merilyn, Gail, Myron, Lolita, and Steve. (Both, THACS.)

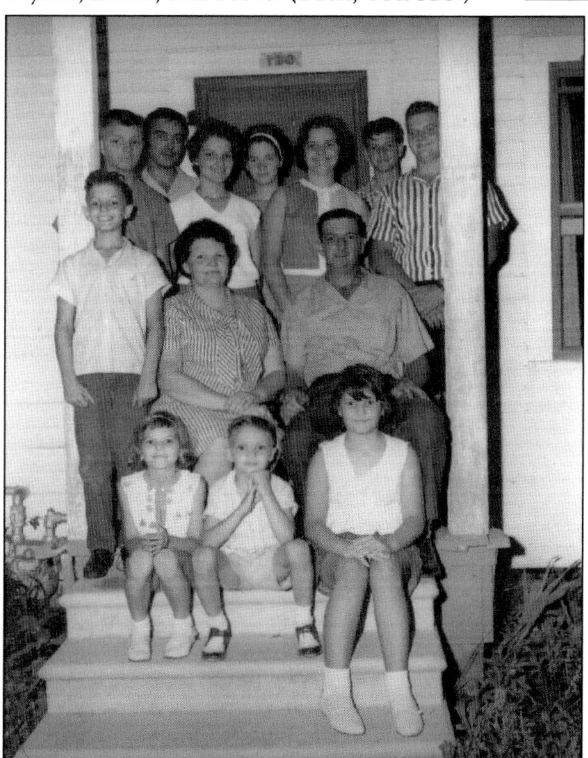

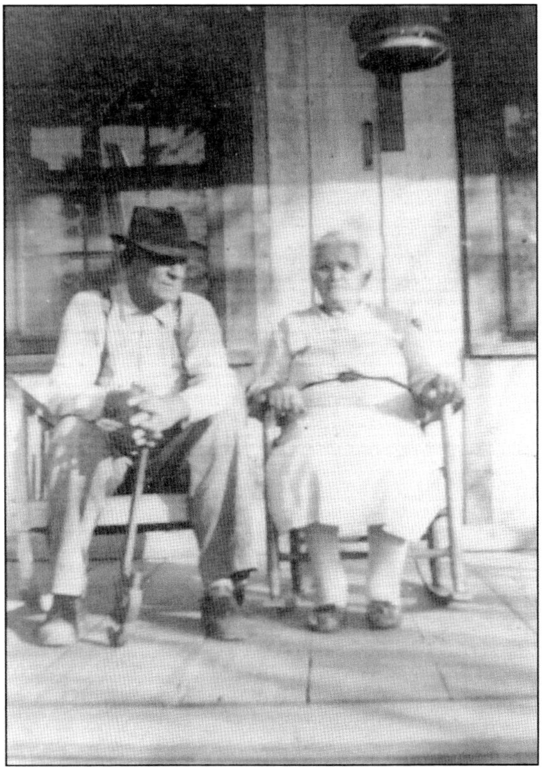

The Freeman family also had a long history at the plantation. Pictured are Joe and Alfreda Freeman. The family of Joe's brother Olden Freeman occupied the top floor of the manor house for many years and also worked at the mill. It was said that another Freeman, Clinton Freeman, lived in the old slave quarters on the property, which has now been converted into a gift shop. (THACS.)

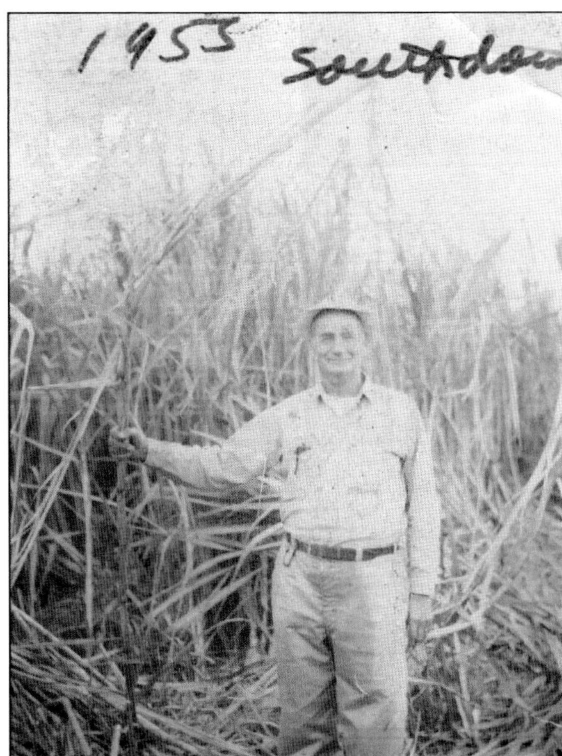

Prosper Toups Sr. was made overseer of Southdown Plantation in 1955. He had previously been overseer for many years at Greenwood Plantation, where he also raised his family. His son Prosper Jr. was at one time a board member for the museum and was an active participant in the biannual Marketplace arts-and-crafts show. Toups's assistant overseer was Ernest Daigle, who was at Southdown Plantation from 1950 to 1957. (THACS.)

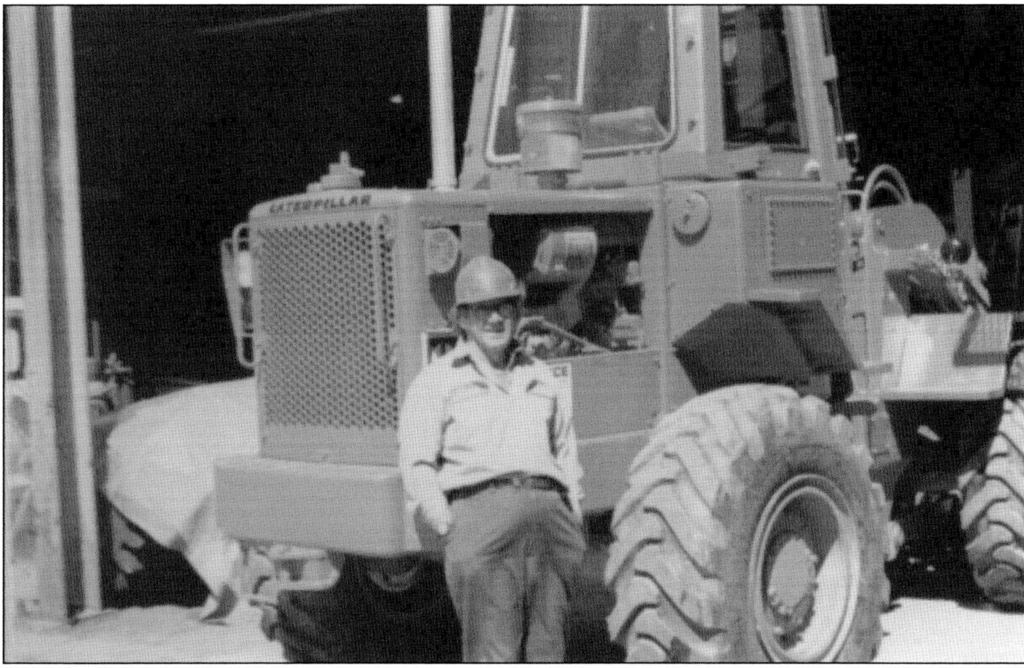

Pictured here standing in front of a tractor, Francisco "Frank" Valdez was a boiler operator. The system used in the early days of Southdown Plantation involved burning the leftovers, or bagasse, as fuel for the boilers. Eventually, natural gas made the boiler operation safer and more efficient. Burning the bagasse would, over time, cause a buildup of the burnt sugar material and could cause fires. (THACS.)

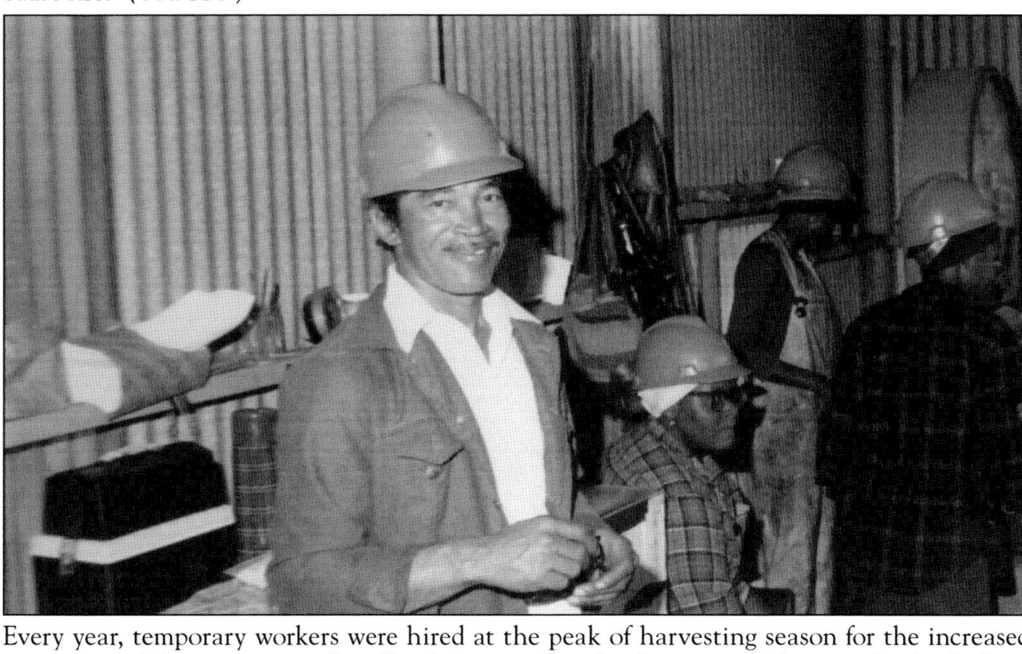

Every year, temporary workers were hired at the peak of harvesting season for the increased processing of the sugarcane, when Southdown mill and refinery ran 24 hours a day (with three eight-hour shifts). Carl "Cuz" Bailey, pictured here, was one of the many longtime workers. A worker was allowed to join the union, but it was not required. (THACS.)

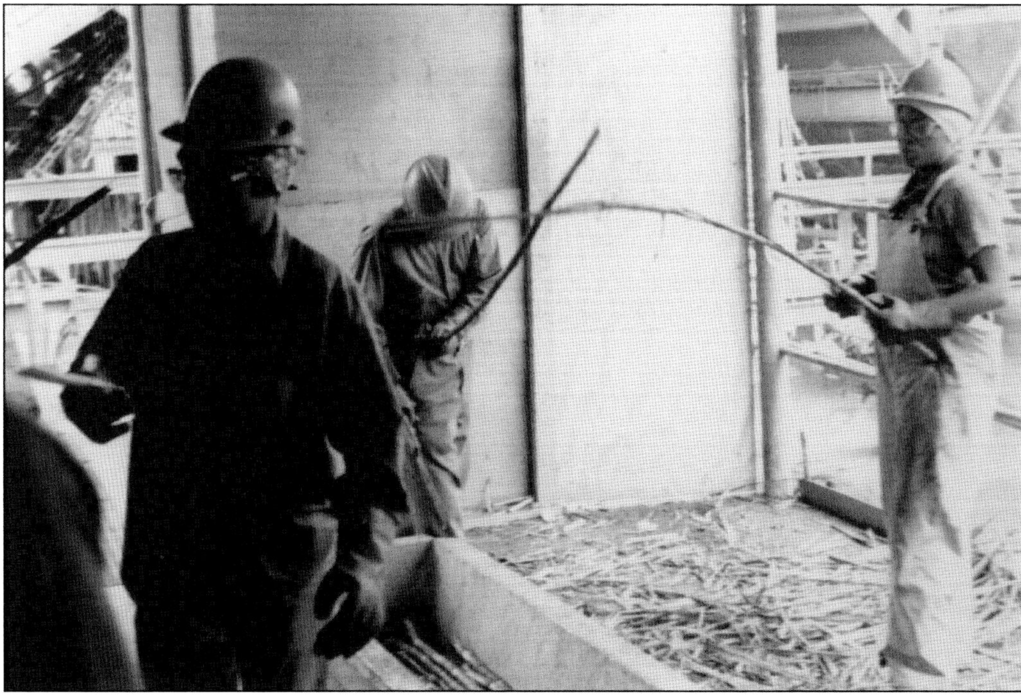

Some operations at the mill and refinery still required manual labor, such as selecting samples of cane during the many stages of the process for testing in the laboratory. Large companies, such as Coca-Cola, that purchased sugar from Southdown required analysis of each shipment before it left the facility. (THACS.)

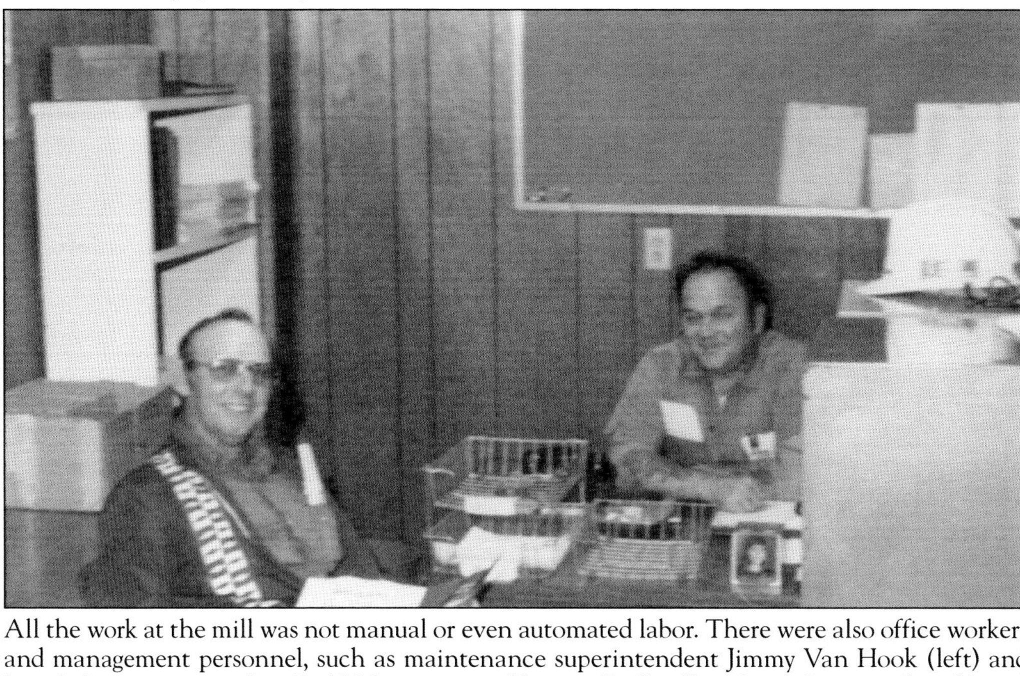

All the work at the mill was not manual or even automated labor. There were also office workers and management personnel, such as maintenance superintendent Jimmy Van Hook (left) and liquid plant superintendent Earl Hebert, pictured here in Earl's office. Southdown produced liquid sugar as well as the crystal form. (THACS.)

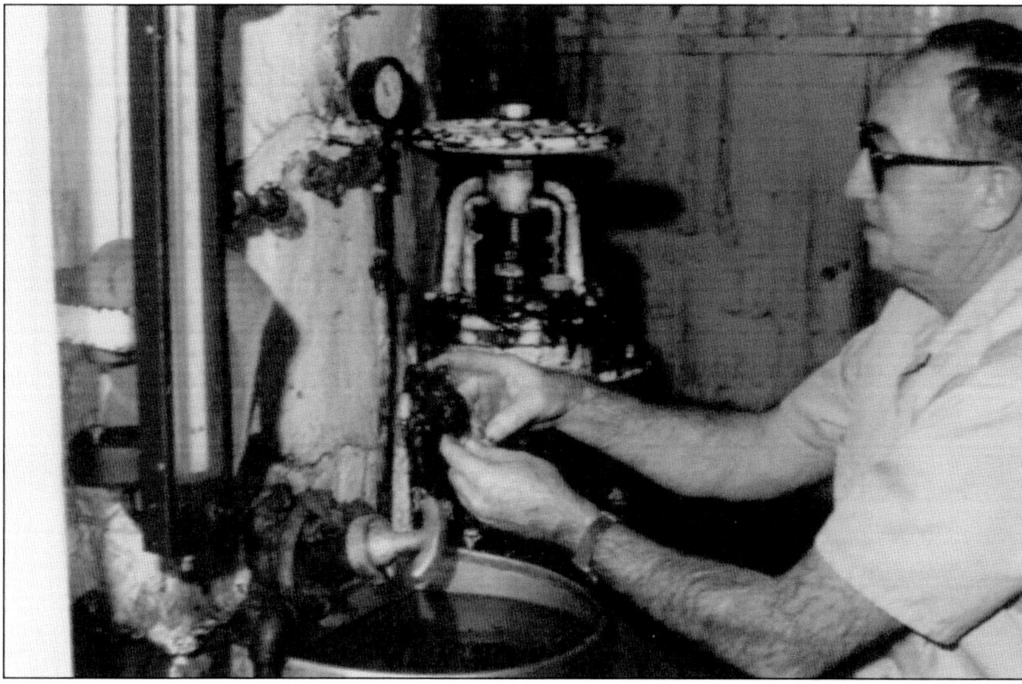

Olden Chaisson is pictured checking the grain in a vacuum pan. Quality control improved crystal size distribution and led to lower sugar color (both distinctions of good sugar) due to uniformity of fluid conditions within the vacuum pan. Good circulation prevents stagnant regions—hot and cold zones that can induce differences in the supersaturation level and crystal growth rate. (THACS.)

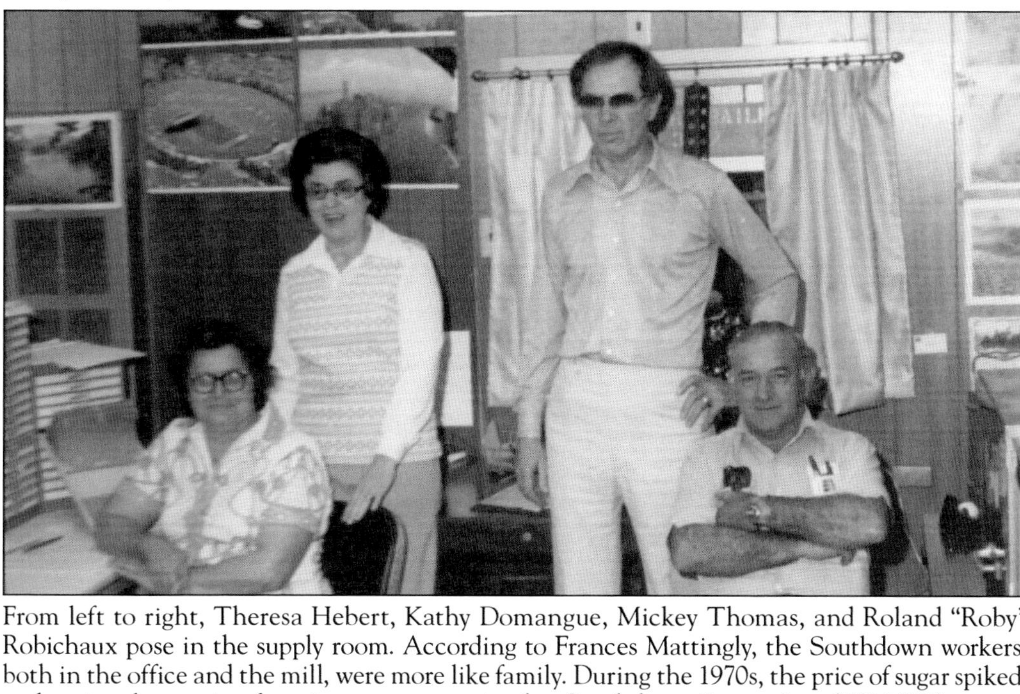

From left to right, Theresa Hebert, Kathy Domangue, Mickey Thomas, and Roland "Roby" Robichaux pose in the supply room. According to Frances Mattingly, the Southdown workers, both in the office and the mill, were more like family. During the 1970s, the price of sugar spiked, and national attention from investors was gained at Southdown Sugars, Inc. (THACS.)

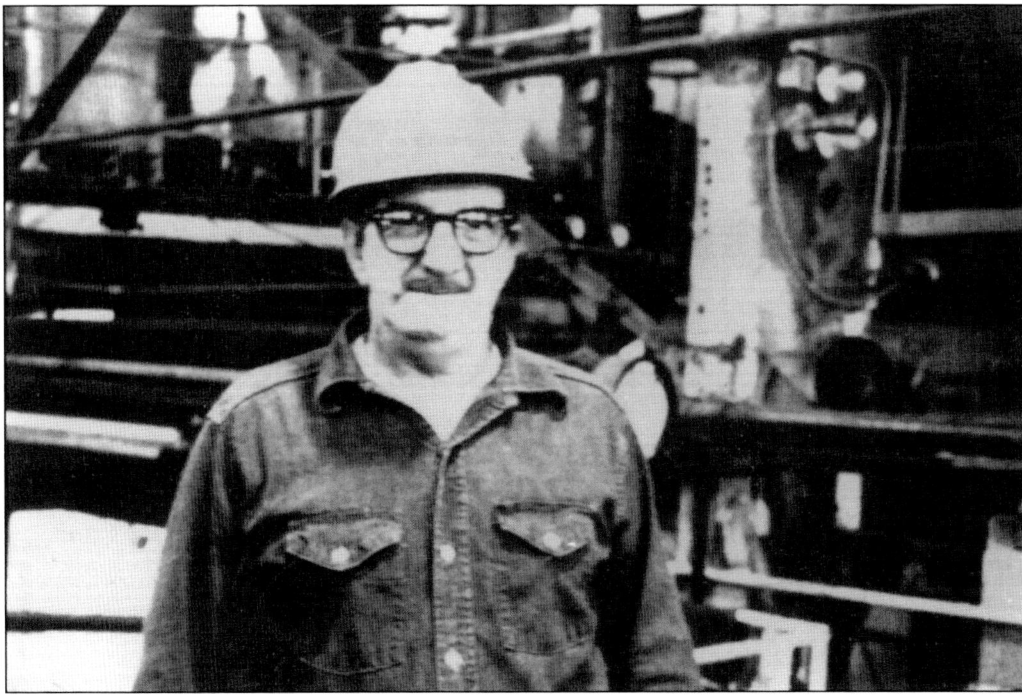

Ivy "Sucrose" Bonvillain, pictured here, worked at Southdown until the mill closed at the end of 1977. He started at Southdown as part of a Bonvillain family tradition. According to members of the Bergeron family, the Bergerons, Bonvillains, and the Eschtes were almost permanent fixtures in the history of Southdown Plantation. (THACS.)

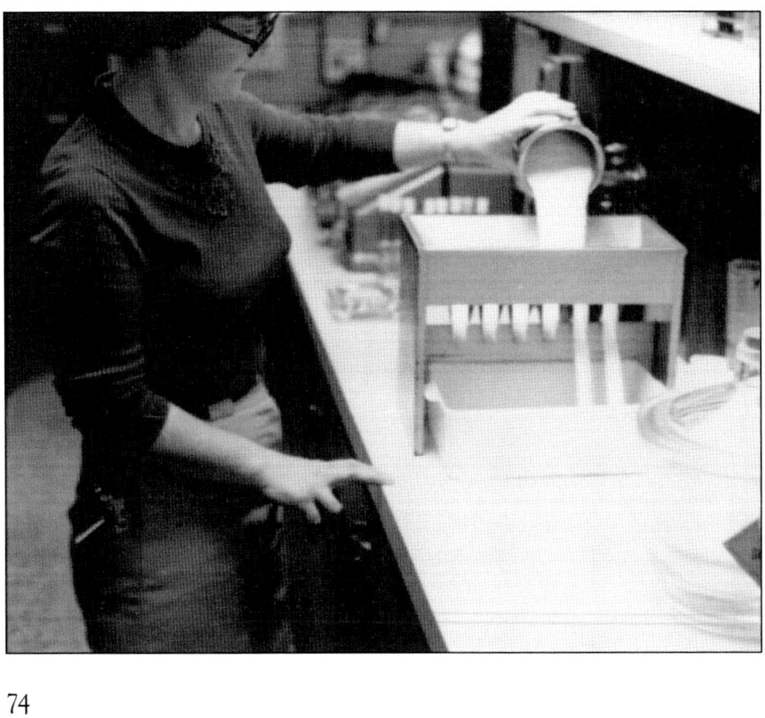

Frances Mattingly, pictured here, was the microbiologist in the testing lab and worked at Southdown Sugars, Inc., from 1974 until the mill's closure in 1978. One of her responsibilities was testing samples of the sugar that would be shipped from the mill. (THACS.)

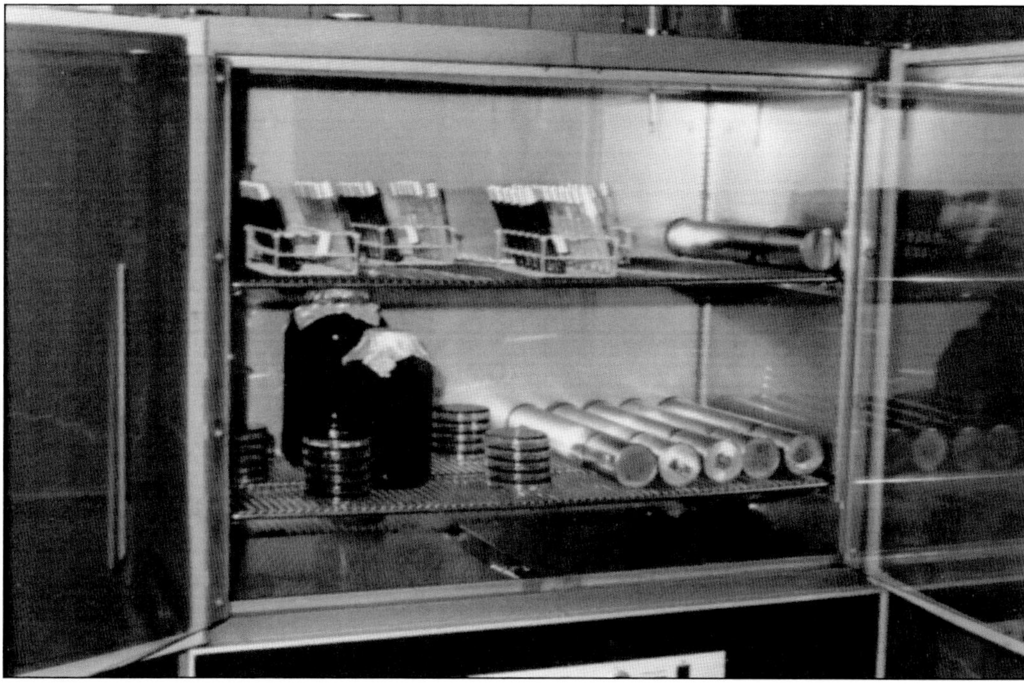

There were two labs at Southdown Sugars, Inc., that routinely tested samples of cane brought in and product going out. The refining of sugar simply removes all impurities and the surrounding plant matter, leaving only the pure sucrose. Raw sugar is approximately 96–98 percent sucrose. The nearly pure crystal is covered by a thin film of molasses, giving it the brown hue. The molasses coating contains sugar, water, plant material, and minerals. Refining the sugar transforms it into granulated sugar or brown sugar. The laboratories were utilized not only to satisfy the customer requirements but also to keep the quality of sugar at its highest. (Both, THACS.)

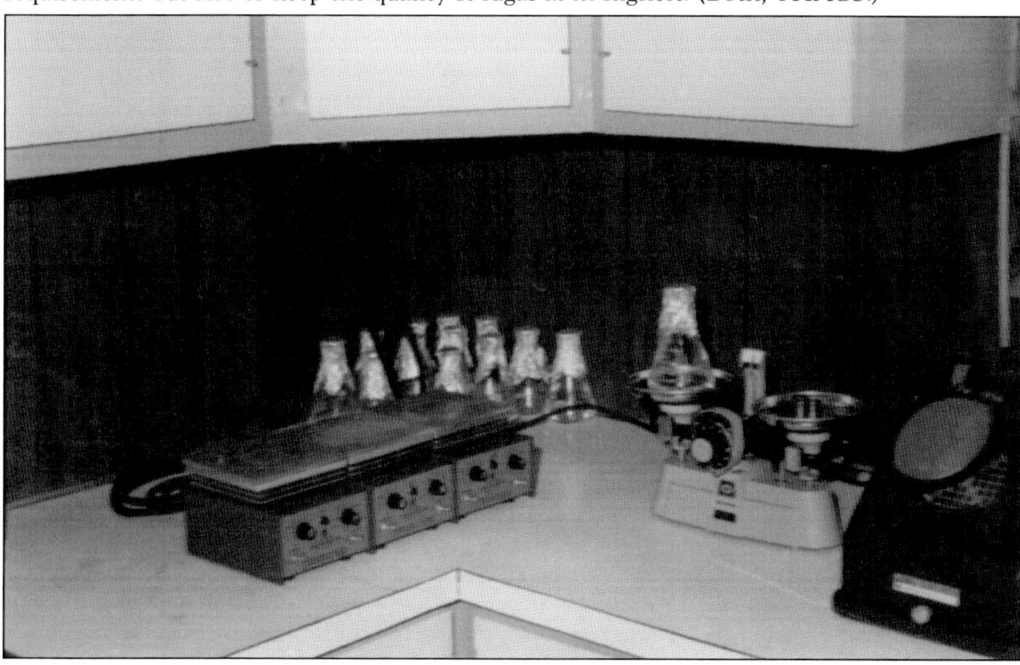

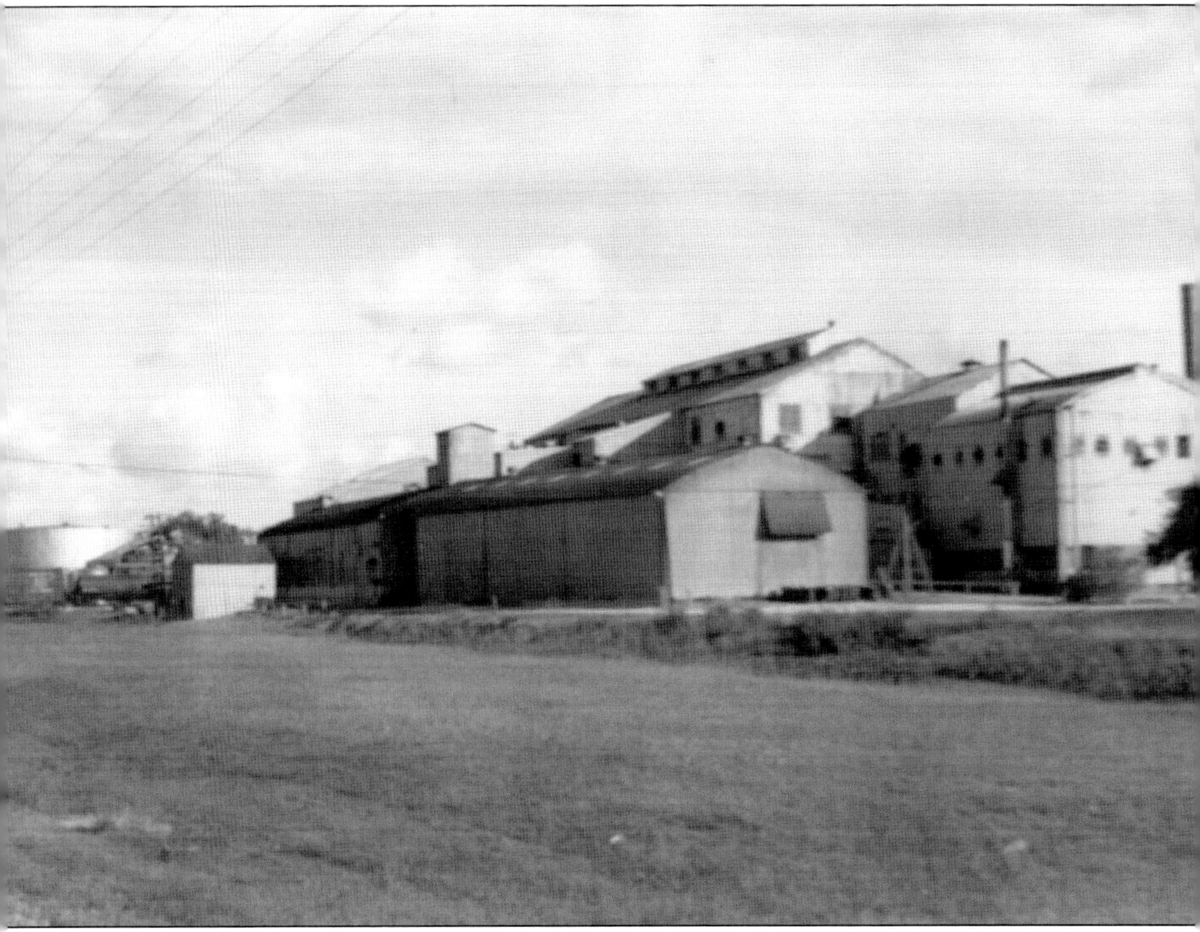

Southdown Sugar is pictured here prior to its closing. With prices of oil and natural gas on the rise in Houma, it was increasingly expensive to run the mill. Pieces of the property were being sold off for the development of nearby subdivisions, such as Southdown West, and eventually, the profit of selling off more property for development won out in the eyes of the investors in Southdown Sugars, Inc. It was announced in 1977 that the mill would be closing at the end of the year, putting at least 175 people out of jobs. Needless to say, the news did not go over well. The original mill builder was William John Minor. Subsequent owners were Realty Operators, Inc.; Houma Sugar Company, Inc.; Southdown Sugars, Inc.; Southdown Lands, Inc.; Southdown, Inc.; Southdown Land Company; and Vahli, Inc. (THACS.)

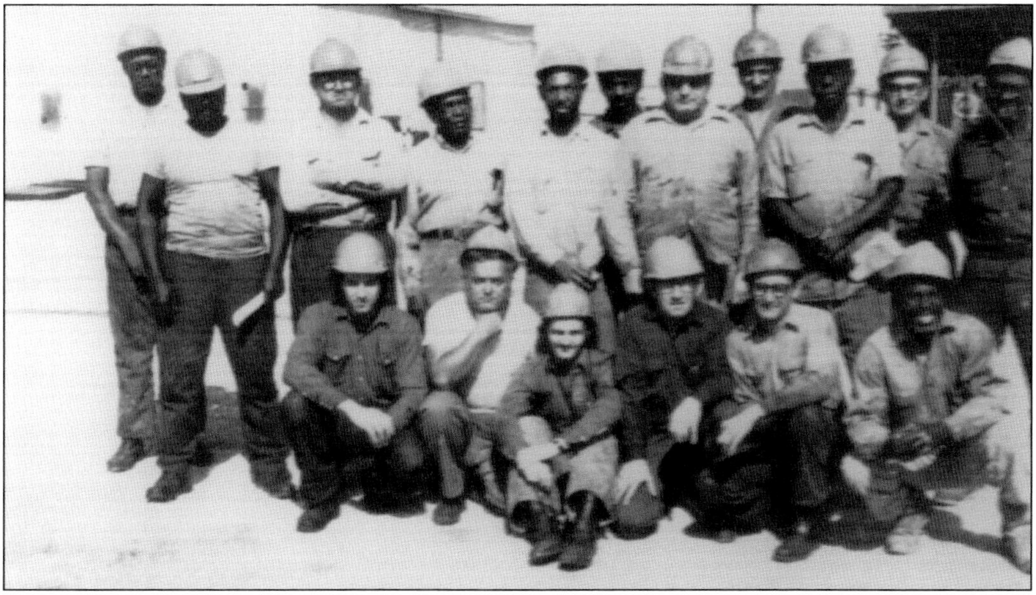

Several generations of families worked at Southdown through the years. Pictured at the exterior of Southdown Sugars, Inc., are Alred "Katin" Charles, Eugene McGuire, Lou Eschete, Nathan Campbell, Francis Bonvillain, Ivy "Sucrose" Bonvillain, Earl White, Arthur Samanie, Henry Jones, Don Freeman, Donald Crochet, Phillip Bonvillain, Alton "Red" Hebert, Earl Brunet, and Joe Lee Taplet. (THACS.)

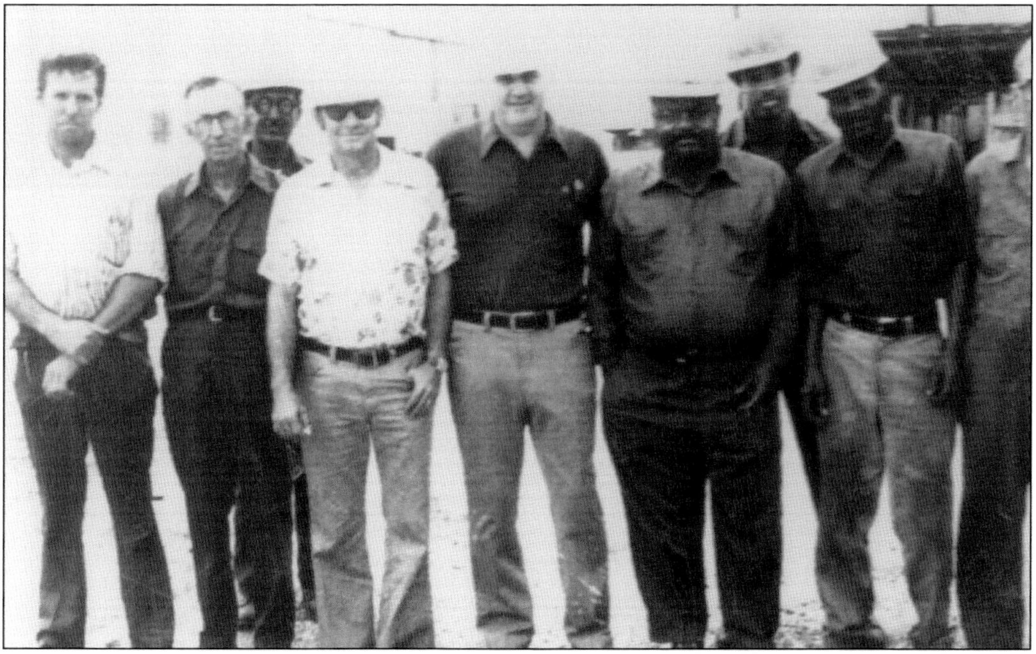

The surnames of employees at Southdown were a virtual history book of surnames for the parish. Slaves that came from Natchez, Mississippi, and Cajuns can trace their lineage through the years by employee rolls. Pictured are, from left to right, Milton Babin, Jack Bergeron, Ed Trosclair, Jimmy Van Hook, John Campbell, Warren Lyons, Anthony Collins, Clarence Scott, and Ivy Bergeron at the Southdown mill. (THACS.)

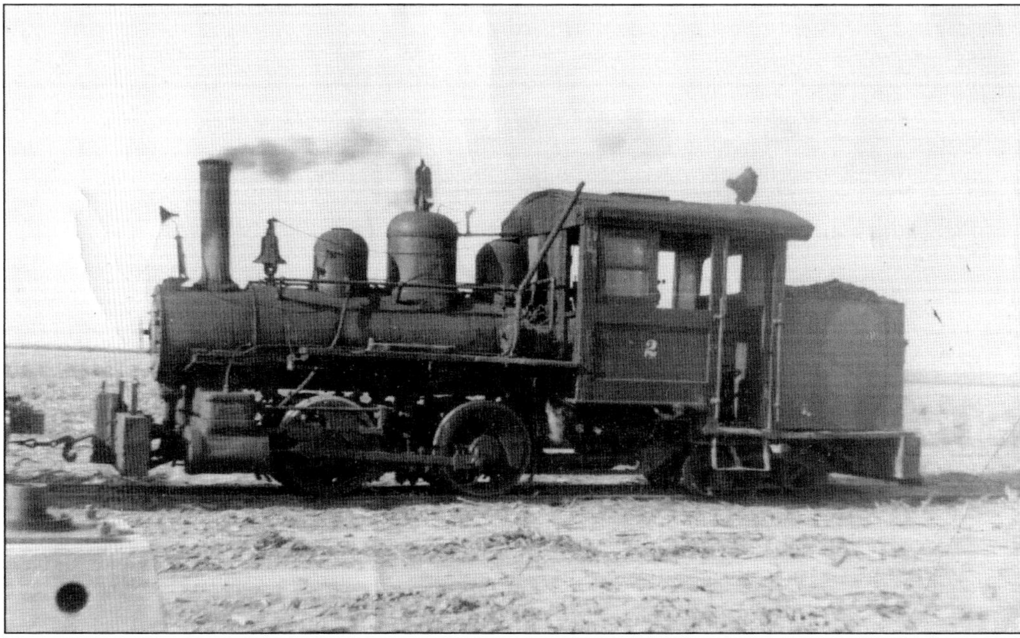

In 1955, Southdown Sugar, as it was called at that time, was still utilizing the older model of trains—the narrow-gauge rail lines that ran from central locations in the fields to the mill—but by the 1970s, newer, more efficient trains were being used at the mill. The newer train pictured was called the Patriot. The largest account during the 1970s was Coca-Cola; it received its product from Southdown Sugars, Inc., by railcar. One single shipment would fill a total of five cars, which held 190,000 pounds of bulk sugar each. (Both, THACS.)

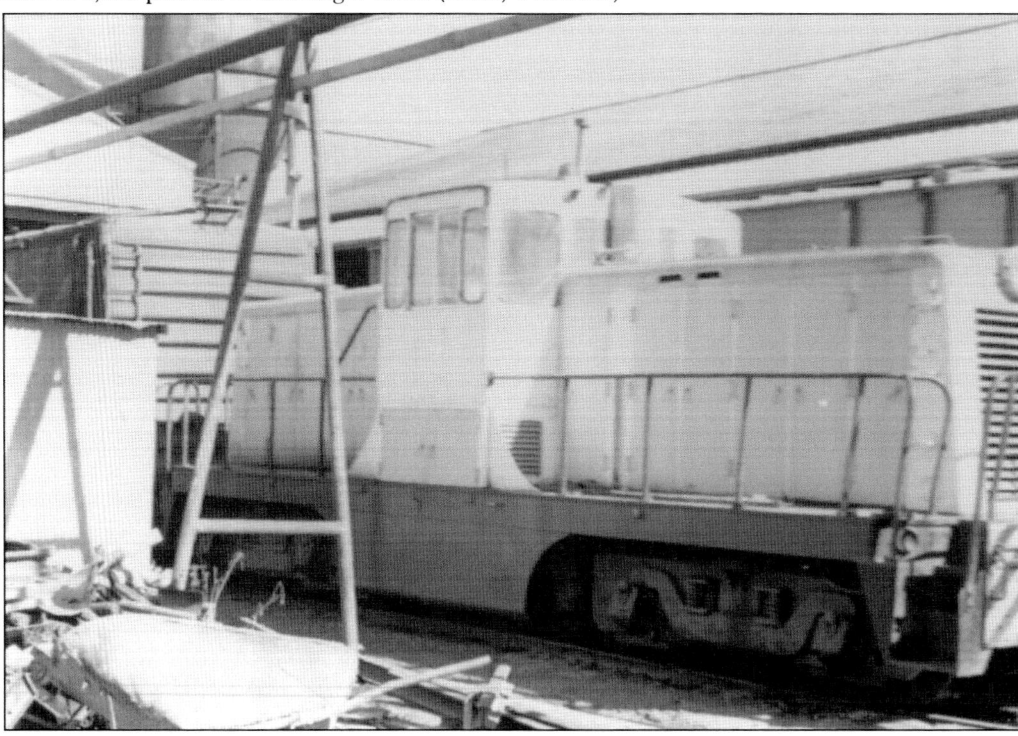

Milton Babin (right), an unidentified person (center), and Frances Mattingly (left), a microbiologist at the mill, are pictured at the mill discussing the samples tests to be taken. In 1931, the US Department of Agriculture built a sugarcane research center on property donated by the H.C. Minor Company approximately a mile from Southdown. The standards and tests established in this facility were the basis for the testing done at the sugar mill. (THACS.)

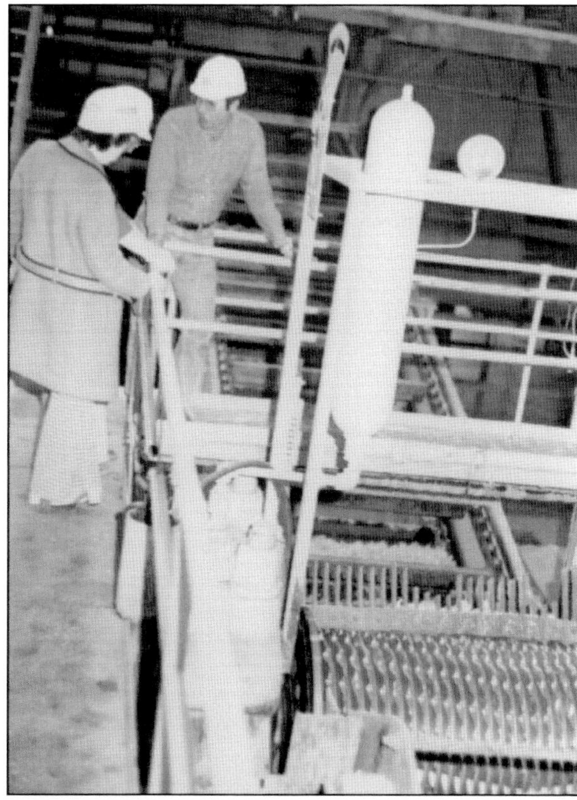

The crusher is the second part of the process for extracting the juice that will become sugar. First, it is washed. The first rollers are the crushers, and the next process is milling. Water is sprayed on the mat of crushed cane as it goes through the series of mills. (THACS).

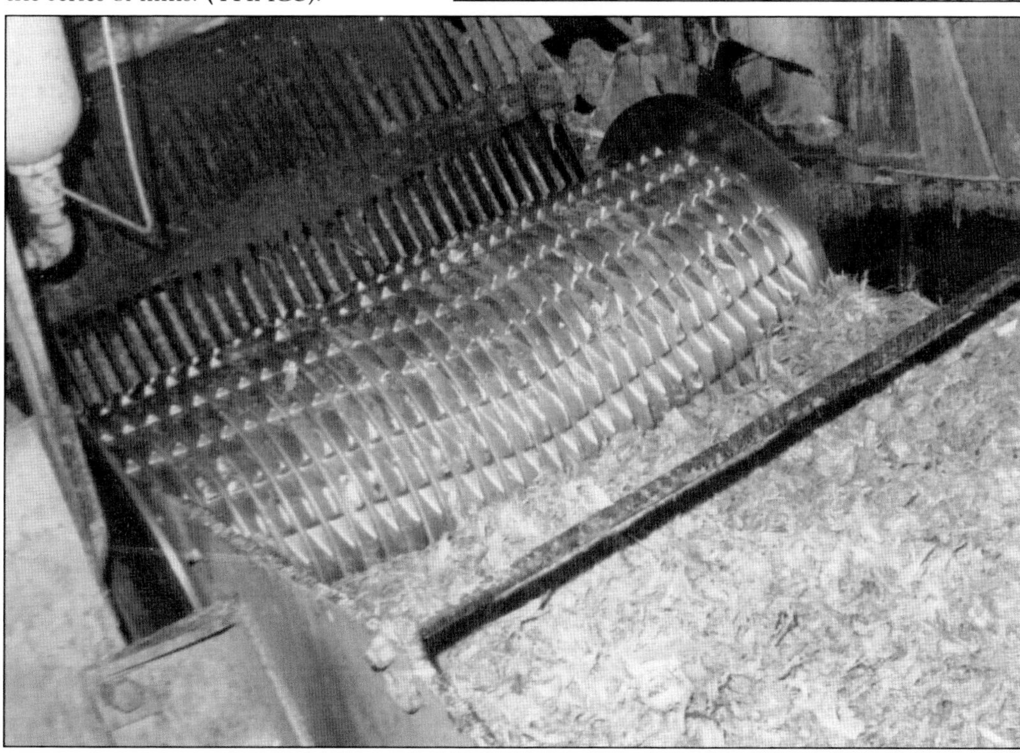

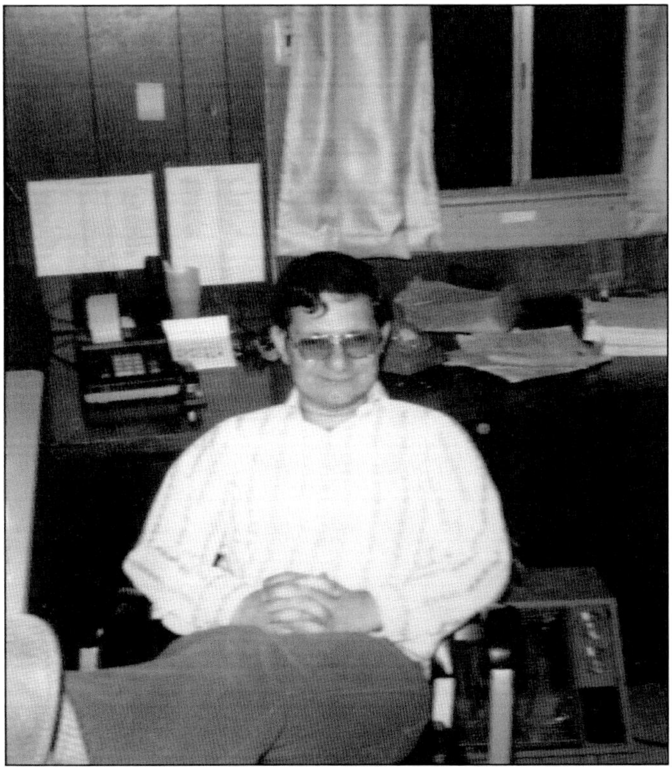

Hubert "Radar" Oncale (left) and Elphy LeBlanc (below) are pictured here in the office. Many people were adversely affected by the closing, but Southdown management kept several people around. In 1978 and 1979, the slow process of dismantling the mill began. The sale of properties around Southdown Plantation continued, and a group of citizens formed the Terrebonne Historical and Cultural Society to save the manor house adjacent to the property. The Valhi Company, which held Southdown Sugars, Inc., at that point, donated 4.5 acres of land and the buildings around the house. It was placed in the National Register of Historic Places soon afterward. (Both, THACS.)

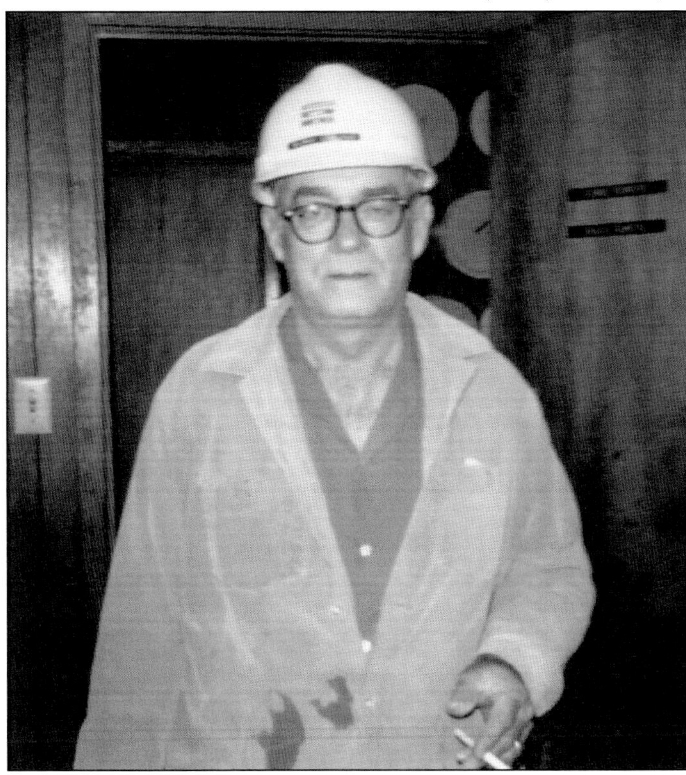

Six

Sen. Allen J. Ellender

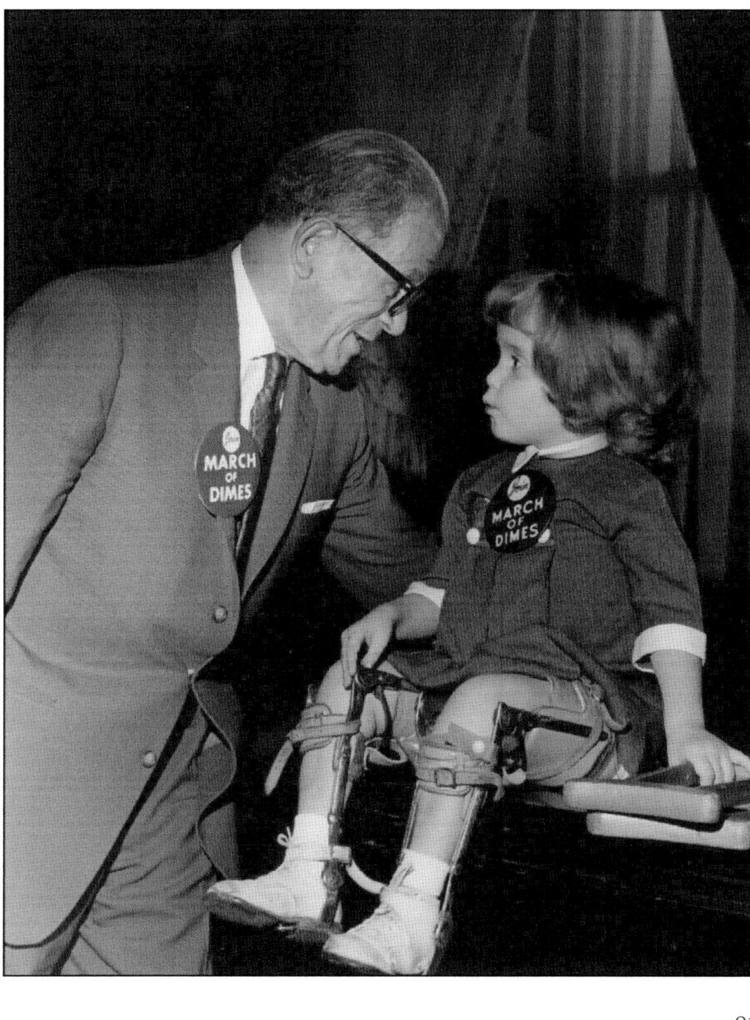

Sen. Allen J. Ellender is pictured with an unidentified girl who received assistance from the March of Dimes. During Ellender's extensive political career, he served under US presidents Franklin D. Roosevelt, Harry S. Truman, Dwight D. Eisenhower, John F. Kennedy, Lyndon B. Johnson, and Richard M. Nixon—through the Great Depression, World War II, the Cold War, McCarthyism, the Korean War, the civil rights movement, and the Vietnam War. (THACS.)

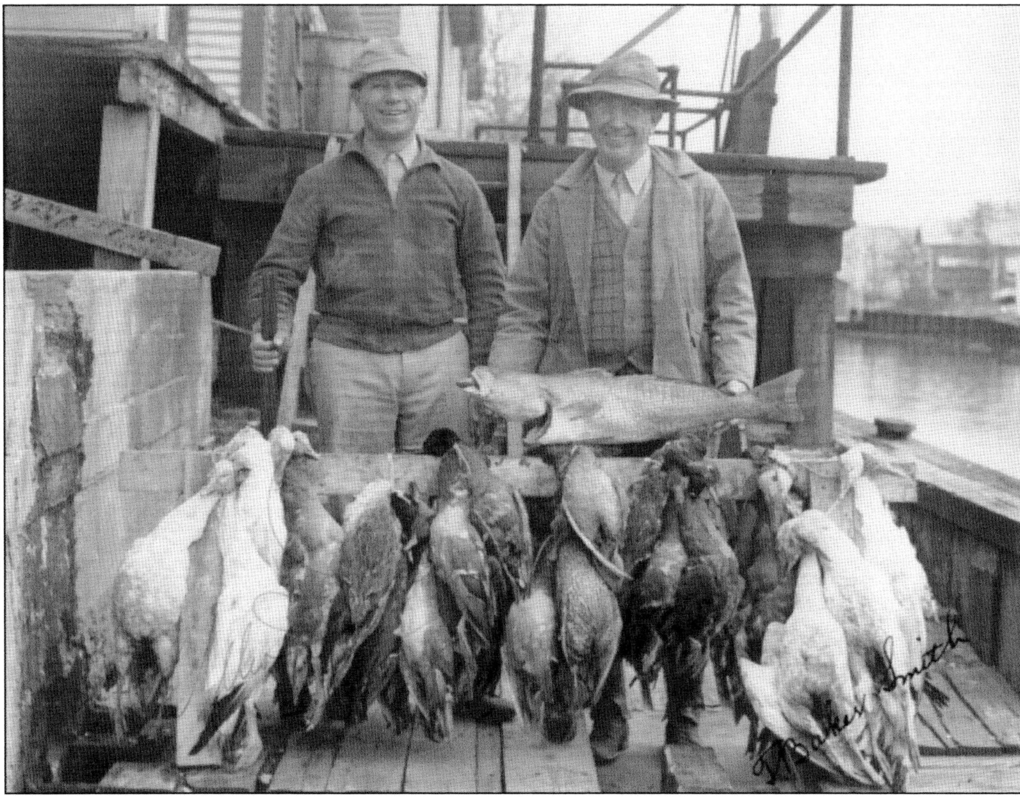

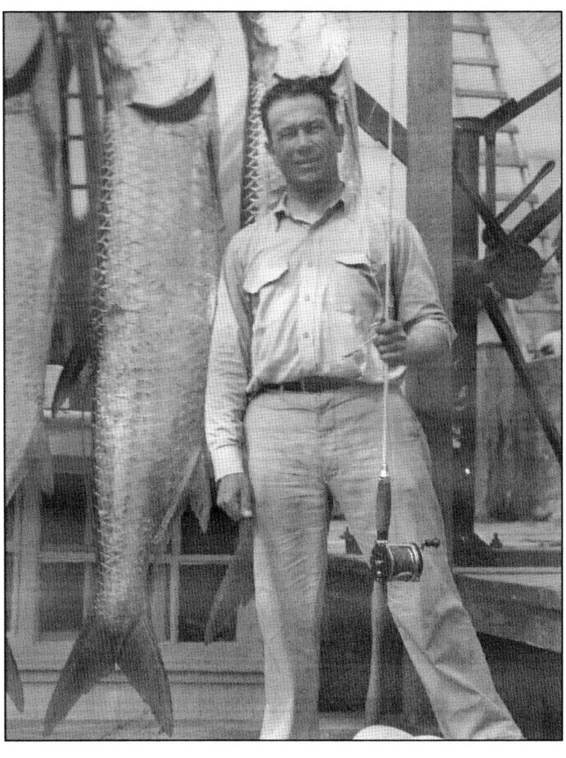

Like many young men who grow up in south Louisiana, Allen Ellender enjoyed the activities of what is today known as "Sportsman's Paradise." He is pictured above (left) with T. Baker Smith after a successful hunt of fowl and fish. Smith founded an engineering and surveying company in Houma in 1913, and it is still thriving in multiple parishes today. Deepwater fishing and hunting are a tradition—if not a rite of passage—in the area. Tarpon fishing in the Gulf of Mexico can lead to catches up to eight feet long and weighing 280 pounds, as shown here. The monster fish is usually sought from July to September. An avid cook, Ellender was known for preparing south Louisiana dishes such as gumbo and jambalaya in Washington, DC. (Both, THACS.)

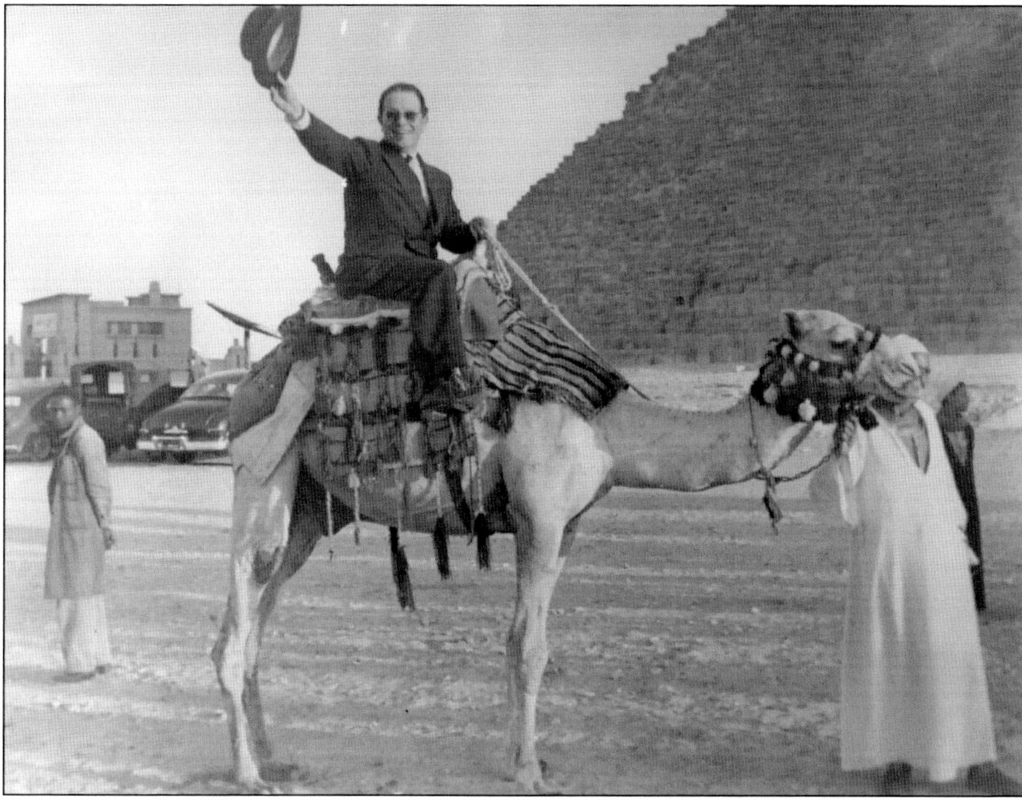

One of the longest-serving US senators, Allen Ellender was very well traveled. In his lifetime, he went to every country in the world with the exception of two—Albania and Bulgaria—bringing home souvenirs and trinkets from each of the places he visited. These items are on display in his re-created U.S. Senate office at Southdown Plantation House and Museum. He often flew with presidents on Air Force One, met with foreign dignitaries, and accompanied Richard Nixon on travels to foreign countries. Pictured here in Egypt in 1949, Ellender first rides a camel (above) and later a famous racehorse (right). (Both, THACS.)

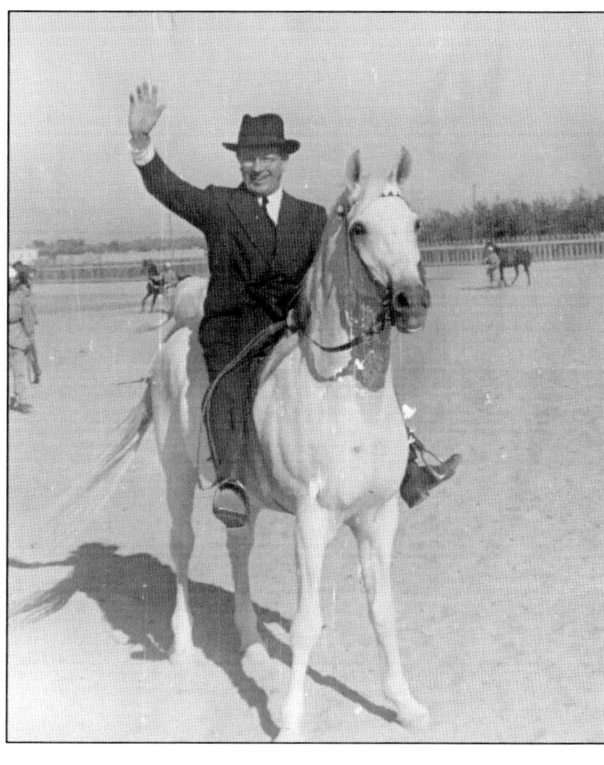

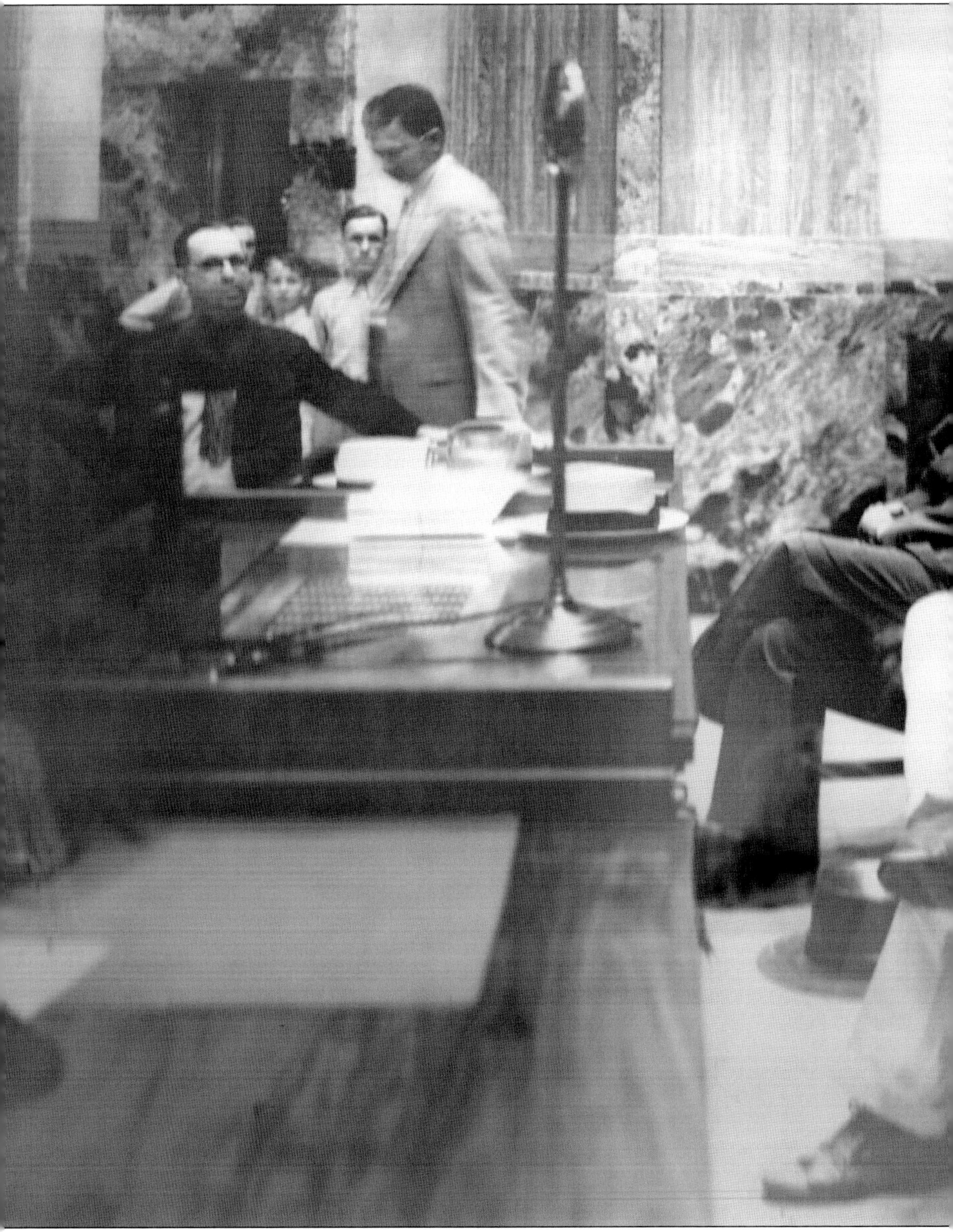

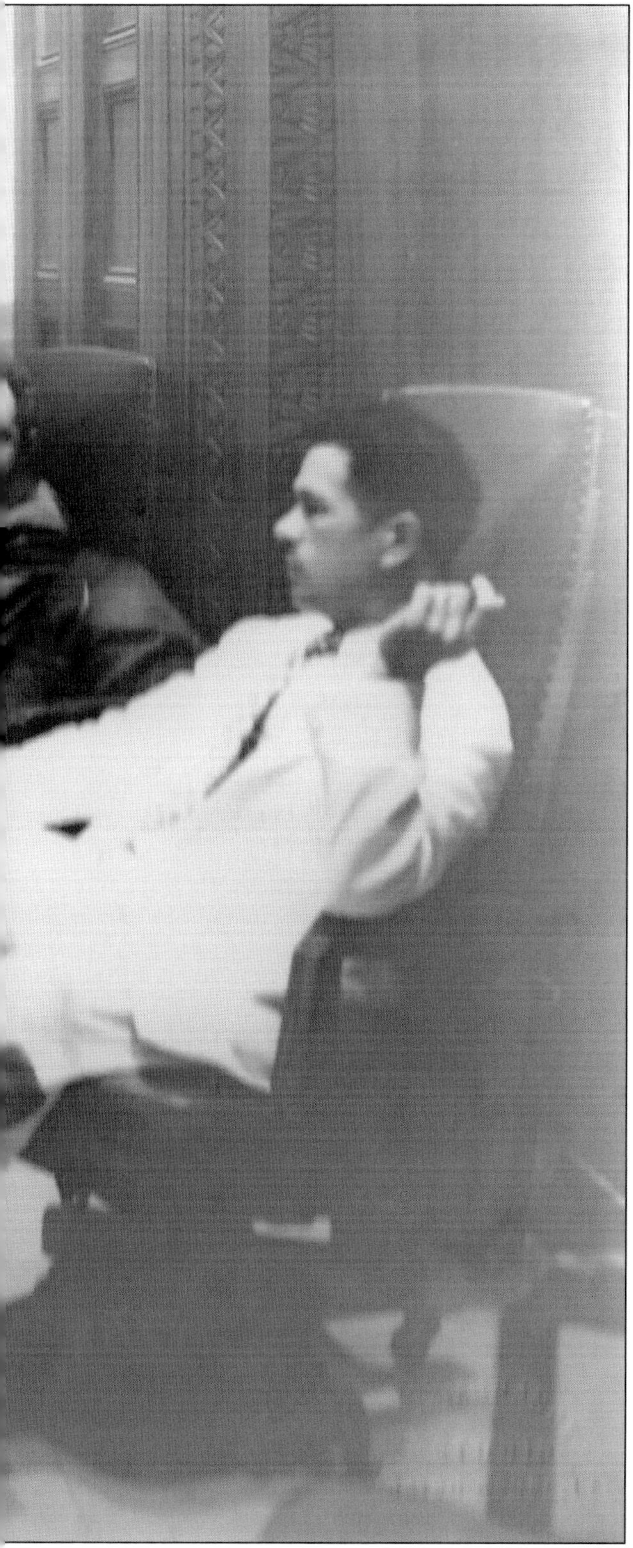

This is the last photograph taken of Gov. Huey P. Long (second from right). Allen Ellender (right), then Speaker of the House of Representatives for Louisiana, is pictured beside Long in Baton Rouge in 1935. Just 10 minutes later, Long would be shot at the age of 42. Long's political opponents formed a group called the "Square Dealers"; it is believed that this organization was responsible for his death. Originally an opponent of Long's, Ellender converted to Longism after Long became governor in 1928. Still, Ellender was opposed to the scandal that surrounded Long's questionable practices with oil leasing on state lands. In 1936, Ellender was elected as a Democrat to the US Senate. (THACS.)

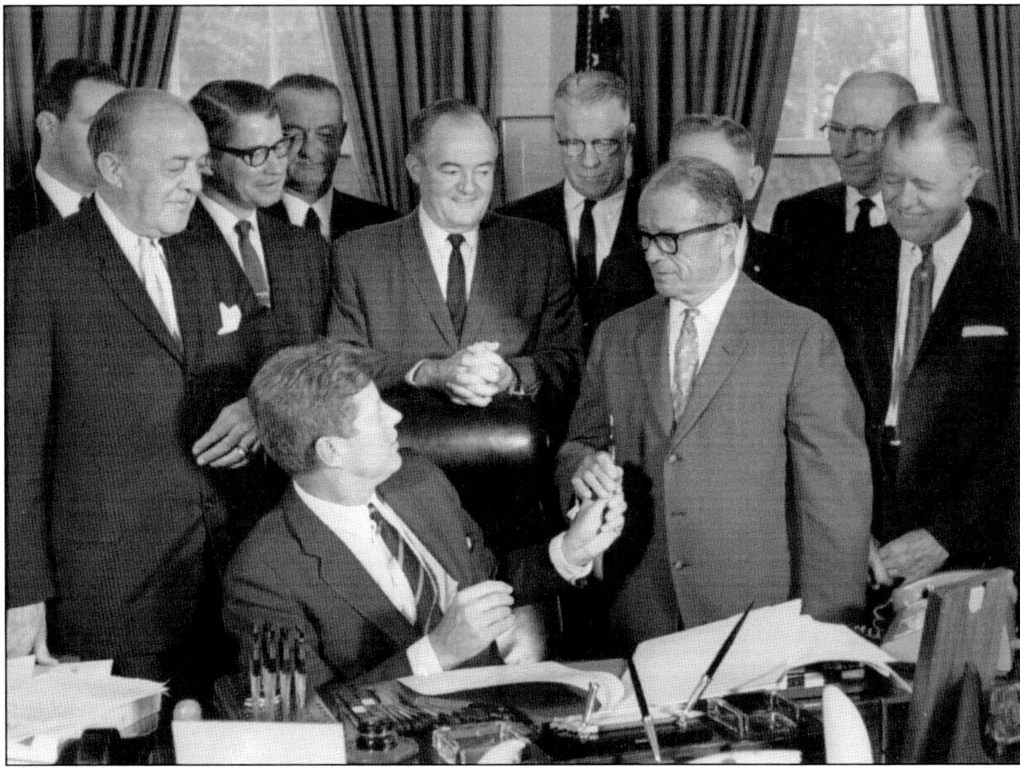

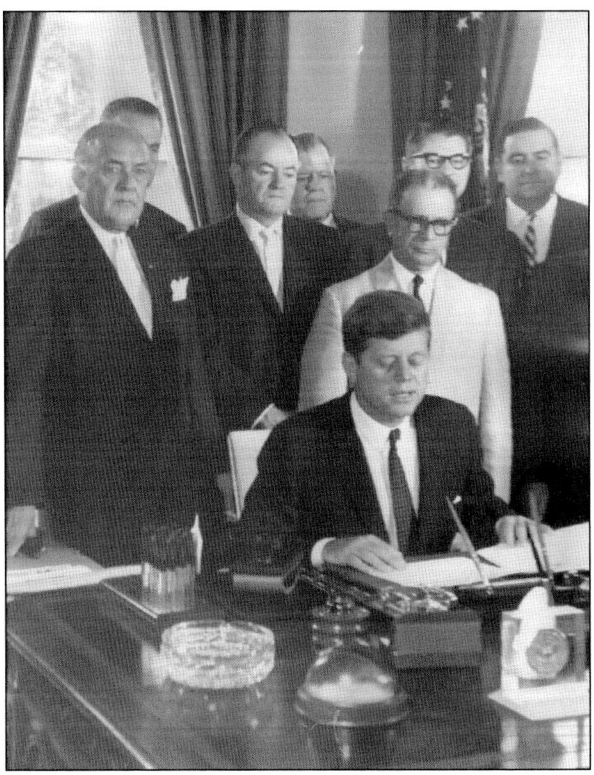

Senator Ellender served as chairman of the Senate Agriculture Committee from 1951 to 1953 and 1955 to 1971, using his powerful influence as a defender of sugarcane production in the South. In the 1950s, Ellender authored several versions of the Farm Bill to replace the Agriculture Act. Finally, in 1957, Congress passed a condensed version of his bill. With great support from President Kennedy and Secretary of Agriculture Orville Freeman, a more satisfactory Farm Bill was passed in 1962. Pictured is President Kennedy signing the bill. Written on the back of the image above is "President hands me first pen used by him in signing the 1962 Farm Bill." (Both, THACS.)

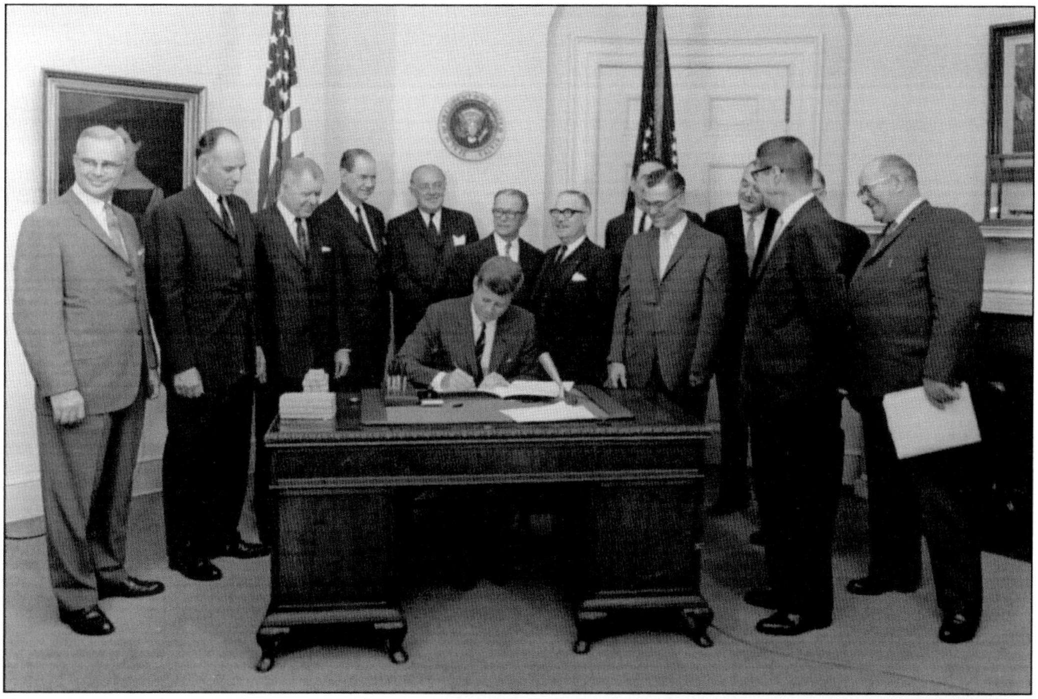

Always outspoken and committed to his political views, Ellender was on the Senate floor defending a library bill when Pres. John F. Kennedy was shot. Kennedy's assassination and Lyndon B. Johnson's presidency would create a different relationship between Johnson and Ellender. The two men had gotten along through the years, but Ellender questioned the more aggressive methods and views for uniting the nation that the new president presented. They disagreed on race issues, but when Johnson signed the Civil Rights Act in 1964, Ellender decided it would be better to work through the framework of the law. Johnson recognized his positive stand and stated, "Your leadership as the first southern senator to call for compliance with the Civil Rights Act was truly an illustration of statesmanship at its best." Above, Senator Ellender is directly behind President Kennedy, who is signing a bill. At right, Ellender (left) is pictured with Lady Bird and President Johnson. (Both, THACS.)

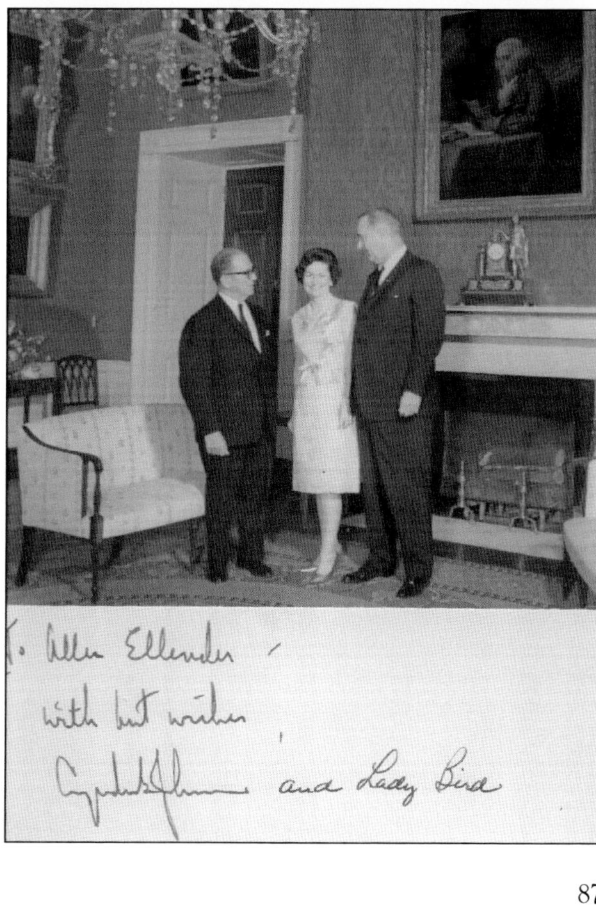

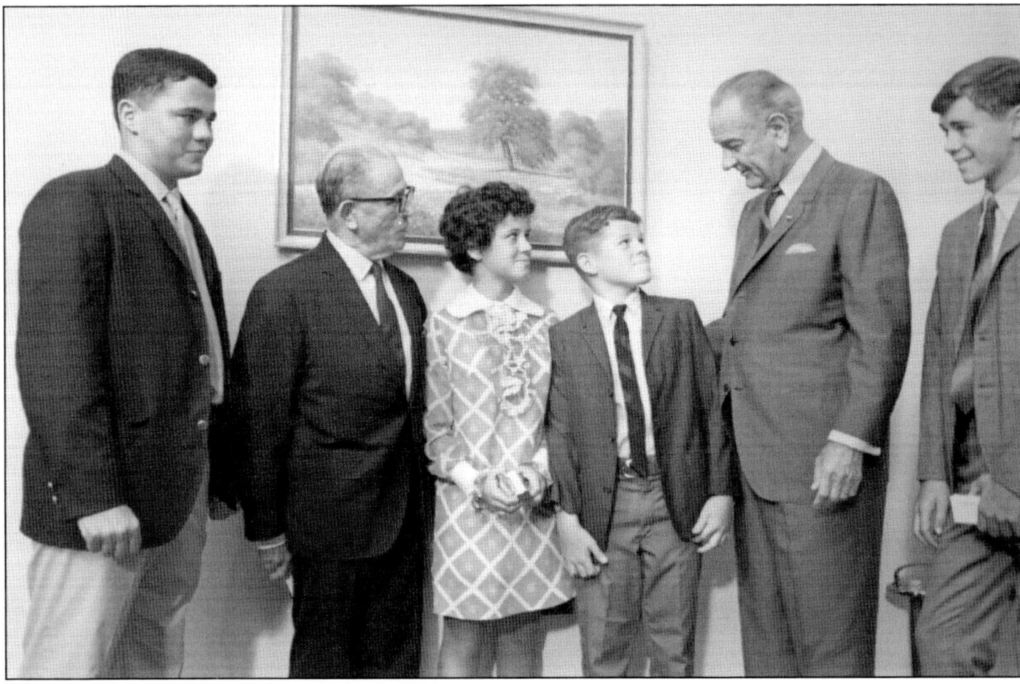

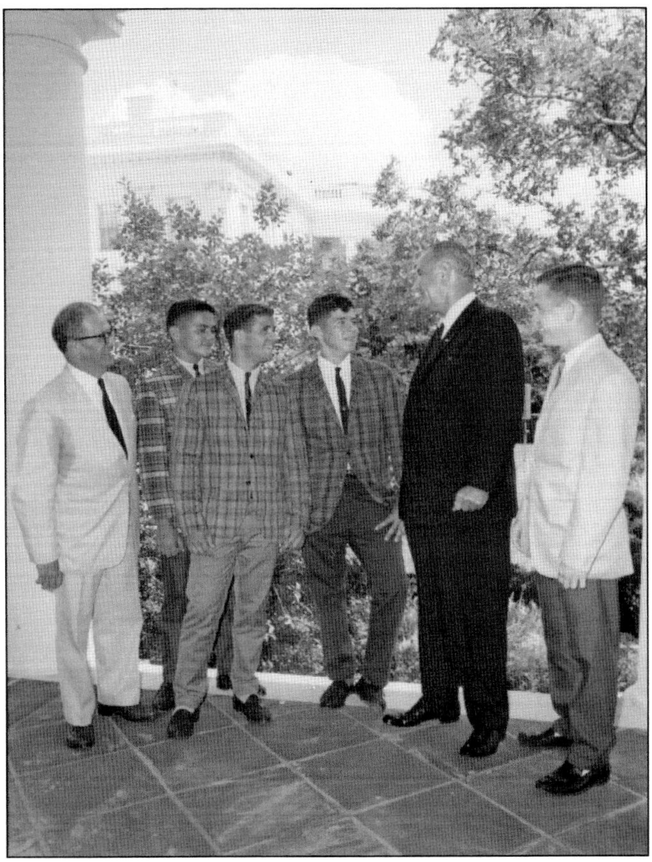

David Ellender, of one 13 grandchildren of Senator Ellender and a member of the Terrebonne Historical and Cultural Society at Southdown Plantation, remembers how his brothers and sisters would visit Washington, DC, in the summers when they were growing up. On such occasions, they would often have the opportunity to meet with dignitaries, presidents, and other politicians. On several occasions, Ellender cooked for the Johnsons. While looking for Lady Bird one day, President Johnson was told she was eating lunch with Senator Ellender. Johnson later stated, "So I put on my hat and invited myself. I went up there and I was the only man there except Ellender, and he had all the pretty women in Washington up there in the room eating with him!" President Johnson is pictured with Ellender's grandchildren. (Both, THACS.)

According to Thomas A. Bechnel, the author of Sen. Allen Ellender's biography, the senator and Pres. Richard Nixon were of like mind regarding the policies for racial integration and US involvement in Vietnam. Nixon "courted" Ellender and other Southern leaders who held important committee appointments. Likewise, Ellender supported Nixon, which undoubtedly led to lucrative economic grants for Louisiana. Ellender visited Nixon in July 1970 and cooked for the president. He also accompanied him on Air Force One to New Orleans, where Nixon presented him a certificate declaring him "Chef Supreme." Ellender is pictured speaking with Nixon as he presents travel journals to him (right) and again at a meeting at the White House (below). (Both, THACS.)

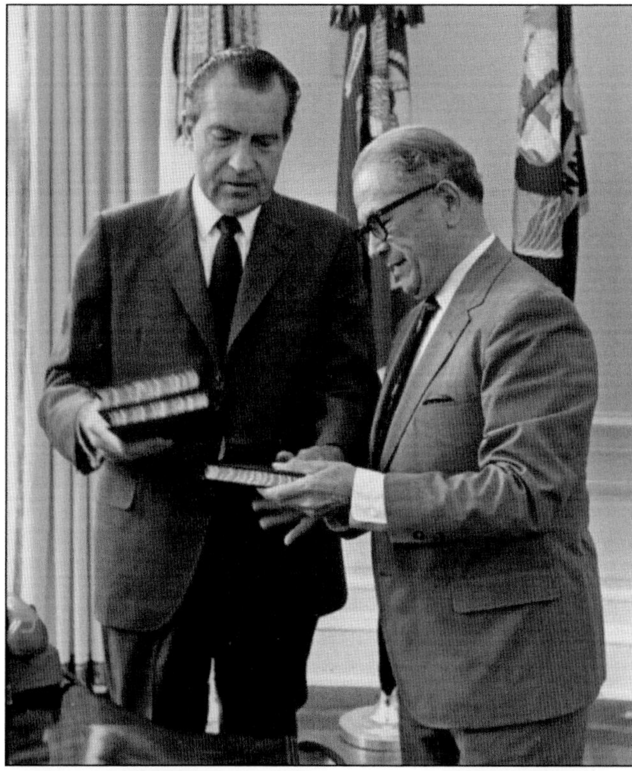

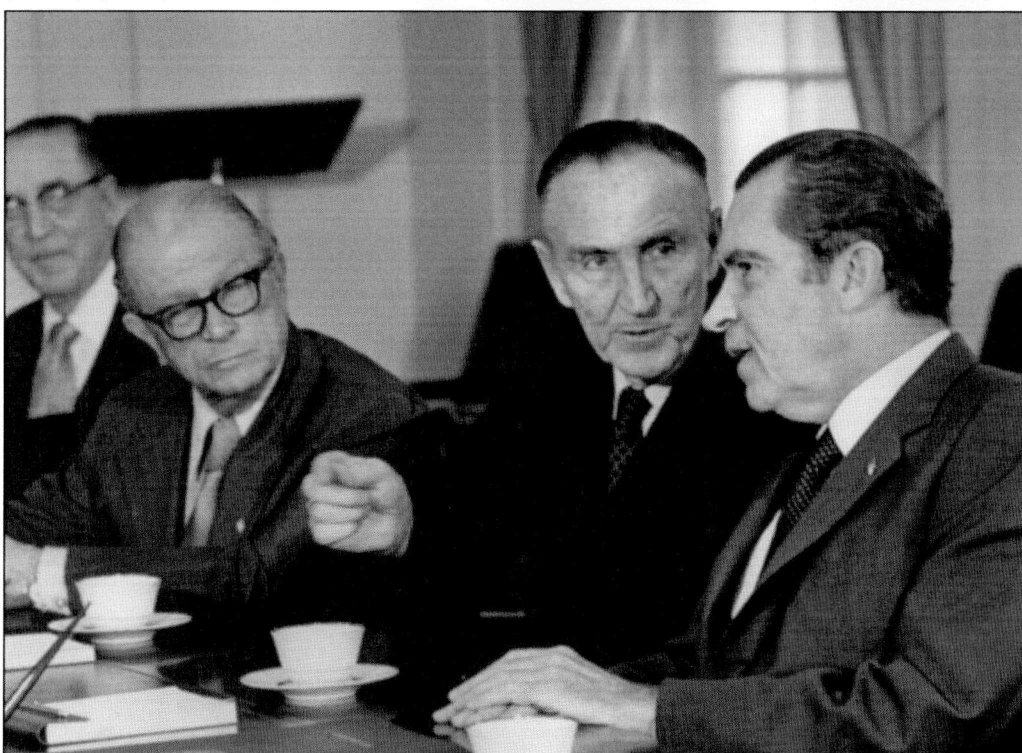

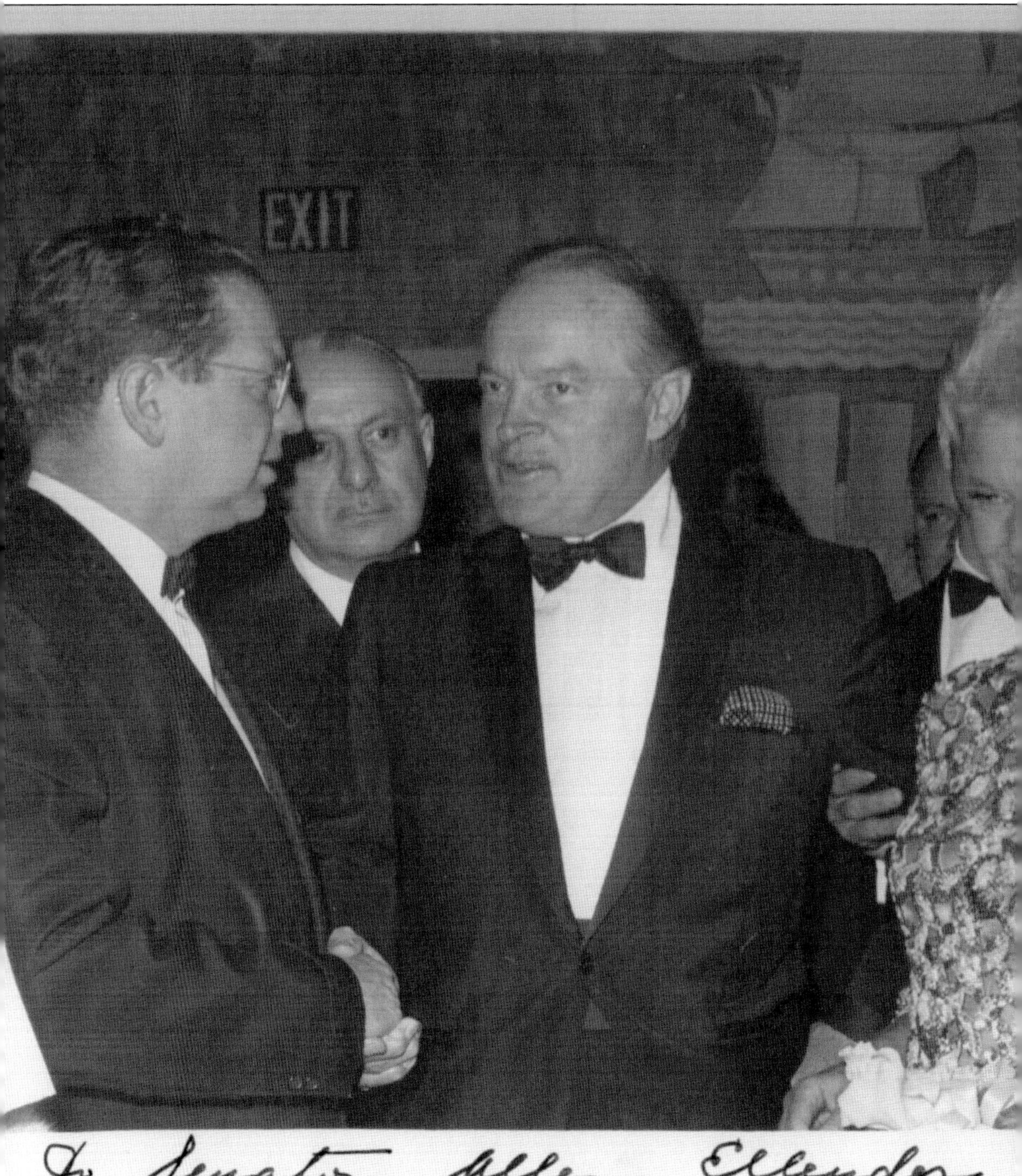
EXIT
To Senator Allen Ellender,
With my very warmest best
Jane Morgan

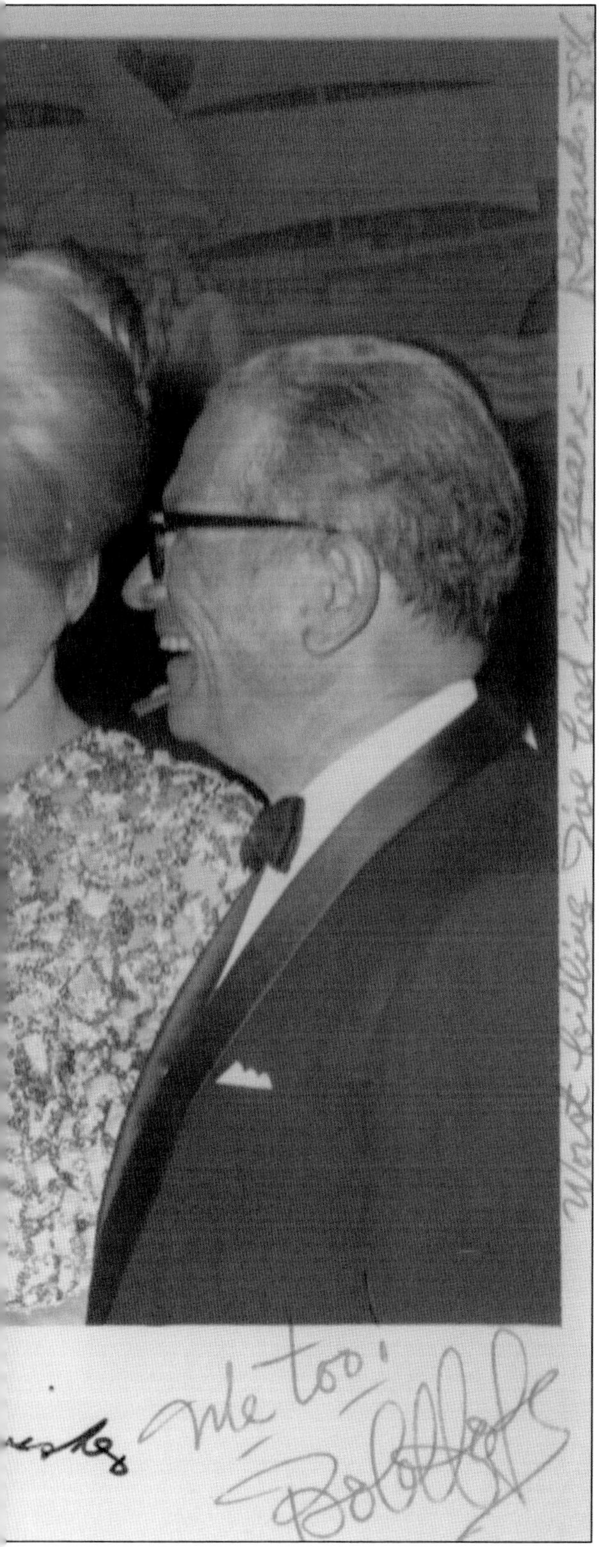

Senator Ellender is pictured on the right, standing next to singer Jane Morgan. Bob Hope is to her left. Morgan signed "To Senator Ellender, with my very warmest best wishes." Hope followed with "Me too!" and his signature. He then added to the side of the photograph, "Worst billing I've had in years—regards—B.H." Given the nature of his personality, his upbringing, and his early years in Houma and the bayous, it is no surprise that Ellender found himself surrounded by famous people during his lifetime. A frequent host of seafood boils and other Cajun-flavored events, Ellender was able to congregate with dignitaries, politicians, local Houma people, and family in his true nature: generous and genuine. He even insisted when in Houma that he be referred to as "Allen" and not "Senator." (THACS.)

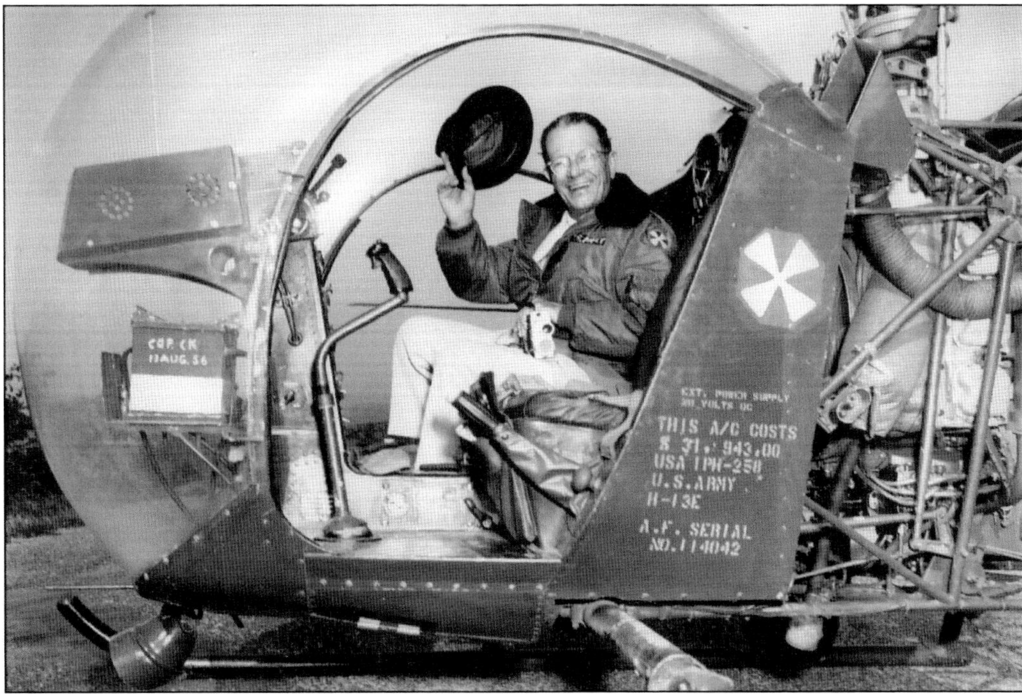

Pictured in a helicopter in 1956 after the Korean War (1950–1953), Ellender wears a flight jacket and raises his hat. The lettering on the helicopter states, "This A/C [aircraft] costs $31,943.00." This particular helicopter, known as the Bell 47, was used in the Korean War to transport medical patients and personnel. Later, it had various other uses, such as transporting the president of the United States. (THACS.)

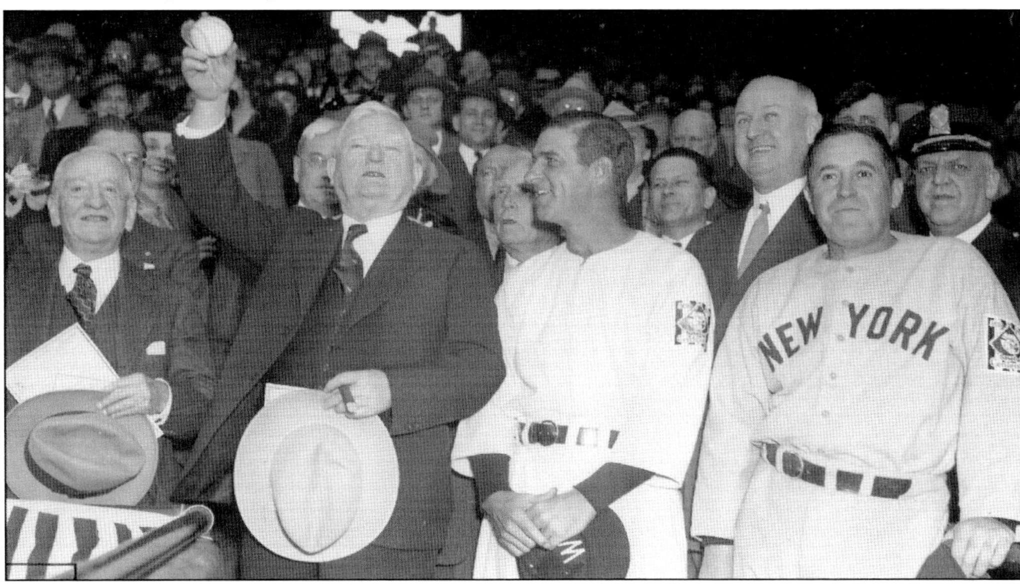

A 49-year-old Allen Ellender can be spotted in the second row, directly behind Lou Gehrig's right shoulder, at a 1939 New York Yankees game. In the foreground are, from left to right, two unidentified New York politicians, Gehrig, and a teammate. The Yankees went on to win the World Series that year. (THACS.)

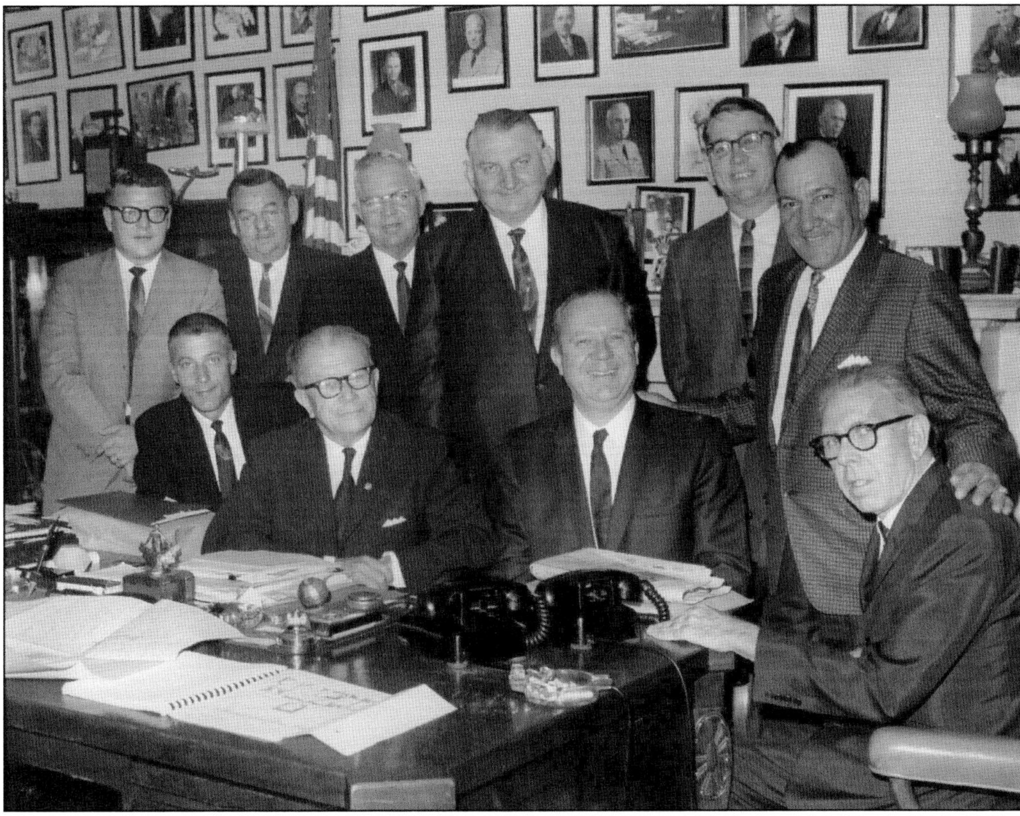

Senator Ellender is pictured in his US Senate office at 245 Senate Office Building in Washington, DC, surrounded by pictures of friends, colleagues, and family. These photographs and all the items from his office are on display at Southdown Plantation House and Museum. At the time of his death—July 29, 1972, at the age of 81—Senator Ellender was campaigning for reelection to Congress for his seventh term. (THACS.)

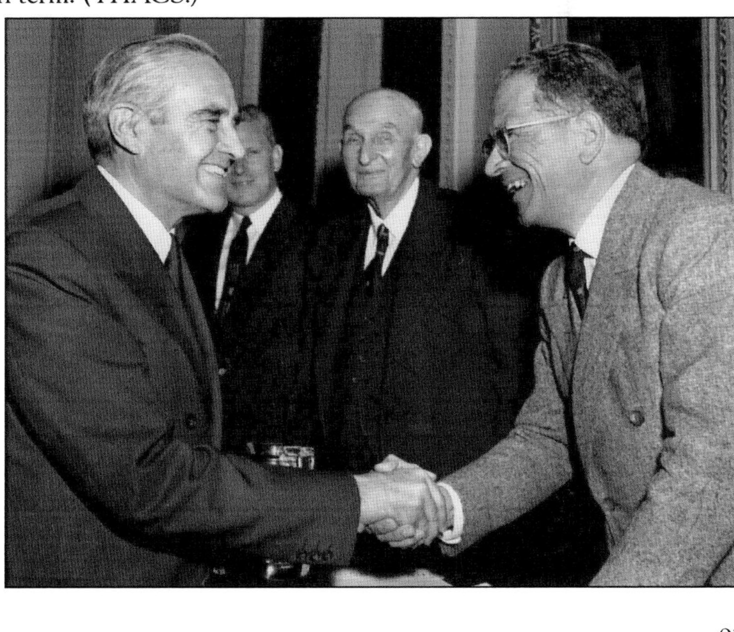

Senator Ellender, right, shakes hands with New York governor Averell Harriman in 1955. Harriman was a Democrat who served as secretary of commerce under Pres. Harry S. Truman and campaigned to be the Democratic presidential nominee in 1952 and 1956, losing each time to Adlai Stevenson. Ellender was one of his biggest supporters. (THACS.)

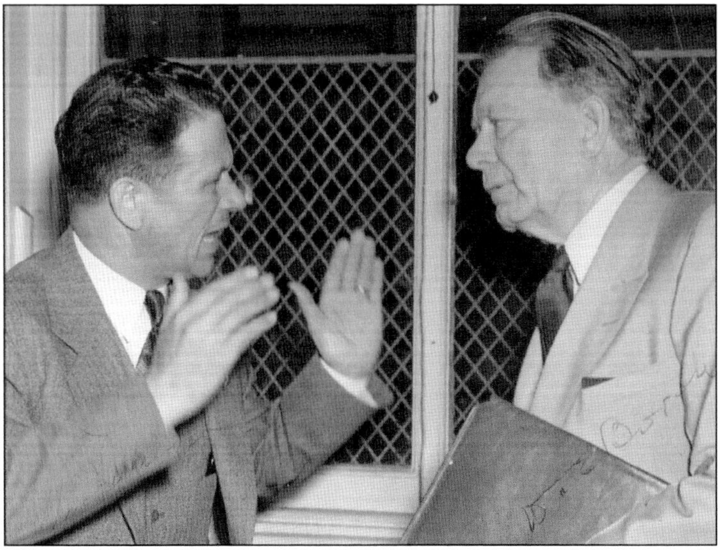

Senator Ellender, left, speaks with Sen. William Borah of Idaho. Known as a progressive Republican, Borah ran as a candidate for the Republican nomination in 1936, the year Ellender entered the US Senate. Ellender's desk was behind Borah's in the senate, and the senior senator once told Ellender, "Huey [Long] was bright and quick and one of the most capable men in the Senate." (THACS.)

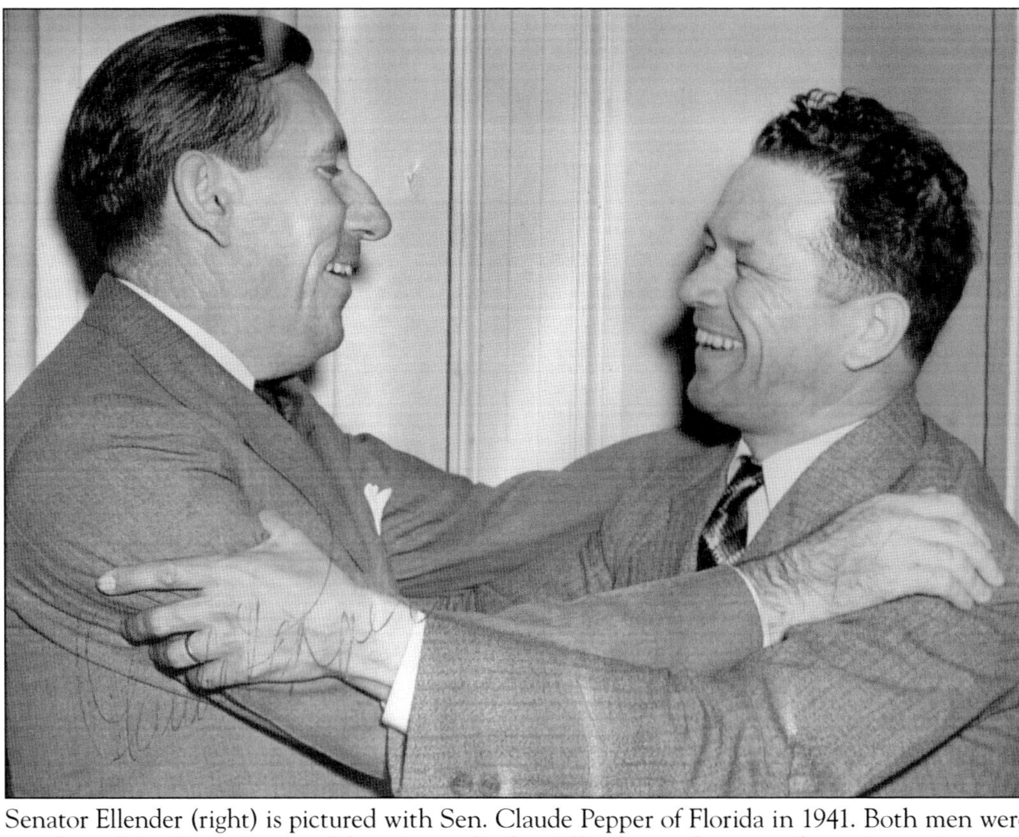

Senator Ellender (right) is pictured with Sen. Claude Pepper of Florida in 1941. Both men were members of the Committee on Education and Labor. Ellender was known to be against unions and the uprisings that they created, calling them "un-American," while Pepper campaigned heavily on a wage-hours bill that would be passed as the Fair Labor Standards Act. (THACS.)

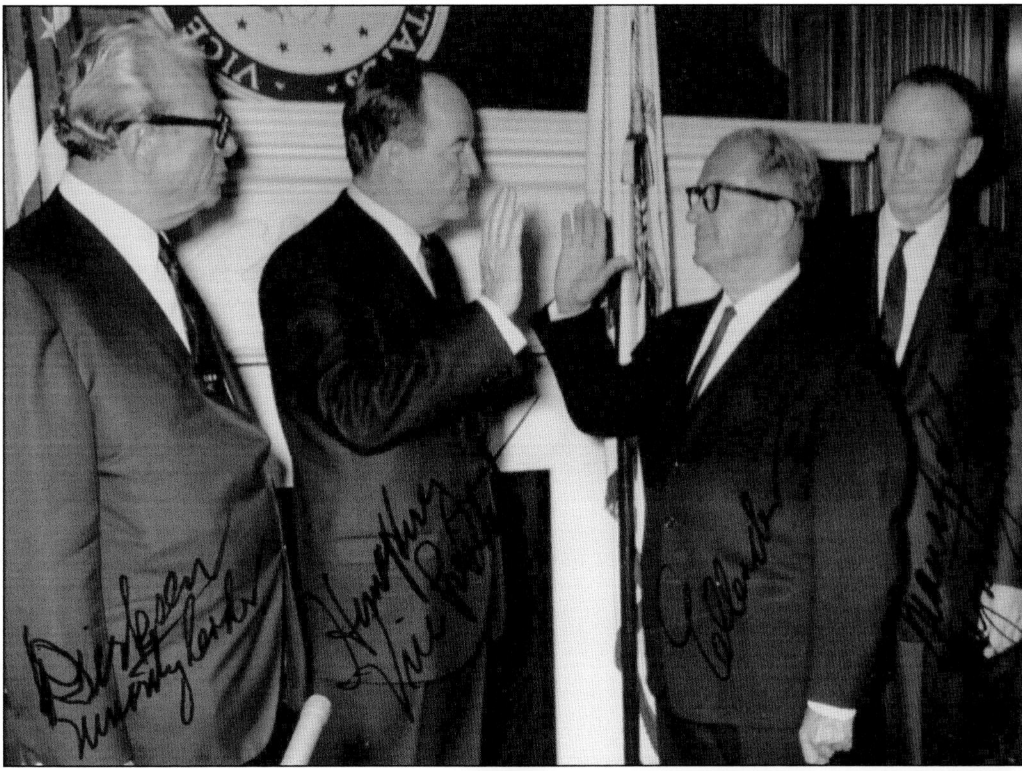

Here, Senator Ellender is being sworn in for his sixth term as a US senator on January 10, 1967. From left to right are Senate minority leader Everett Dirksen of Ohio, Vice Pres. Hubert Humphrey, Sen. Allen Ellender, and Senate majority leader Michael Joseph "Mike" Mansfield. Mansfield, a Democrat, was the longest-serving majority leader of his era (1961–1977). (THACS.)

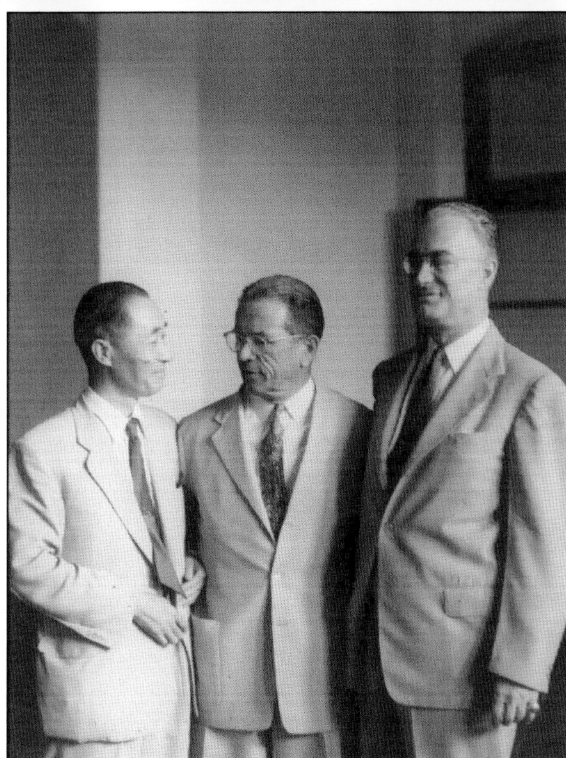

President of the Legislative Yuan of the Republic of China (Taiwan) Chang Tao-fan, left, stands next to Senator Ellender in Taipei in 1955. Chang held several high-profile positions during his lifetime, including president of the Broadcasting Corporation of China, executive vice minister of the Ministry of Transportation and Communications, and Provost of National Chengchi University. (THACS.)

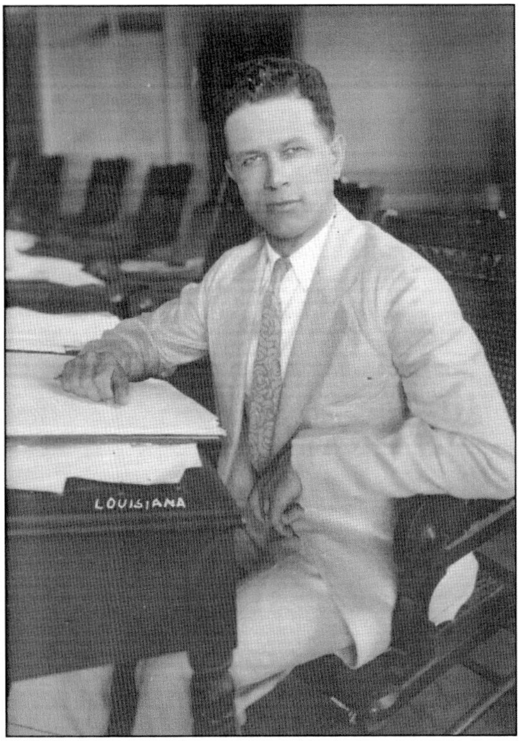

Allen J. Ellender started his career as a lawyer in Houma. He quickly became interested in politics and was appointed district attorney for Lafourche and Terrebonne Parishes. He successfully ran for a seat in the Louisiana House of Representatives and won, holding the position until 1936, when he was elected to the US Senate. He served in this capacity from 1936 until 1971. Senator Ellender served as president pro tempore of the Senate in his last term, as pictured below (top right). Running for reelection in 1972, he suffered a major heart attack on the campaign trail in July. Though he did not live to see the election that year, 10 percent of Louisiana's voters voted for the deceased candidate anyway. (Both, THACS.)

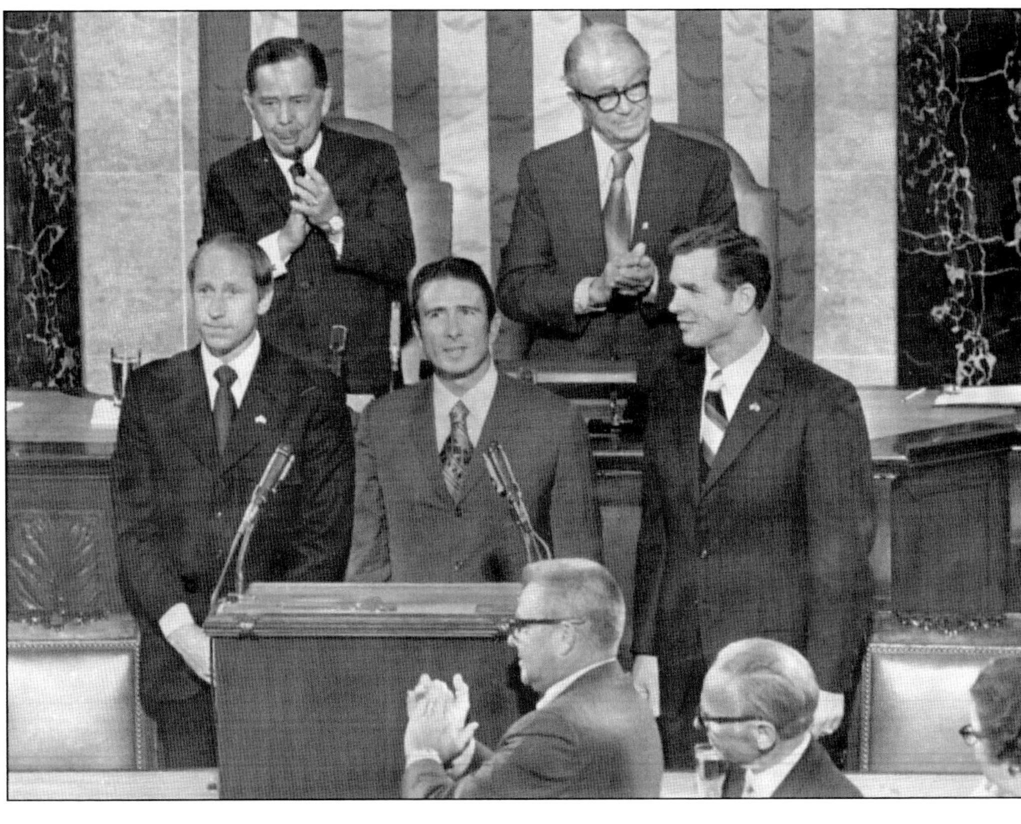

One of the first successful truck farmers in the area, Ellender is shown on the right sitting in a potato field. Below is a photograph of the US Senate that graces the walls of his office. Biographer Thomas A. Becnal writes that the "amiable, congenial and unpretentious" Ellender had represented his constituents for 35 years. Newspaper and television coverage of his funeral alerted people, some for the first time, to his national and world importance. A *Houma Daily Courier* editorial best summarizes local reaction to his death: "Although he was from the bayous, he knew the world. And he left his imprint upon it and upon America. He was our number one citizen and America's number one senator. Few men of his stature ever pass our way. We of Terrebonne are proud and grateful—and sad." (Both, THACS.)

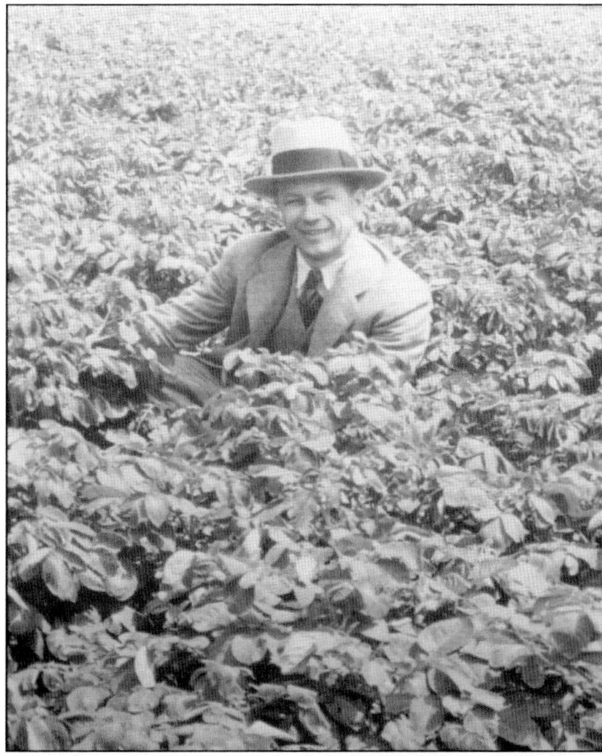

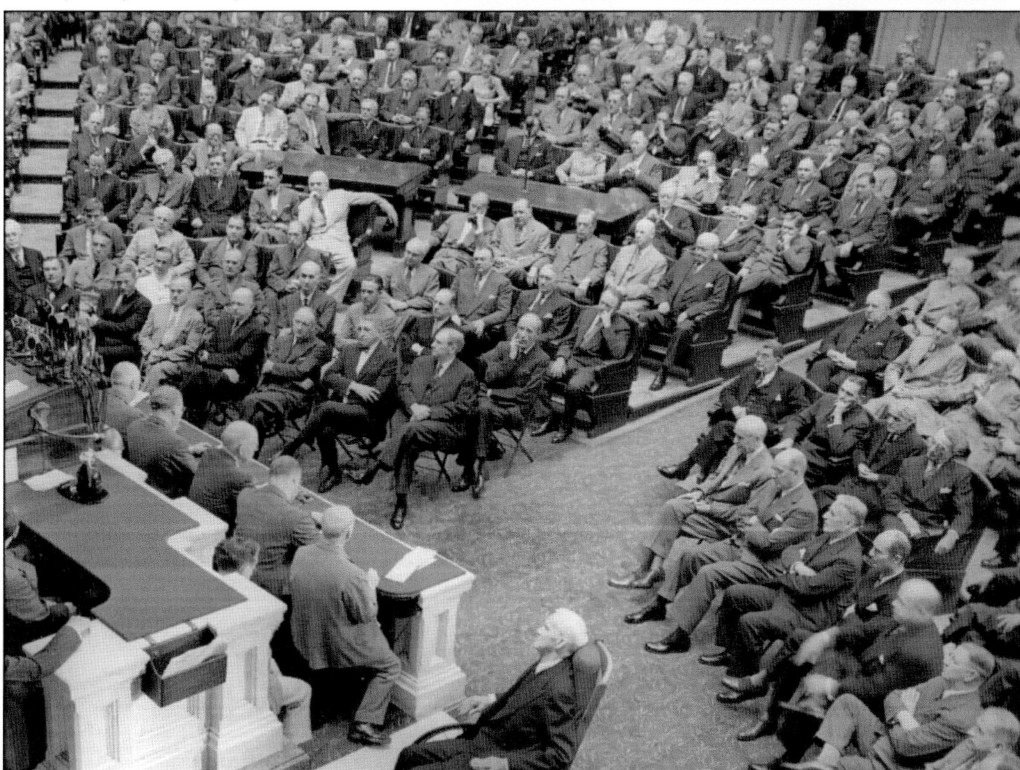

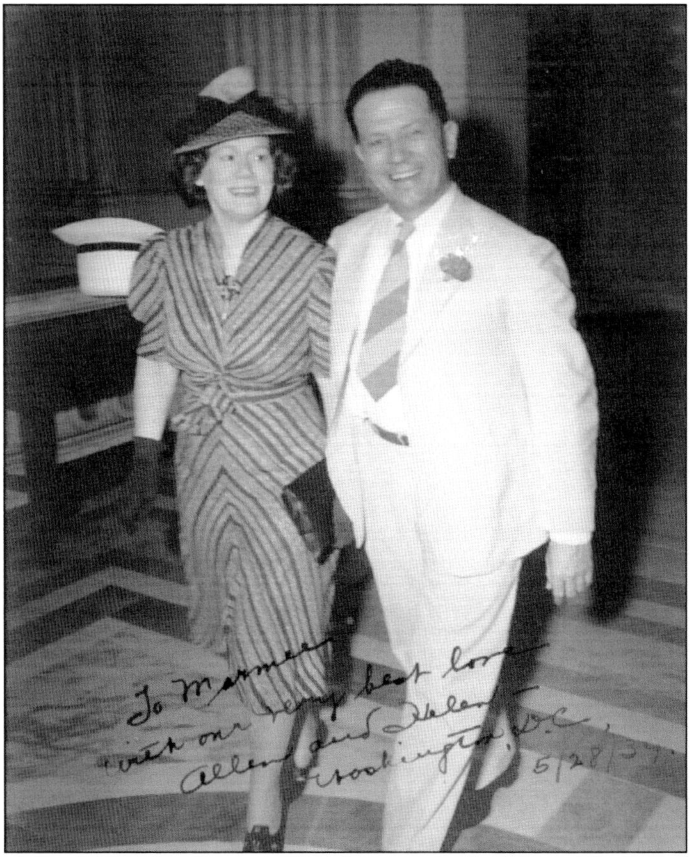

Helen and Allen Ellender are pictured in Washington, DC, in 1939. Helen Calhoun Donnelly was born in New Orleans in 1895. The two married at St. Louis Cathedral in New Orleans on March 19, 1917. Helen gave birth to a boy, whom they named Allen Jr. Since Houma did not have a hospital, it was a home birth, and it turned out to be very difficult for Helen. Because of the pain she suffered, she vowed never to bear other children. Allen Jr., however, made up for a lack of siblings as he and his wife, Ligia Ribas Ellender, had 13 children. Sons were Allen III, Gerald, William, Michael, Claude, Charles, David, Jules, Frank, and Elward, and daughters were Maria, Lucia "Nancy," and Carmen. (Both, THACS.)

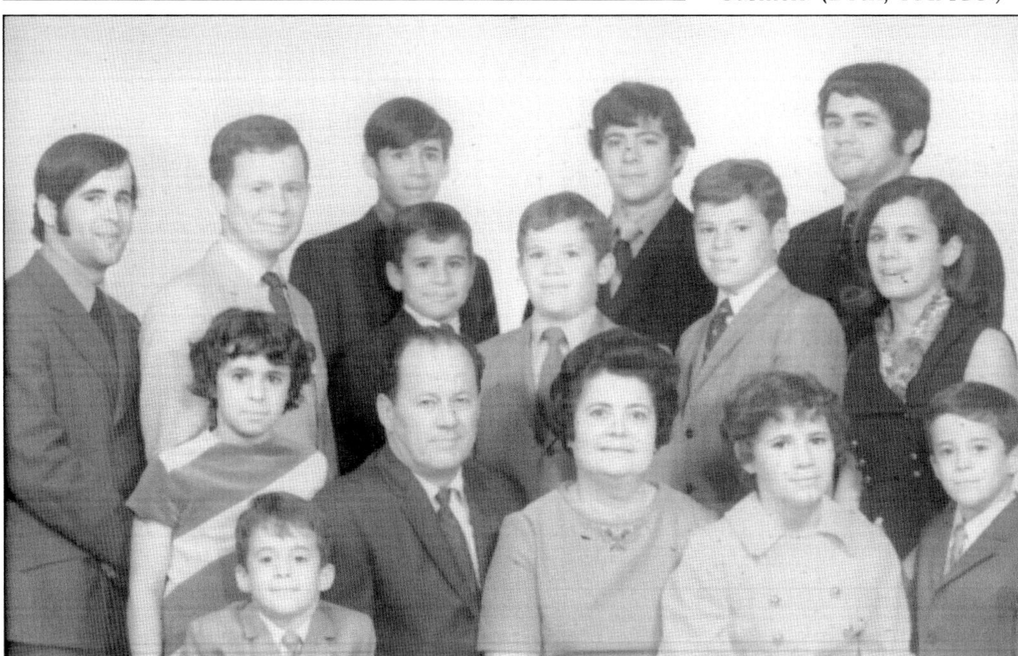

Seven

LAGNIAPPE

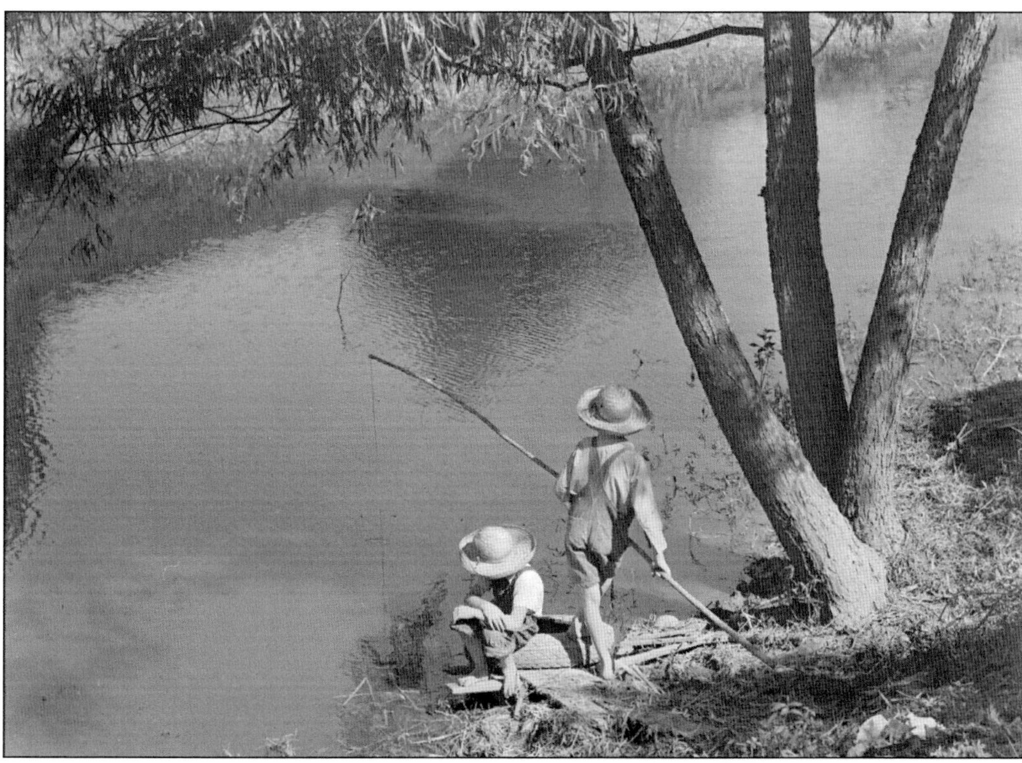

Lagniappe is a Creole/Cajun word meaning "a little something extra." The playful word also brings to mind the recreational aspect of living in Houma and the bayous beyond. This chapter fills in the blanks of activities and events not yet touched upon, like the two boys fishing here. It is just a lagniappe. (THACS.)

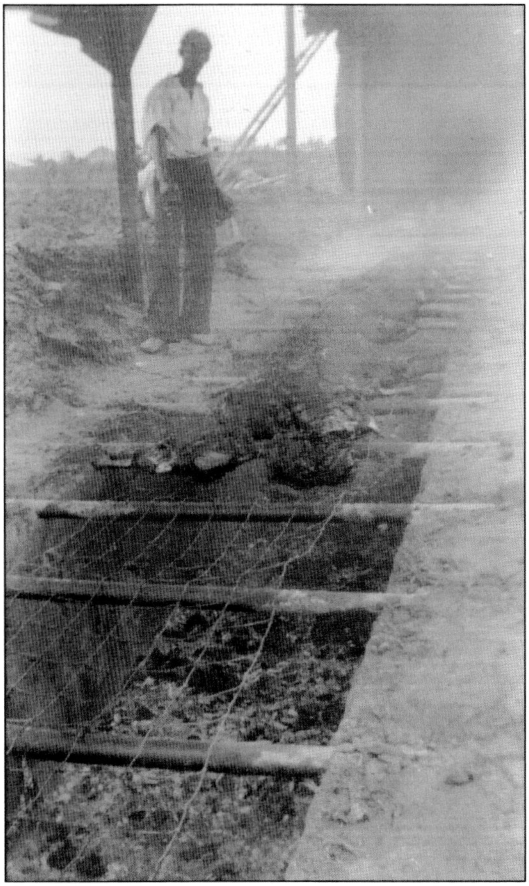

Sunday, May 13, 1934, the last day of Houma's Hundredth Celebration, featured a barbecue and picnic on the grounds of the American Legion Park. A parade celebrated the Homecoming Day, which included an invitation for former residents to be part of the occasion. The unidentified man cooking stands over a pit with a wire rack resting on iron supports. (THACS.)

Even in Houma's earliest years, parades were a standard celebration for Independence Day, Mardi Gras, Veterans Day, and Christmas. Horses were brought out in all their finery on these days, but many people used horses for general recreation, as shown in this image of Dora Thatcher getting ready for a ride. (THACS.)

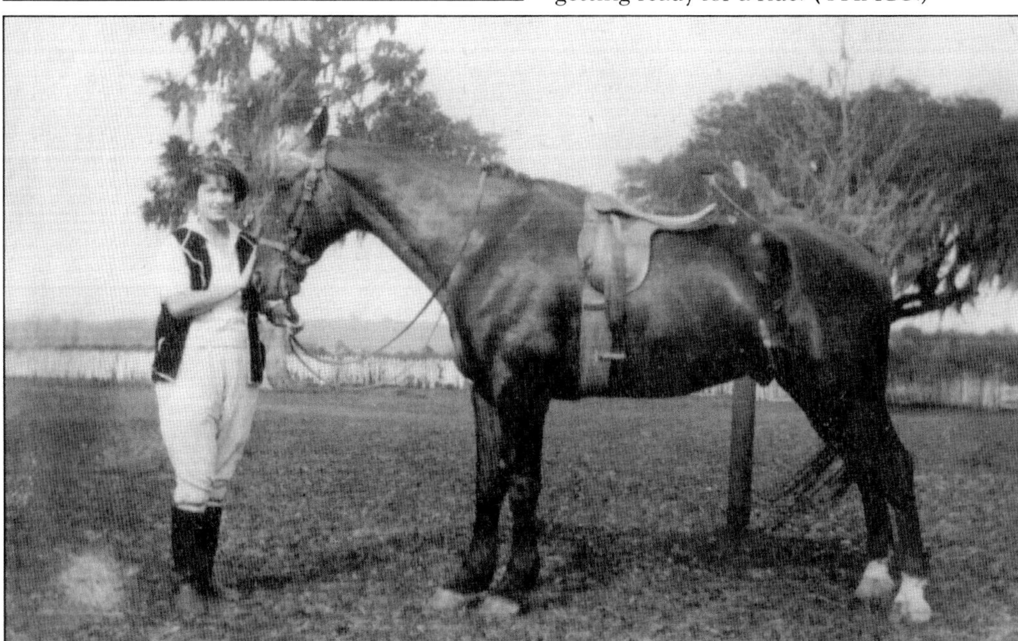

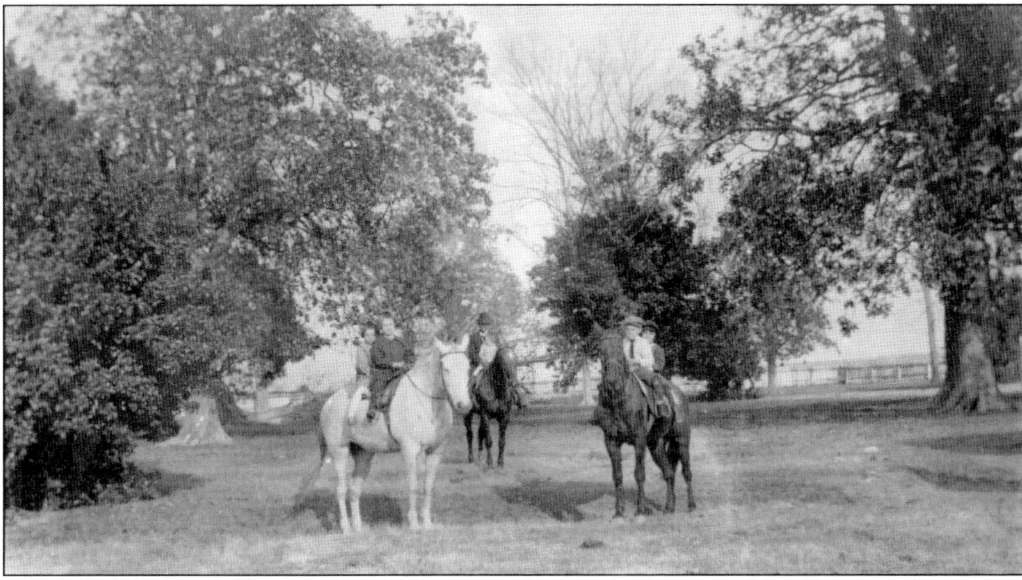

Equestrian training was considered a part of proper education for those growing up on one of the more prominent plantations. William John Minor of Southdown Plantation built elaborate stables and a racetrack on his property, and horse lovers from all over the country would travel for the races and auctions. Yet horse riding was essential for travel, farmwork, and even recreation. In a practice similar to cattle branding, individual owners would use a brand on their horses for identification purposes. This view of children sitting on a horse while it lies on the ground may seem odd, but with that many children around, the horse must be exhausted. (Both, THACS.)

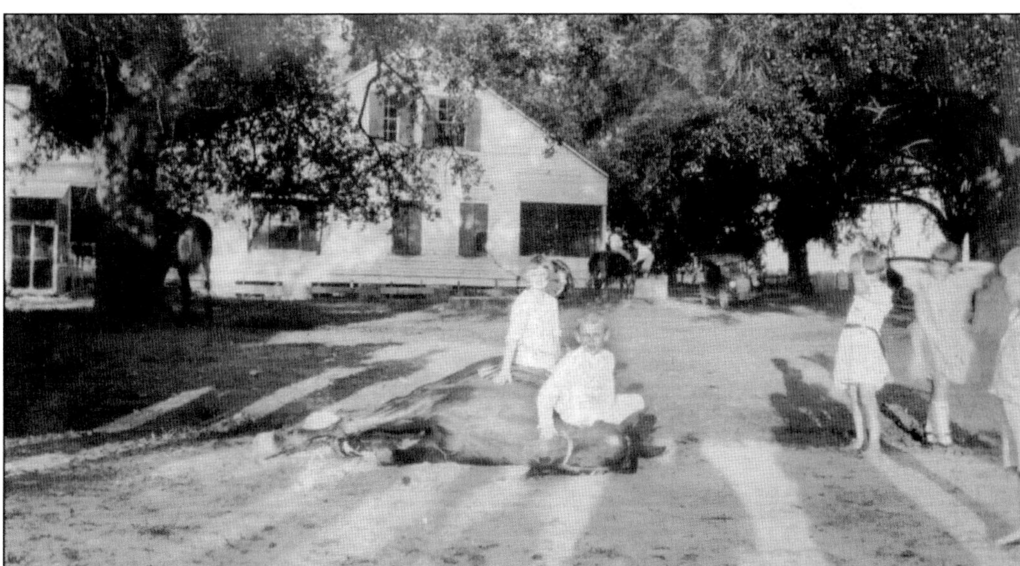

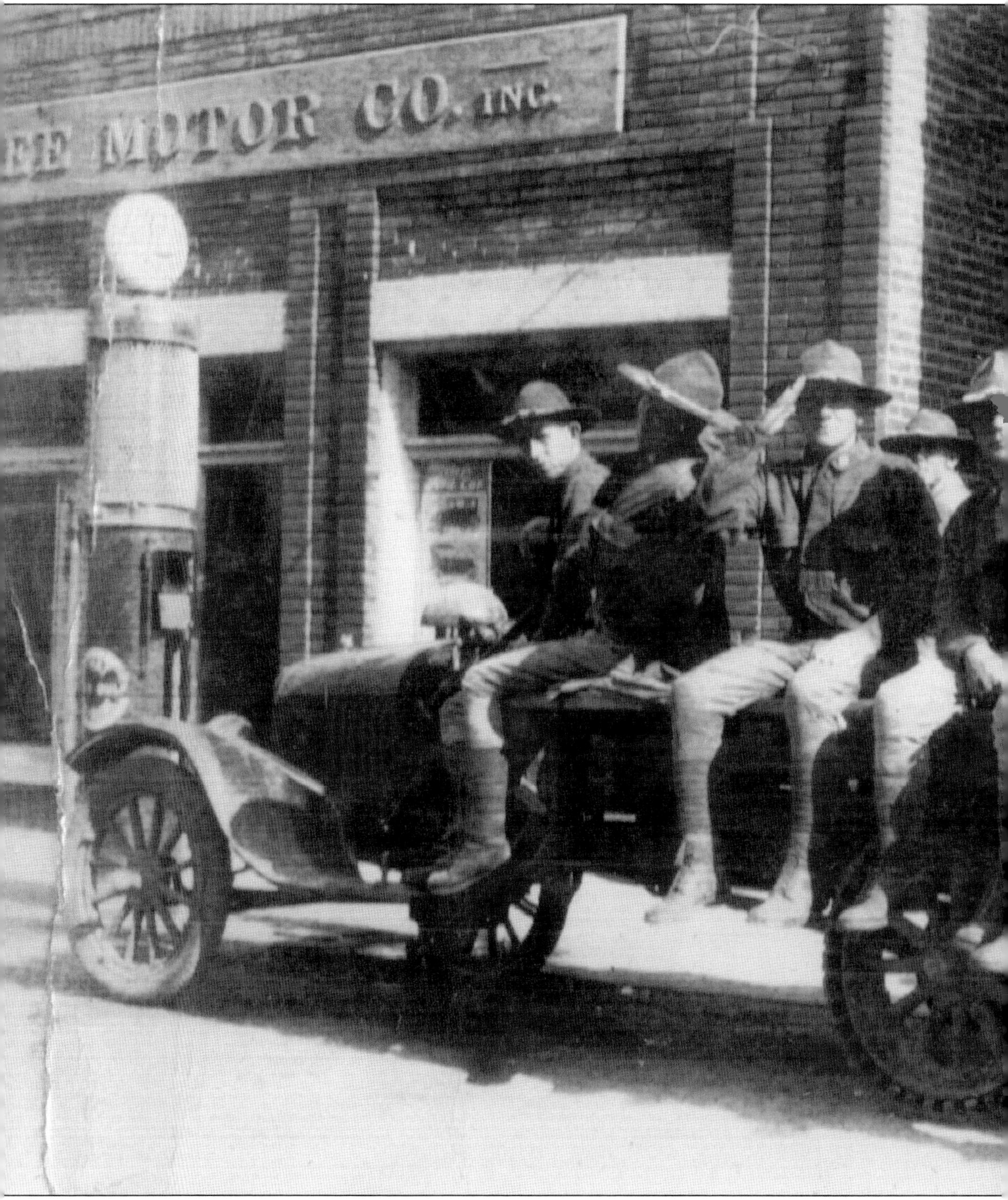

In April 1927, more than 15 inches of rain fell in south Louisiana in an 18-hour period, and the mighty Mississippi River overflowed its banks. Water rose rapidly, and homes on Bayou Black were merely islands. It was considered the worst river flood in the United States and was called the "Greatest Flood of All Time." Nearly everyone in the area was affected. The levees broke in 145

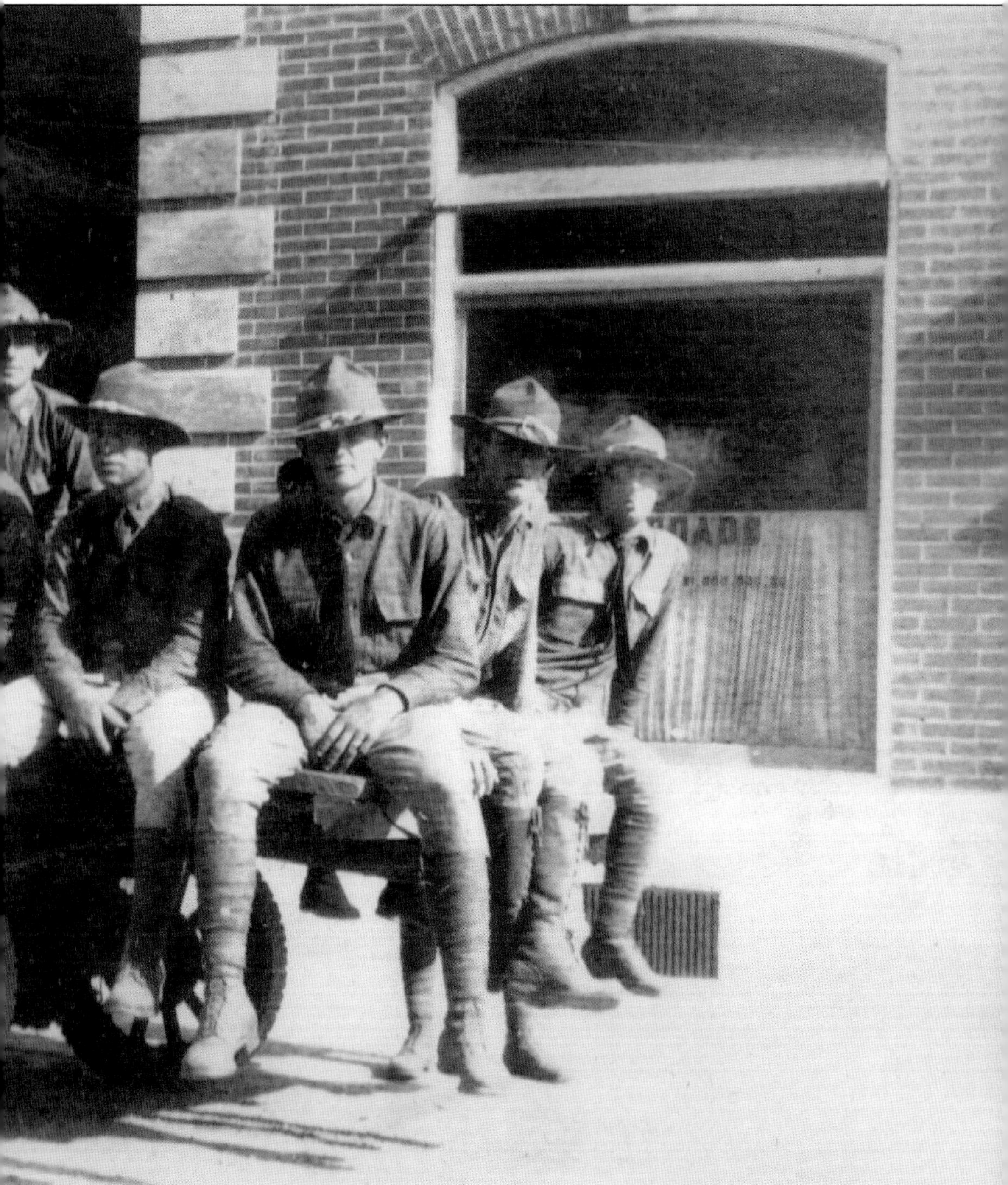

places and flooded more than 27,000 acres of land, such as Bayou Black Road in Houma. National Guardsmen arrived in Houma to help with the rescue and cleanup efforts. Troops, under the command of Captain Wright, camped at Aragon Plantation, which had rail access. (THACS.)

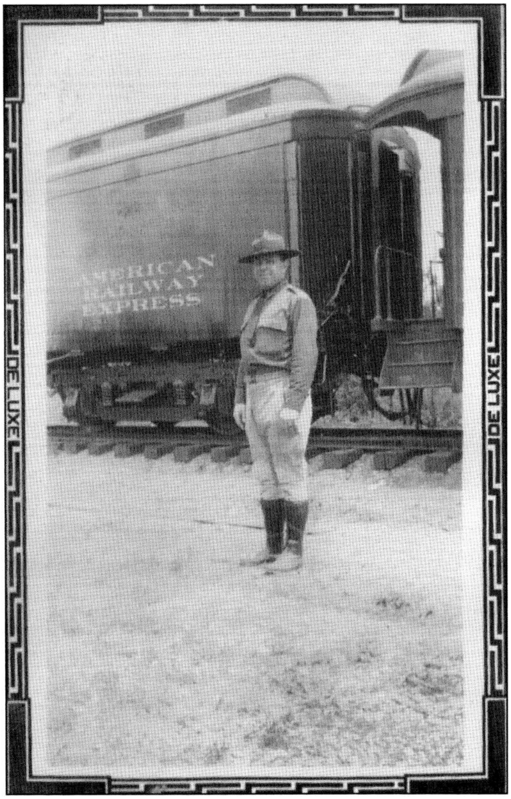

On the left, Captain Wright stands next to the railcar that was used to transport the troops and supplies. The main station at Schriever was eight miles from Houma, where much of the flooding was reported. The number of troops was too small to meet the demand of the country. Many citizens were left to their own devices, and plantations, such as that of Robert Ruffin Barrow Jr., suffered great losses. Still, the citizens of Houma welcomed the soldiers and made accommodations for them when possible. Pictured below are Captain and Mrs. Wright in all their finery, attending a social event in Houma. (Both, THACS.)

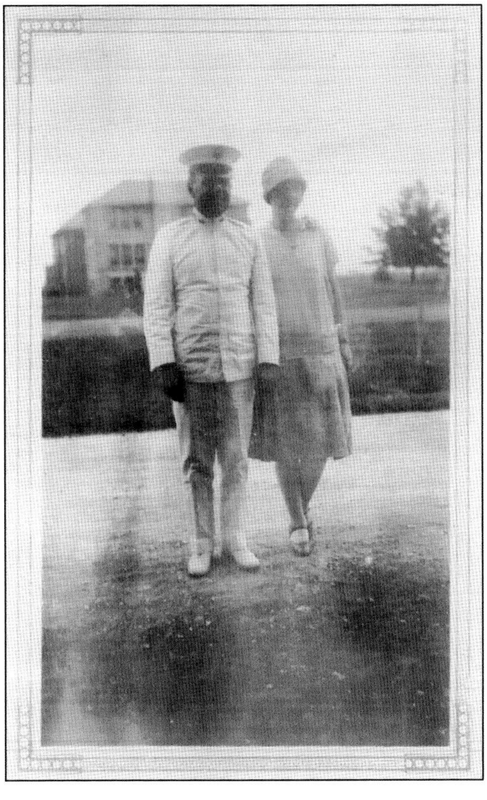

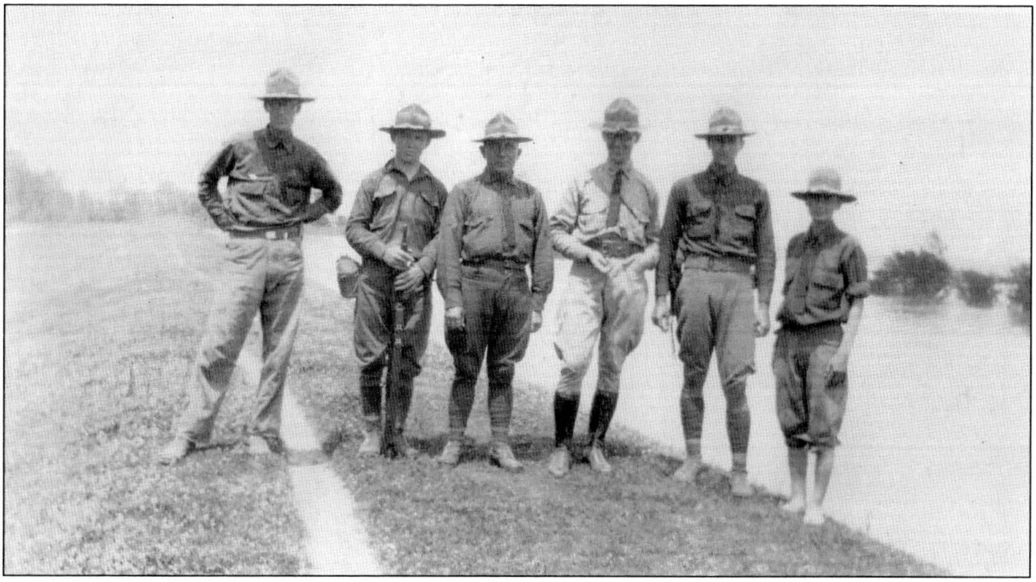

Levees are the best method of protection from flooding in south Louisiana. Pictured are some of the soldiers assigned to Houma posing on the levee and relaxing there as well. The US Army Corps of Engineers spent many months detailing the flooded areas, destruction of levees, destruction of property, and loss of life. It produced maps of its investigations to help in future problems with flooding. In some instances, additional canals dredged by the new oil companies were to blame for flooding in the parish. Eventually, the Terrebonne Levee and Conservation District would be established to engage in flood-control works as related to hurricane protection and tidal or river flooding. (Both, THACS.)

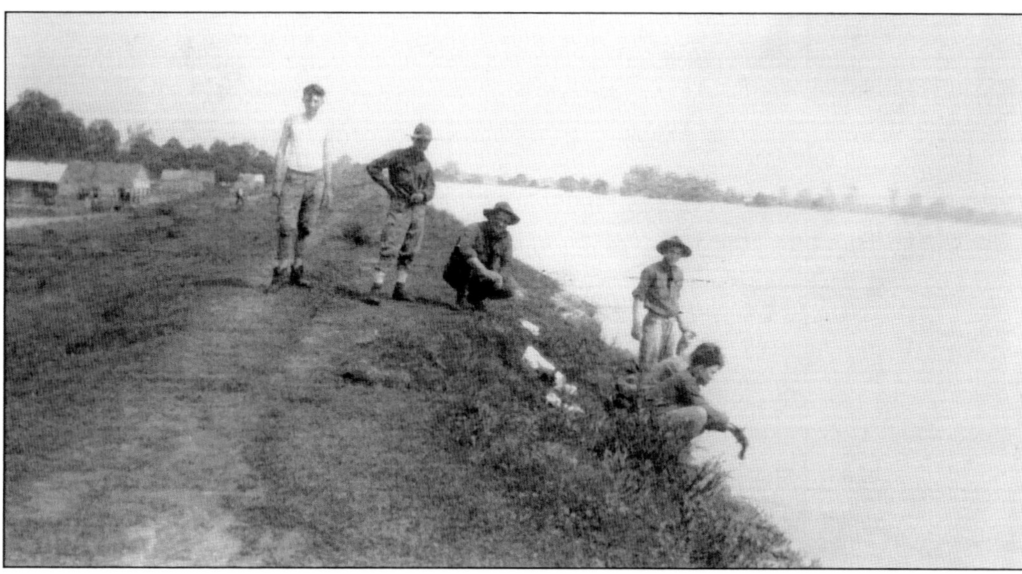

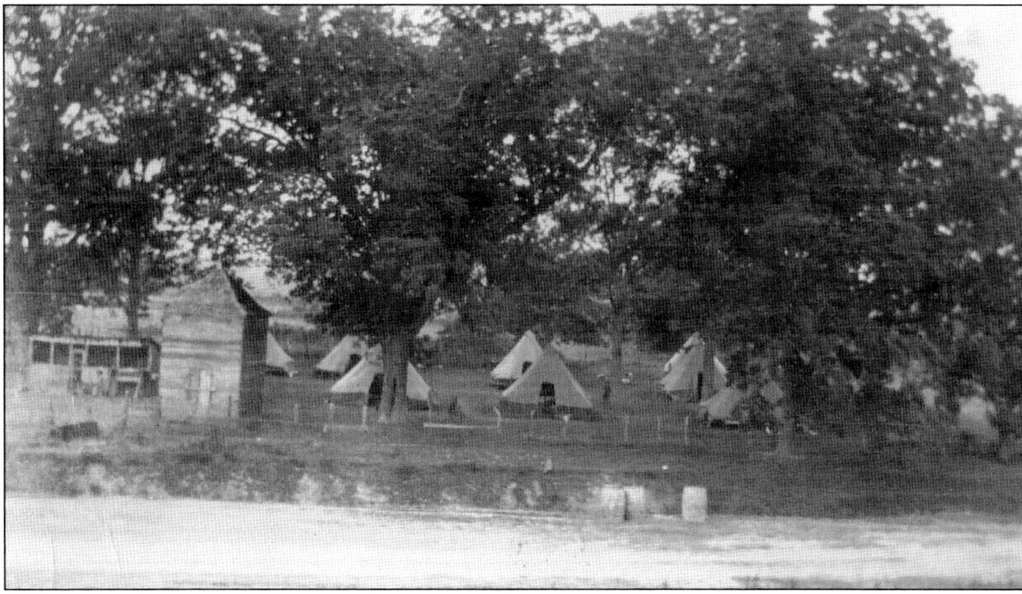

Camps like these pictured were set up all along the path of the Mississippi River–flooded area, housing not just soldiers but also those displaced by the floodwaters. Since government land was not designated for such use, individuals and landowners with available spaces were petitioned and, in some cases, compensated by the government for the use of their land. Many homes, like the one pictured above, had suffered from the tropical hurricane in August the previous year. Survivors were ferried from isolated pieces of land when they found themselves with no other route to the mainland. In some instances, those who owned private boats were recruited in the efforts. (Both, THACS.)

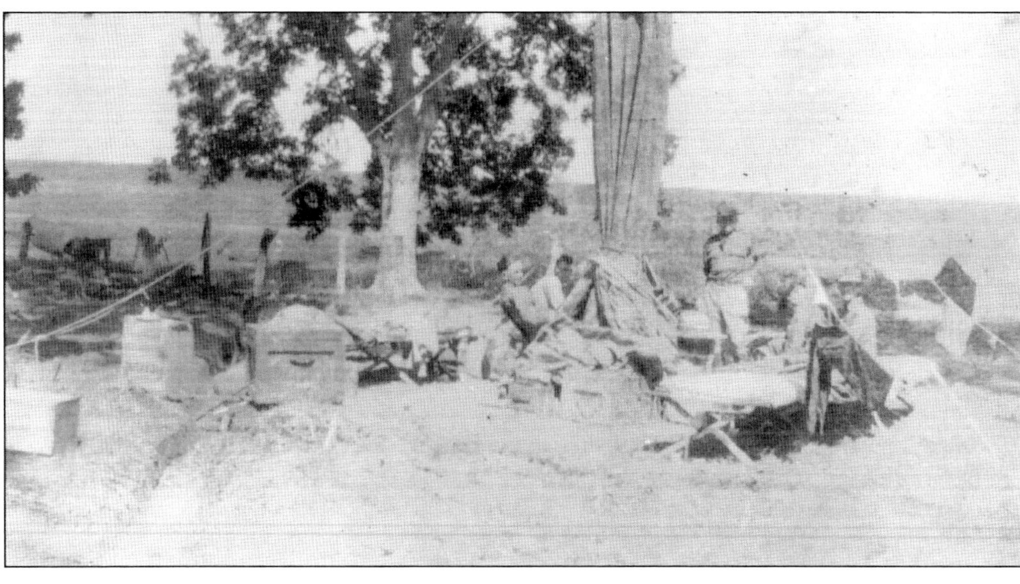

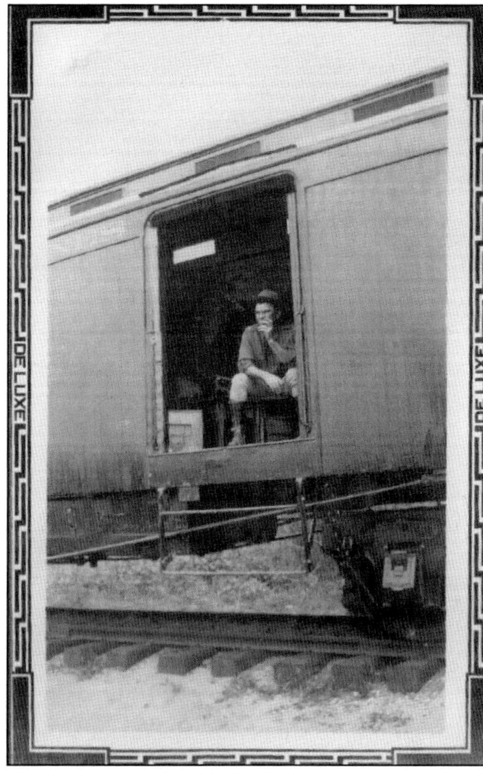

Lieutenants Connelly and Wright are pictured in their designated areas of command. Lieutenant Connelly is standing near the railcar, and Lieutenant Wright, on a levee with the high waters behind him. The depth of the water can be gauged by looking at the barely exposed treetops in the background. Railways were utilized extensively during the flooding. A rail line from Opelousas to New Orleans enabled the soldiers to ship needed supplies and personnel to the affected areas. In some cases, with the shortage of living space, the soldiers could use the railcars as sleeping quarters. (Both, THACS.)

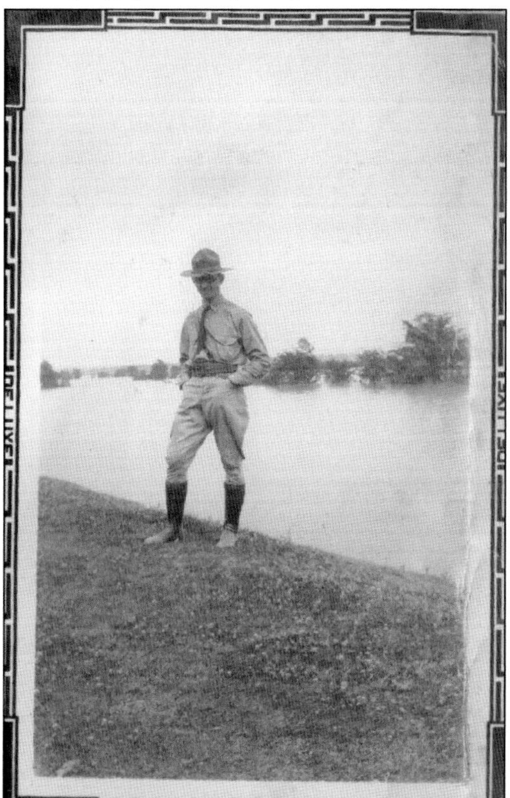

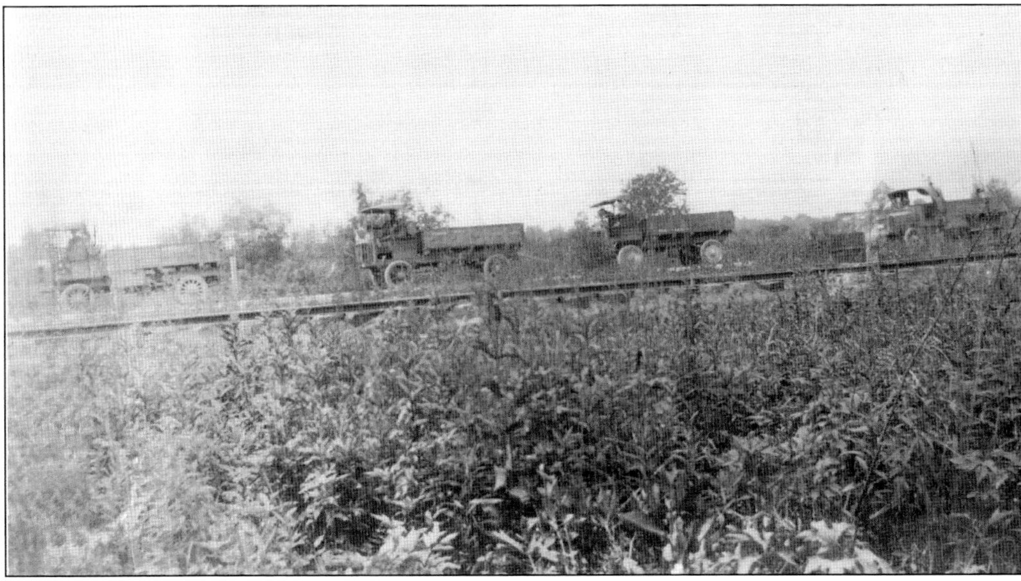

The trucks pictured are fitted with special wheels in order to travel the raised rail lines. In total, more than 100,000 people in the region known as Acadiana were displaced by this flood. The soldiers shown here are creating a makeshift outdoor grill for their accommodation near the rail lines. The flood had changed the face of Louisiana and of America. The total loss and destruction led to the most comprehensive legislation the government had ever enacted, touching the entire Mississippi River valley from Pennsylvania to Montana. In its aftermath was laid the foundation for the New Deal of Franklin D. Roosevelt. Still, it was not only the large rainfall that caused the rising waters in lands so far from the river; man had caused much of the trouble with dredging, clearing land, and years of logging the trees from the swamps. (Both, THACS.)

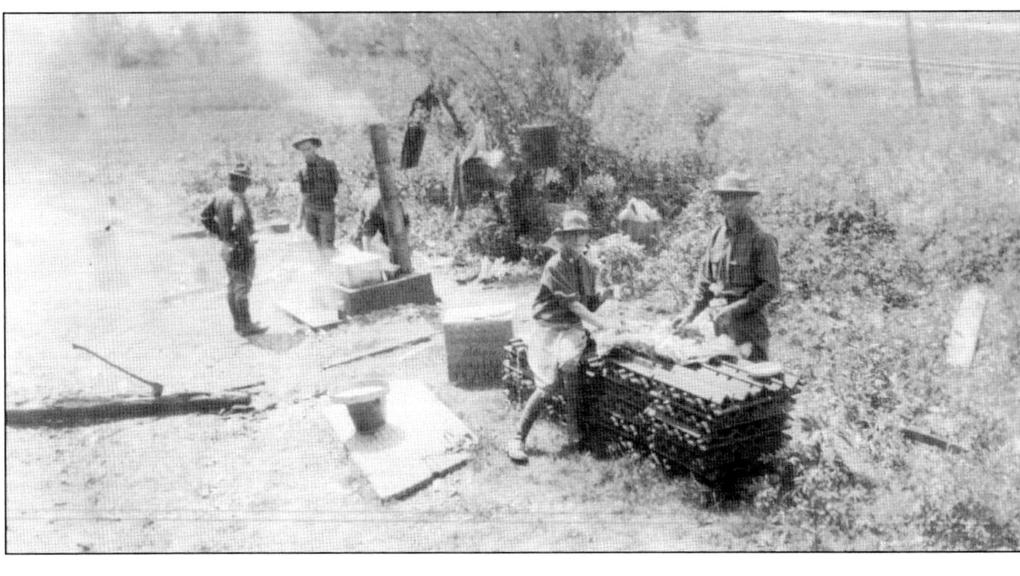

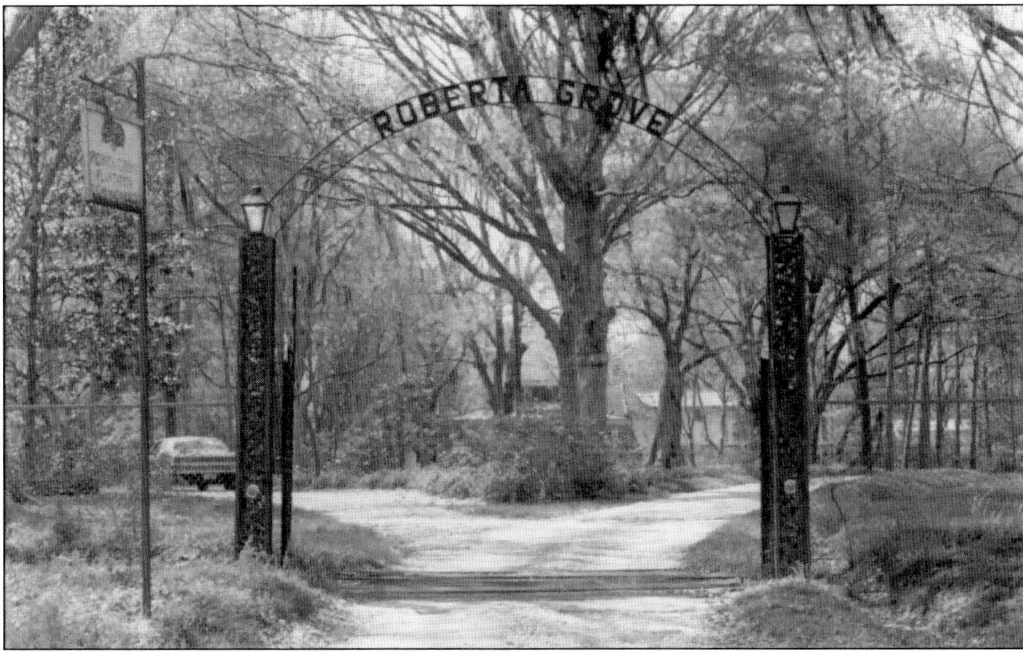

Roberta Grove, the ancestral home of Robert Ruffin Barrow Jr., stood proudly on 14 acres on the east side of Houma. The last owners of the property were Dr. Christian Grenes Cole and his wife, Hallette Barrow Cole. Pictured above is the entrance to the grand house, adorned with foliage and beauty. The Coles lived here and also had a home in New Orleans on St. Charles Street and another grand mansion on a hill in Birmingham, Alabama. Dr. Cole, seen here sitting in his rocking chair, was the coroner for New Orleans for more than 30 years. Originally from Greensburg, Louisiana, he graduated from the Tulane School of Medicine. (Both, THACS.)

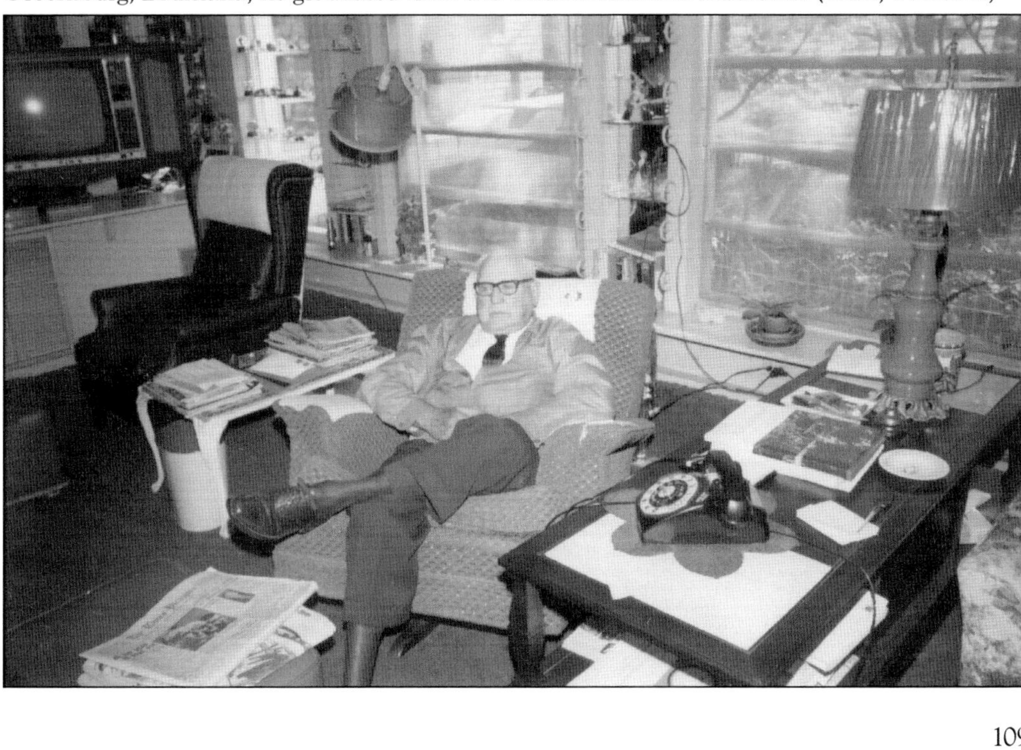

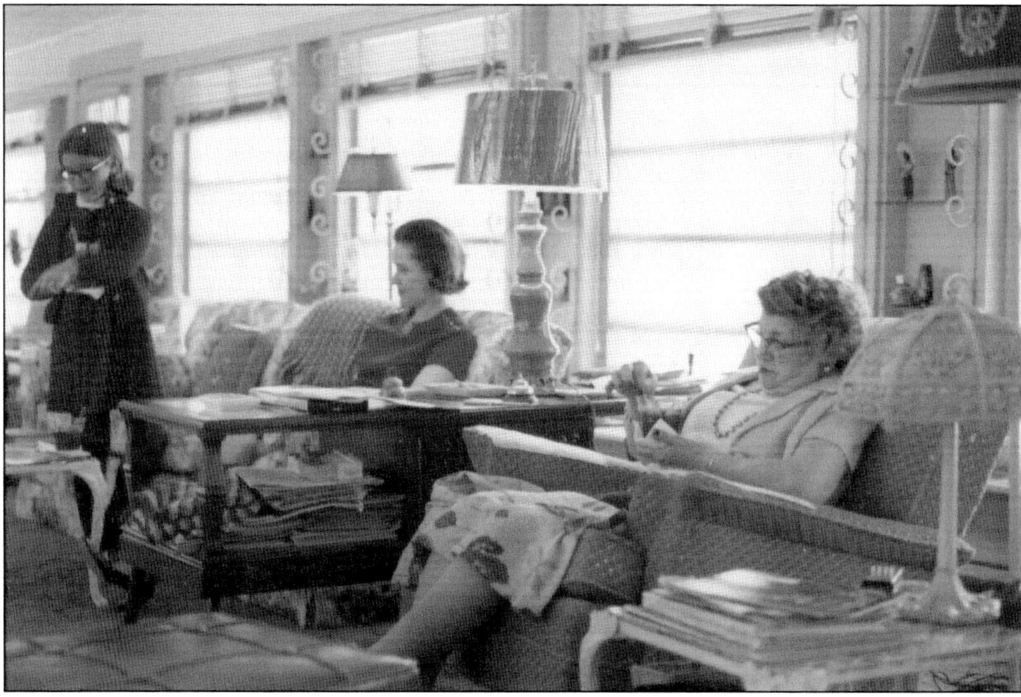

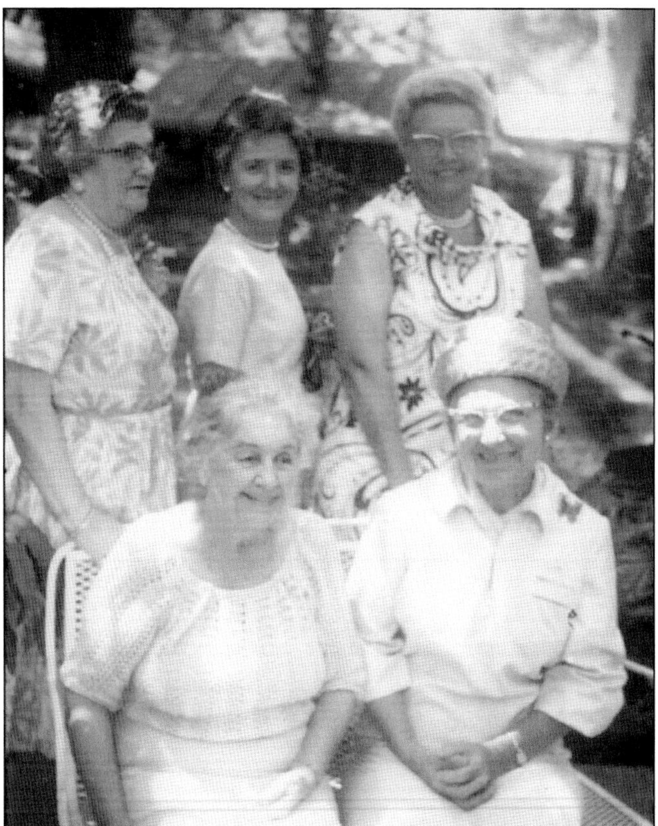

Although the Coles did not have children of their own, they were frequently surrounded by family and friends. Hallette Cole, on the far right in the image above, was descended on her mother's side from the lineage of the last Spanish governor of Louisiana, Manuel Gayoso de Lemos. Her paternal grandfather, Robert Ruffin Barrow, was among the first and the wealthiest sugar plantation owners in Houma. Born to Houma society, Cole was known throughout the region, especially as a collector of limited-edition porcelain. At left, she poses with members of her Garden Society in March 1968; from left to right are (first row) Cecile Pellegran and Thelma Ellender; (second row) Cole, Clothilde Darsey, and May Bazet. (Both, THACS.)

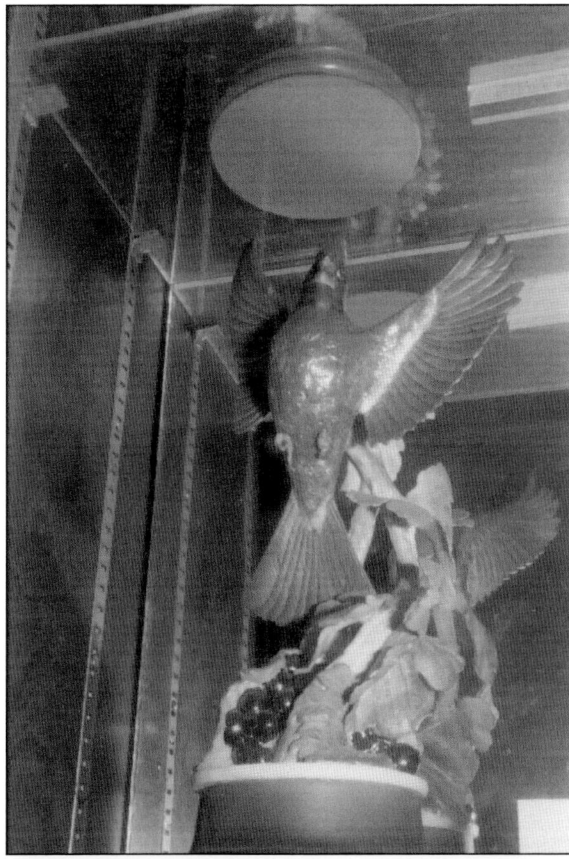

Amongst the treasures Hallette Barrow Cole kept at her Roberta Grove plantation was a collection of 43 Boehm porcelain birds, flowers, and animals. Her collection also included 84 birds (like the cardinal pictured here) by Dorothy Doughty of England, made by the Royal Worcester company. All pieces were limited editions made in the 1950s, 1960s, and 1970s. She commissioned a series of cases (seen below) in which to showcase her porcelain. A great lover of art, Cole donated some of the pieces to the Louisiana Art and Science Institute. After her passing, the rest of the collection went to the Terrebonne Historical and Cultural Society at Southdown Plantation. (Both, THACS.)

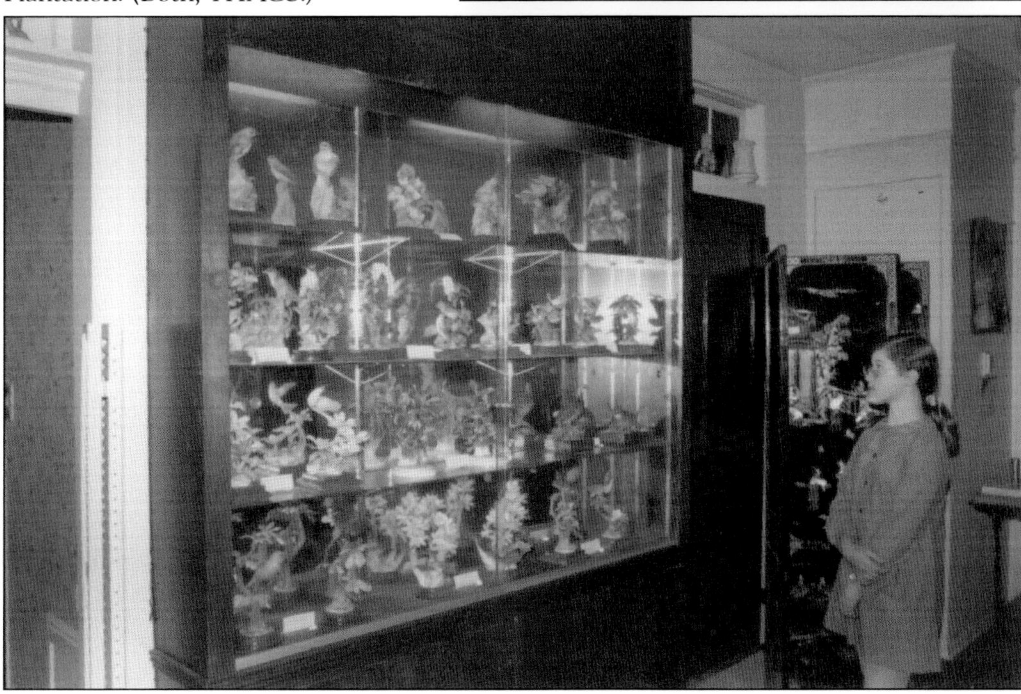

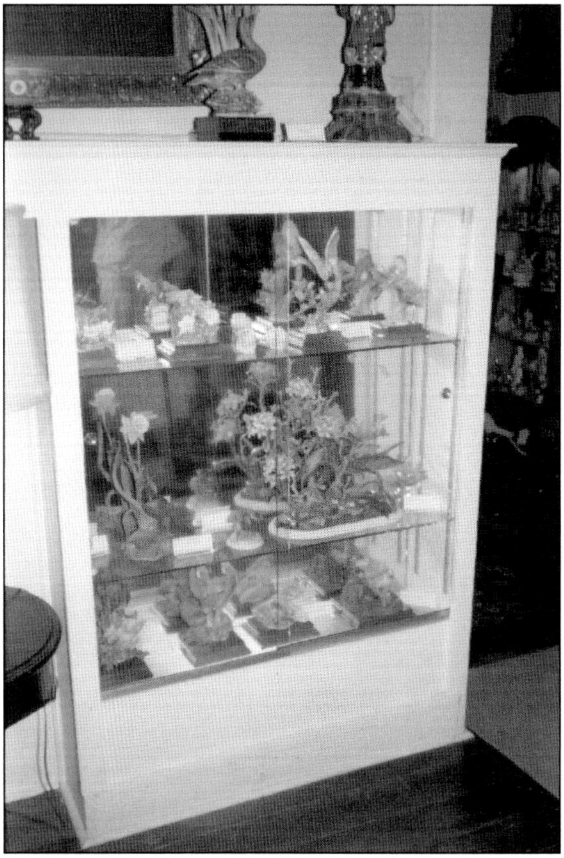

The porcelain figurines graced all surfaces in the house, but Roberta Grove was more than just a showplace for them. The antiques that filled the rooms could be traced back to the 1790s in Portugal, before Governor Gayoso transported them to America. Gayoso landed in New Orleans with a young wife—a Portuguese princess—and a daughter. They traveled to Natchez, Mississippi, where he would take the position as governor. Unfortunately, his wife and daughter died of yellow fever shortly after they arrived. Gayoso would go on to marry again, beginning the line that became Hallette Barrow Cole's ancestry, but he himself died in 1899 of yellow fever in New Orleans. (Both, THACS.)

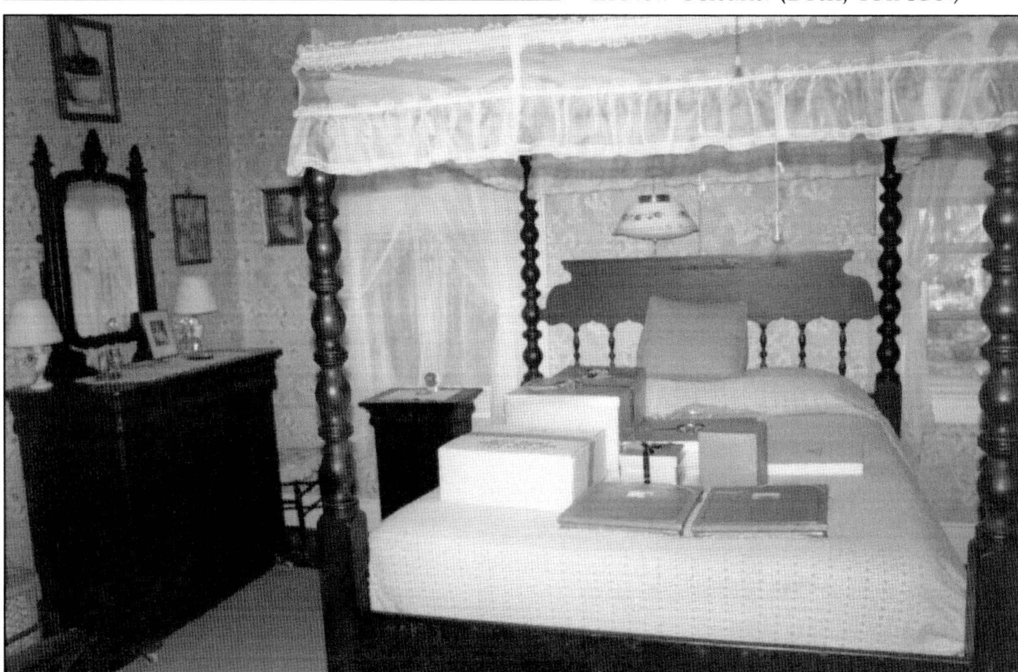

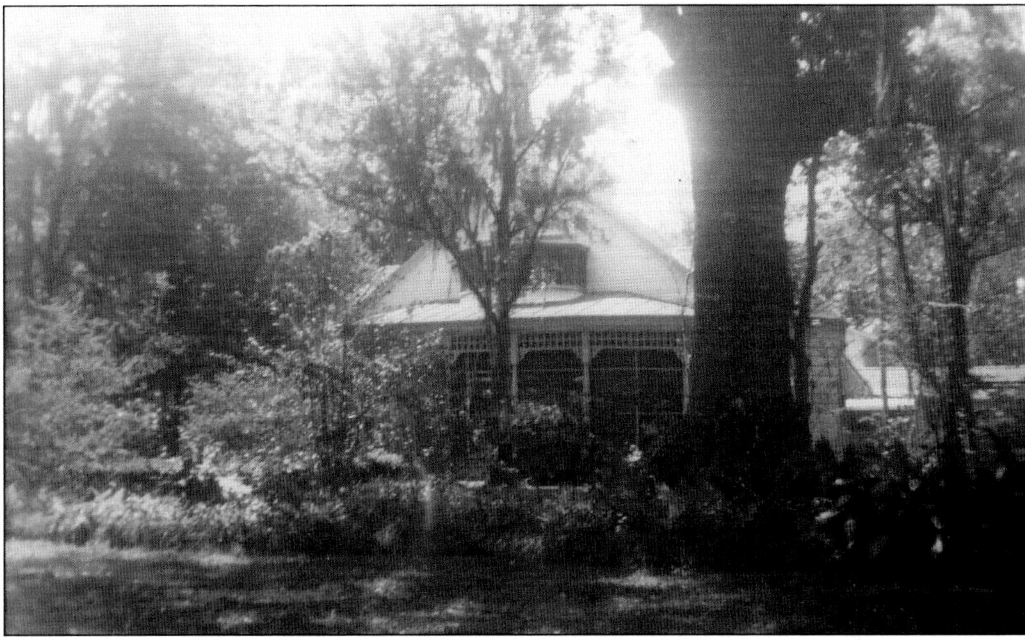

Roberta Grove Plantation is pictured here in the 1960s. Hallette Barrow Cole passed away in 1976, leaving in her will all the contents of the house and her belongings to Dr. Christian Grenes Cole, her husband. When Dr. Cole passed almost exactly a year later, his will divided the estate between four nephews and one niece. Several items were donated to the Terrebonne Historical and Cultural Society at Southdown Plantation, but a dispute between the heirs held much of the property in court for several years. Eventually, things were divided, but there were still issues with the decision of what to do with Roberta Grove. Several years after the Coles' deaths, a fire broke out and destroyed the house, as pictured. The fire marshal declared that the fire was caused by arson. (Both, THACS.)

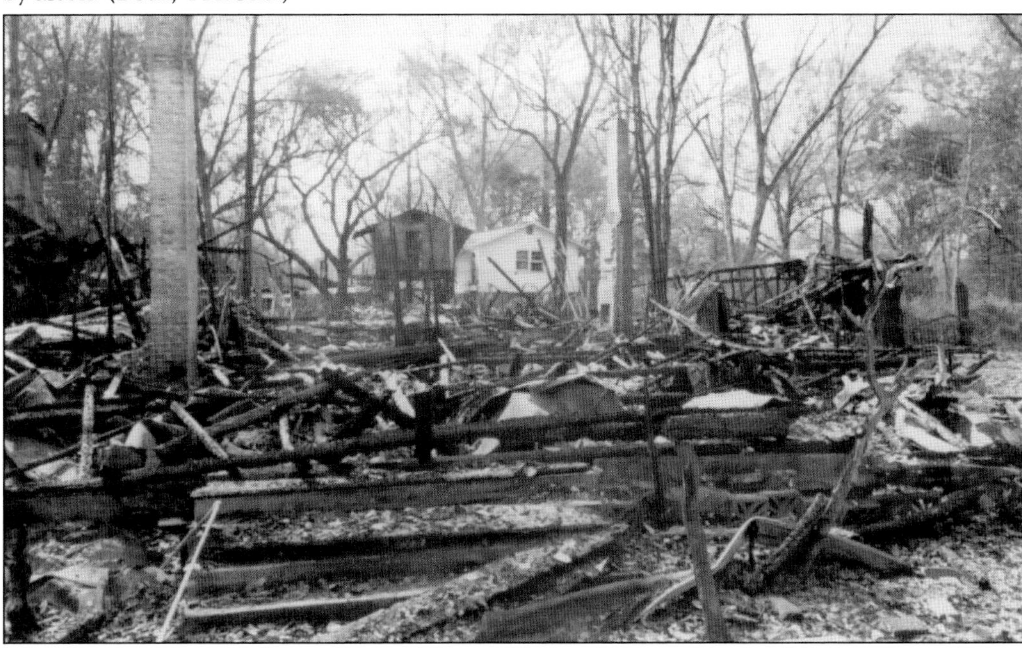

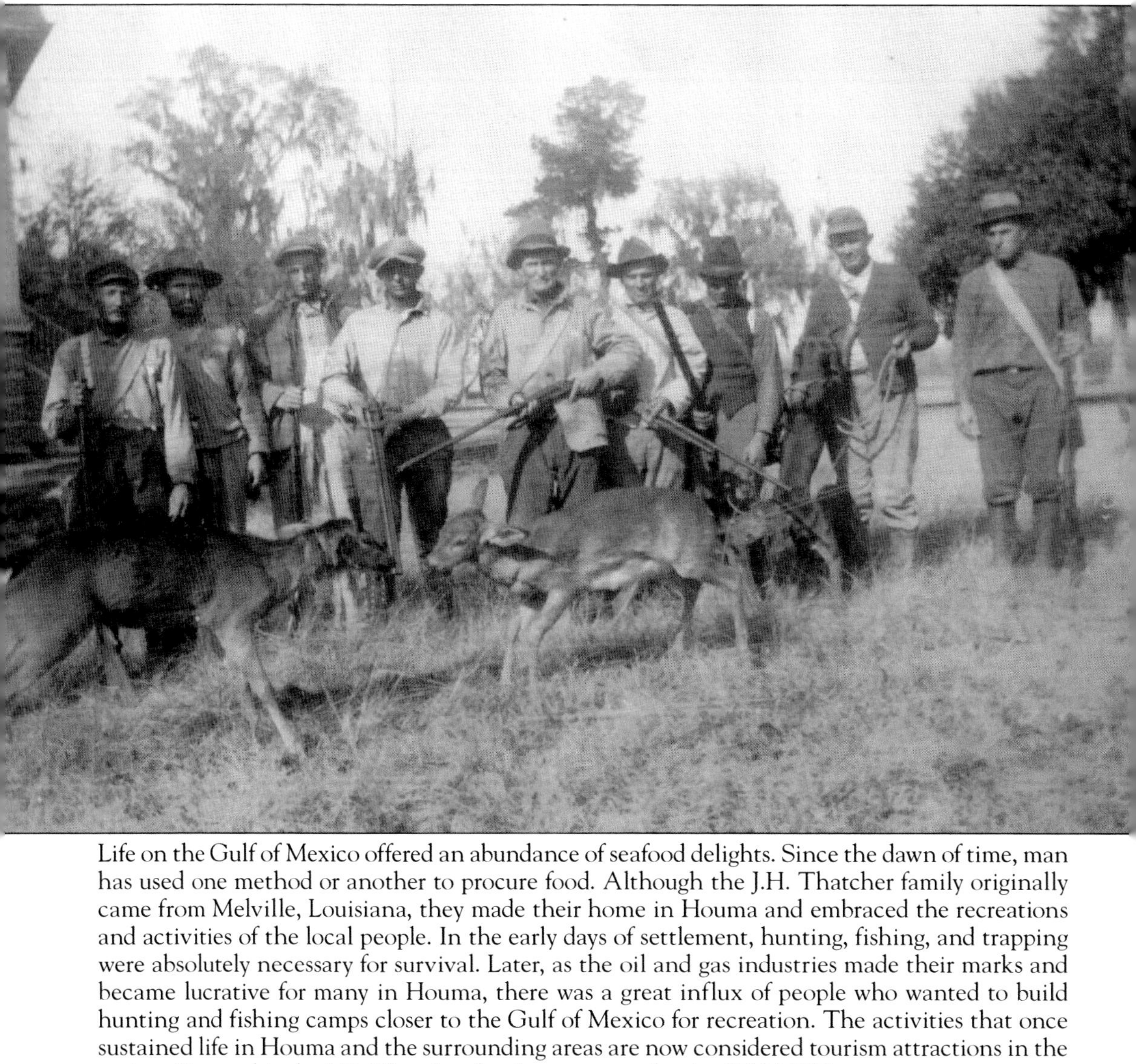

Life on the Gulf of Mexico offered an abundance of seafood delights. Since the dawn of time, man has used one method or another to procure food. Although the J.H. Thatcher family originally came from Melville, Louisiana, they made their home in Houma and embraced the recreations and activities of the local people. In the early days of settlement, hunting, fishing, and trapping were absolutely necessary for survival. Later, as the oil and gas industries made their marks and became lucrative for many in Houma, there was a great influx of people who wanted to build hunting and fishing camps closer to the Gulf of Mexico for recreation. The activities that once sustained life in Houma and the surrounding areas are now considered tourism attractions in the region. Pictured is the J.H. Thatcher family on one such trip. (THACS.)

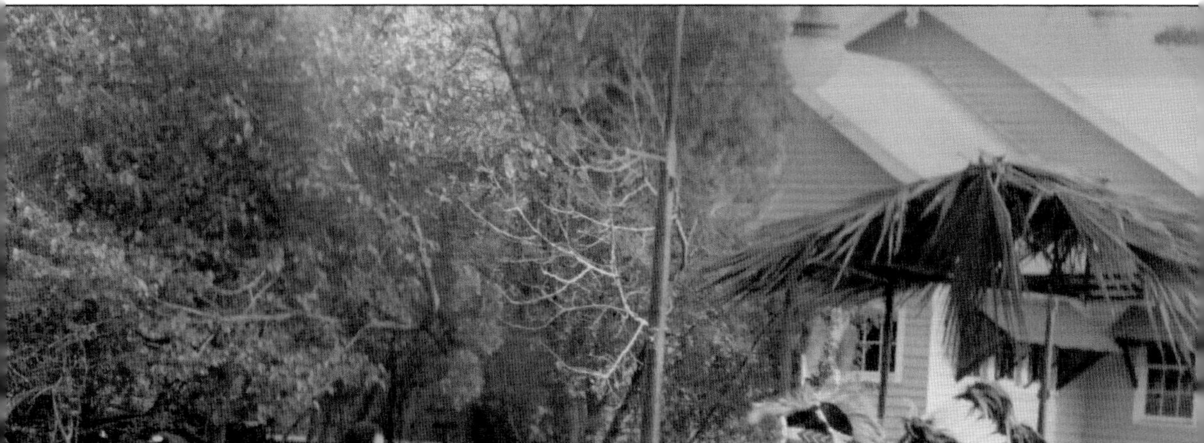

Pictured is a Houma Indians powwow in downtown Houma. The Houmas celebrate their culture with traditional dance, music, arts, crafts, and cooking. "Dancing is our way to come together," said Louise Billiot of Dulac. She has been performing tribal dances for decades and now helps teach youths. "They have to be very elegant and poised," she has noted. "It's like ballet." Dancers dress in beaded formal tribal clothing, full of color and energy. Most recently, there has been an Indian princess contest, in which young Native American girls vie for the title and the opportunity to represent the tribe in other powwows across the country. Along with the celebrations of the Houmas, there are festivals and events depicting Cajun, French, and other traditions through foods, histories, religion, music, customs and crafts, hunting and fishing tournaments, and the wetlands-awareness music festival called Voice of the Wetlands. (UHN.)

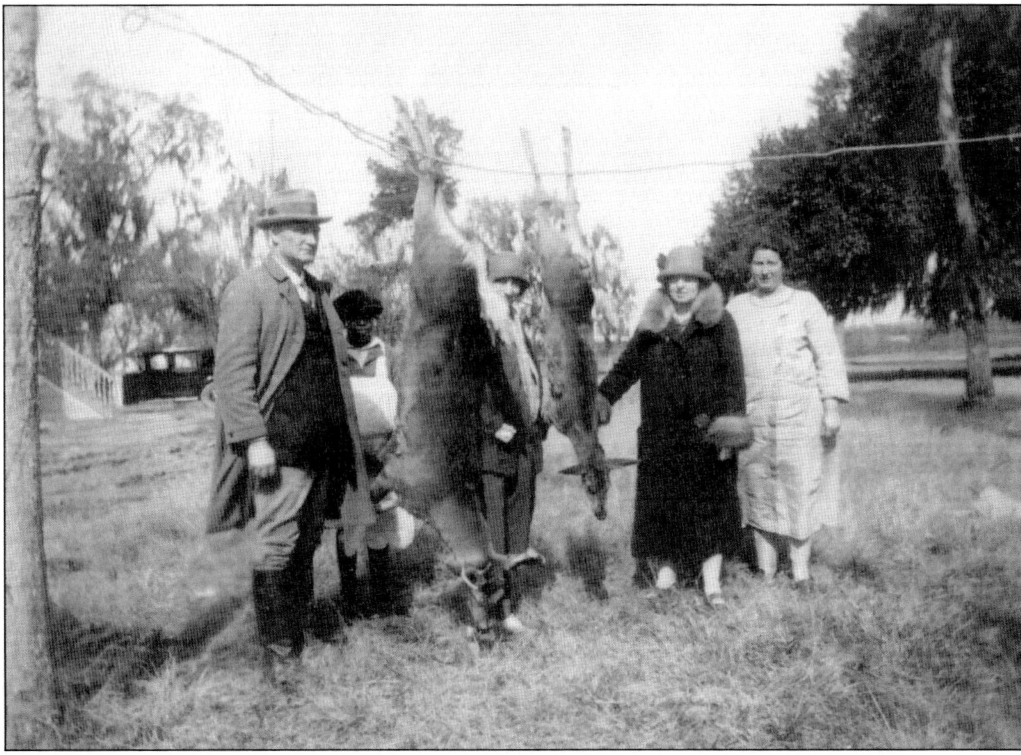

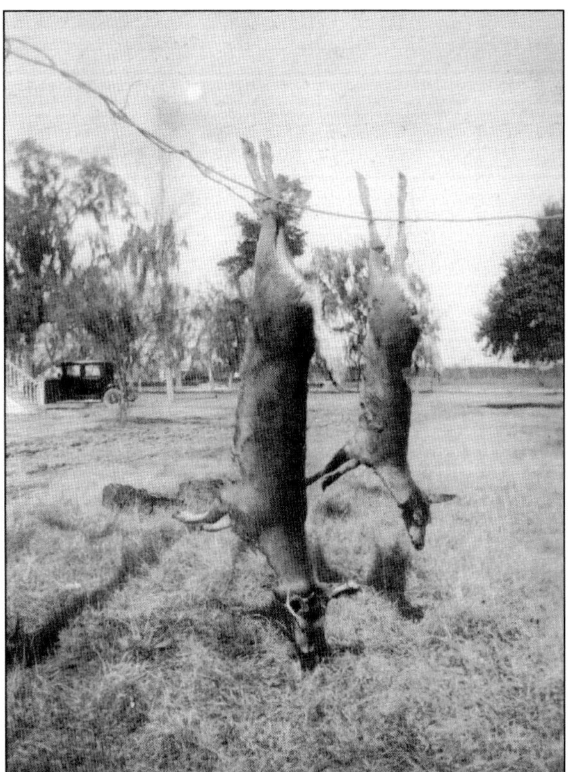

Above, J.H. Thatcher is pictured on the left, with Dora Thatcher (in the coat) to the right. Helen Wurzlow, who was a writer for the *Houma Courier* and eventually put her articles into a collection called *I Dug Up Houma, Terrebonne* (published in 1984), writes, "Man, in his greed for gold, has ruined what was one of Terrebonne's most productive fur-bearing areas Point au Fer Island. This area started a trapper's war that lasted 20 years." She adds, "You can no longer see the stag at eve drinking from his natural stream. The wild deer have to go to the logging canals for drink." (Both, THACS.)

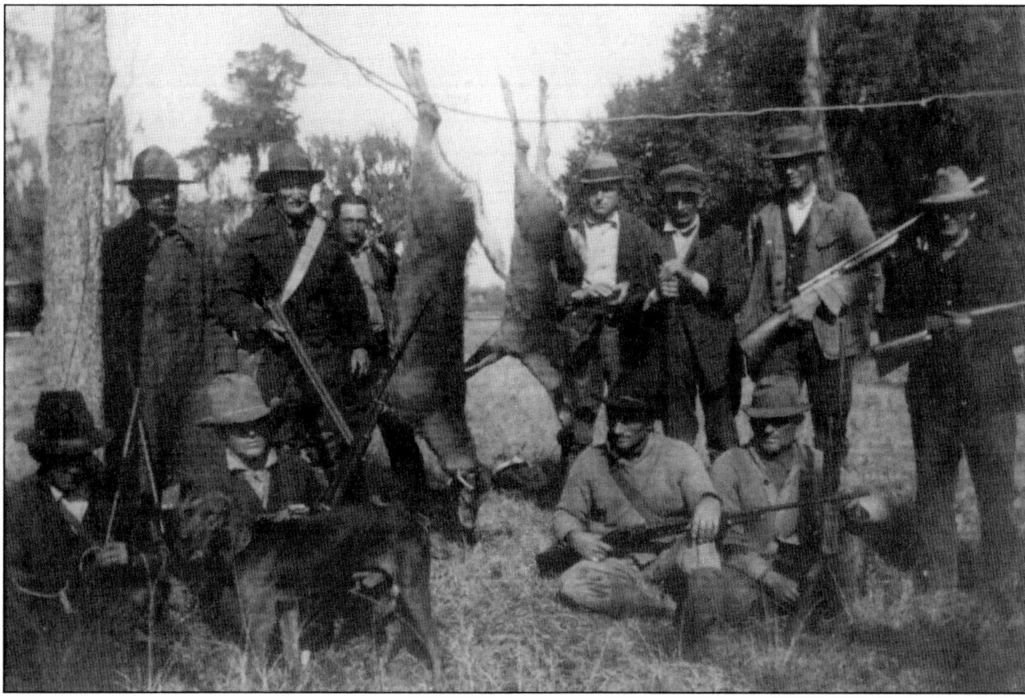

Poaching became a problem in this era as well, since the poachers knew the deer were relegated to drinking from the logging canals. They killed many a wild deer and other animals illegally. Still, there were good, honest men and women who undertook hunting as recreation, and it eventually became a vehicle for a better economy. Businessmen with the oil and gas industry in particular purchased lands down the bayou and built elaborate camps to entertain clients and dignitaries. Business surrounding the hunting industry developed, with tours and trips specifically to experience the "Sportsman's Paradise." (Both, THACS.)

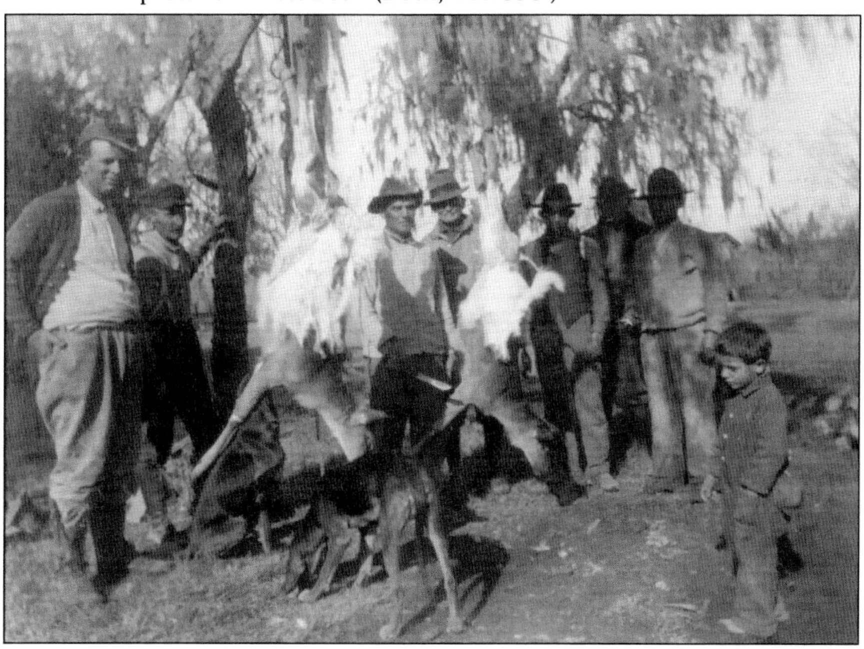

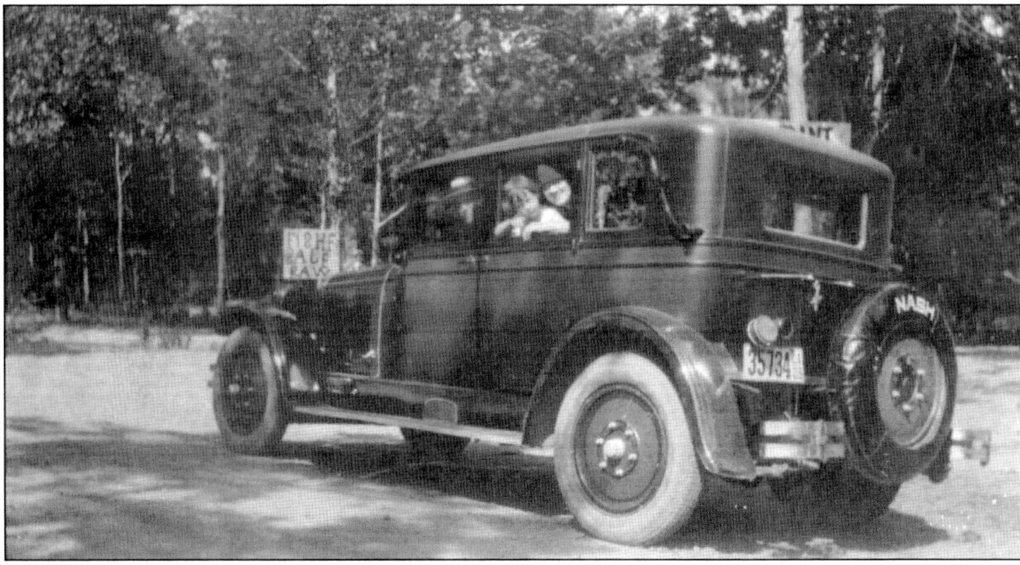

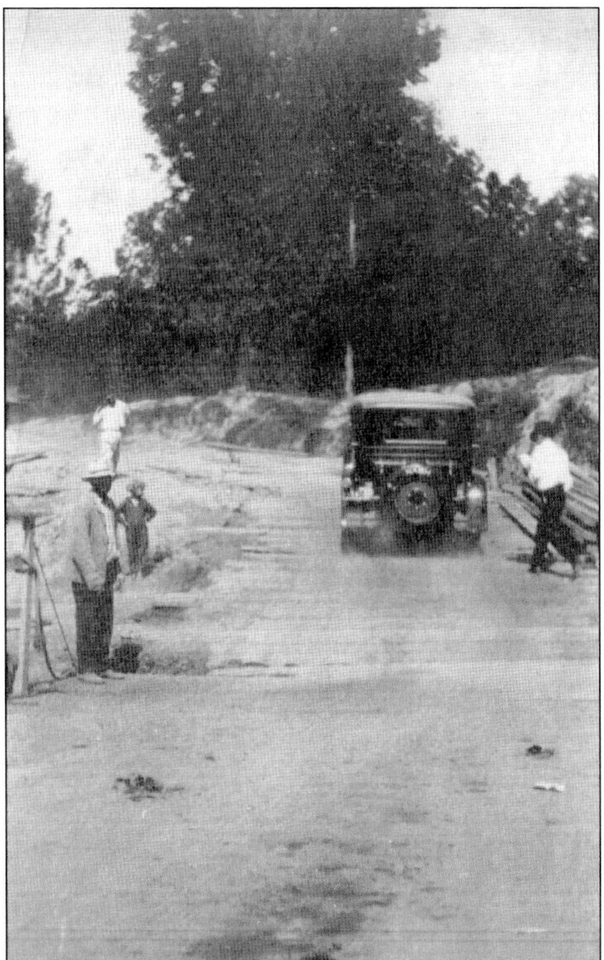

By the 1930s, the modern world was taking hold at Houma in what had started out as a remote area of Louisiana. Gone were the days of horses and wagons; the boats on the bayous and canals that hauled sugarcane turned to barges that hauled oil field supplies and equipment. One by one, the grand plantations were divided into oil and gas fields where sugarcane would not grow again. Local freshwater fishing ended because of the many man-made canals dug for the oil and gas industry to access the Gulf of Mexico, which allowed saltwater intrusion to the freshwater of Houma. The water main street in Houma no longer had the life and activity it had once enjoyed, and the native flora and fauna on it ceased to exist. (Both, THACS).

Eight

Vanishing Coast

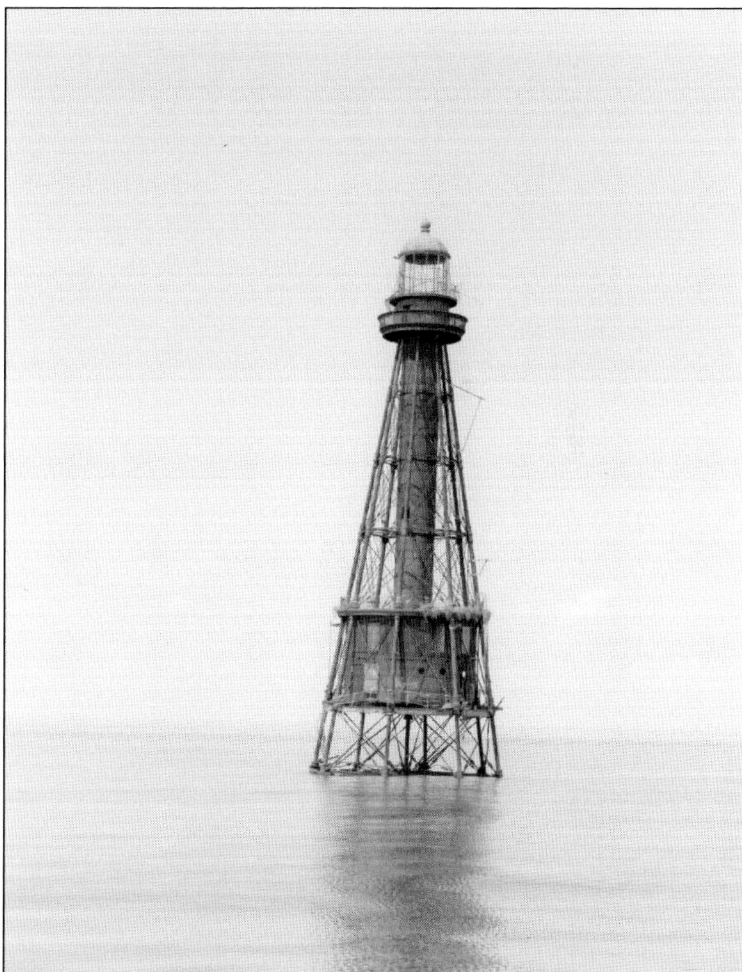

"Vanishing" is the term used for the south Louisiana coast. Like this lighthouse that once stood so proudly as Ship Shoal Light Station at Theriot in Terrebonne Parish, the land is also disappearing. Louisiana is losing 25–35 square miles of land to erosion each year; that is a football-field–sized loss every 15 minutes. (THACS.)

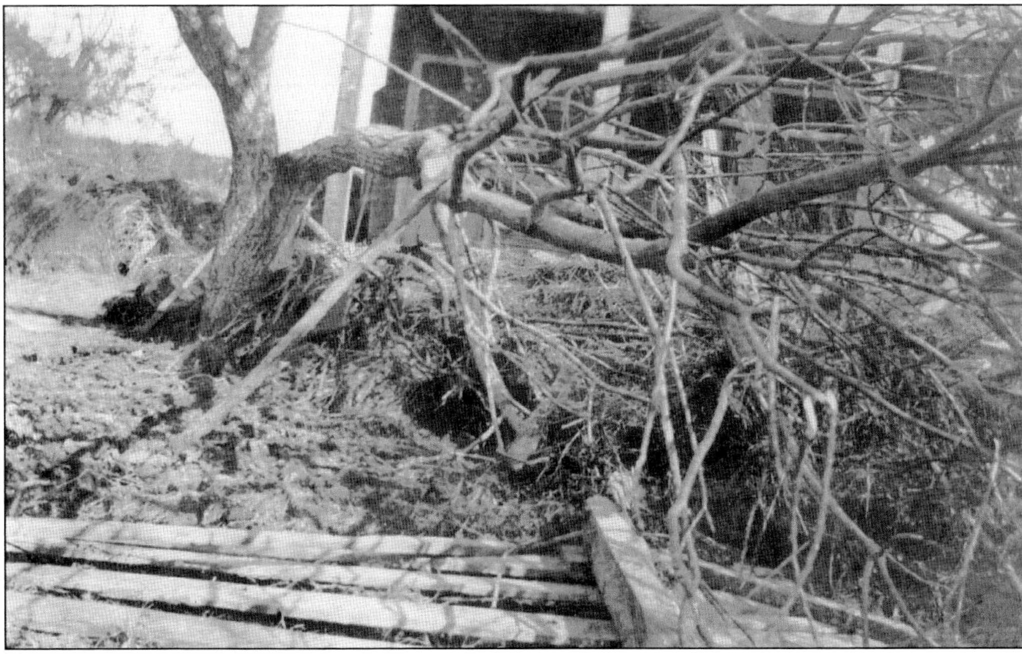

August 25–27, 1926, a hurricane struck near Houma. The steamship *Cody*, lying 220 miles east-southeast of Galveston, reported 75-mile-per-hour winds, while the steamship *Argon* saw northeast winds of 100 miles per hour near N 27 W90.5. The pressure bottomed out at 28.31 inches in Houma, with estimated winds of 100 miles per hour. The destruction was massive, especially in the small communities down the bayou. In the image above, the house in the background was not a casualty; the tree in the foreground luckily fell in the opposite direction. At Houma, the sugarhouse was wrecked at Southdown Plantation, and the Episcopal church was smashed. (Both, THACS.)

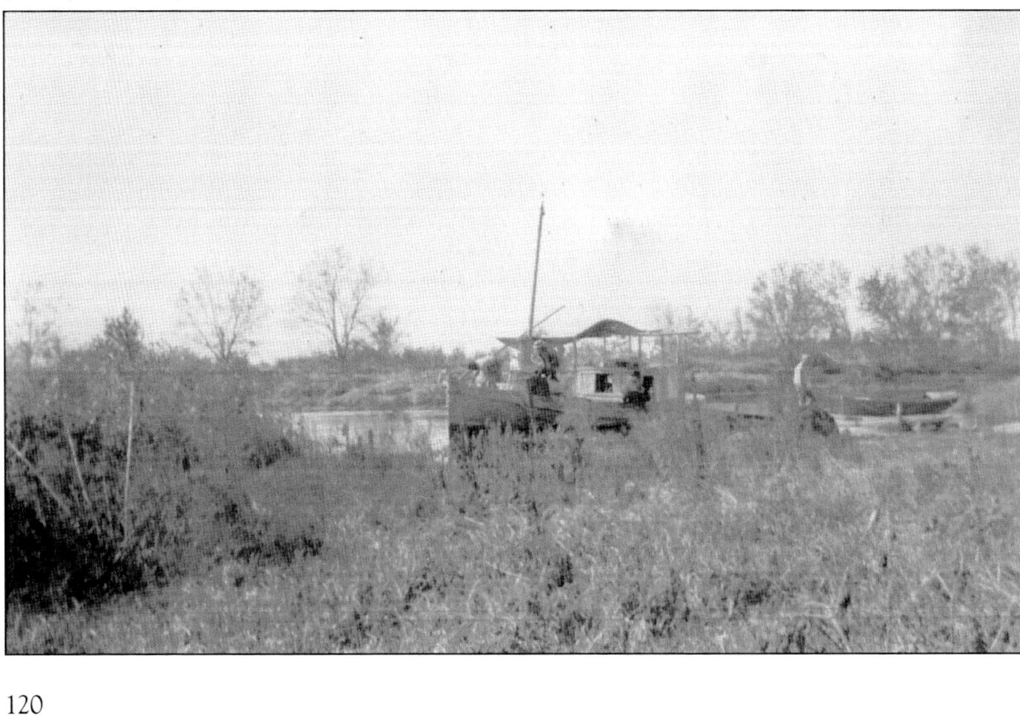

During the 1926 hurricane, the house seen at right on the bayou at Grand Couteau was literally blown into the water, rendering the structure a total loss. Below is a tree that was next to a house in Montegut before the hurricane. The mangled tree remains, but not the house. The situation was grim at Montegut. Days after the hurricane, authorities were still finding bodies. One account states they were "trapped within the walls of their shack and tossed about on the waves until the flimsy structure was battered to pieces sending the fugitives to their death." Bodies of nine of the eleven persons had been recovered and identified, while more than a hundred men in small boats were scouring the waters in search of the missing two. (Both, THACS.)

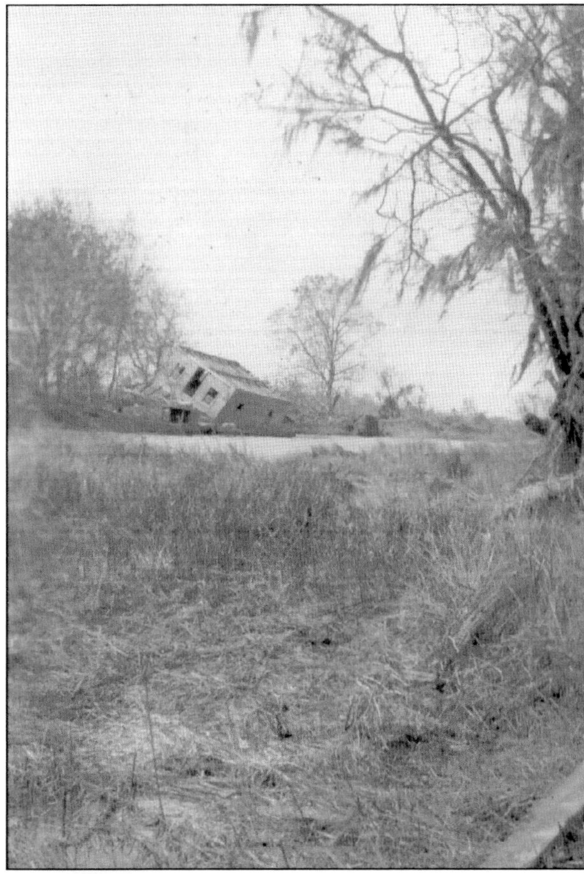

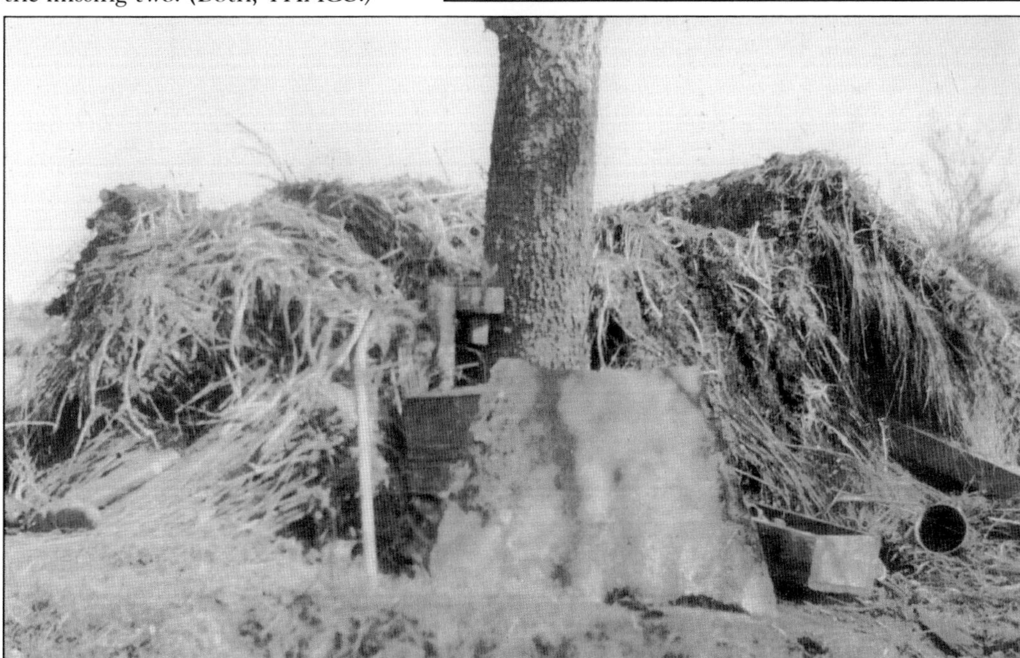

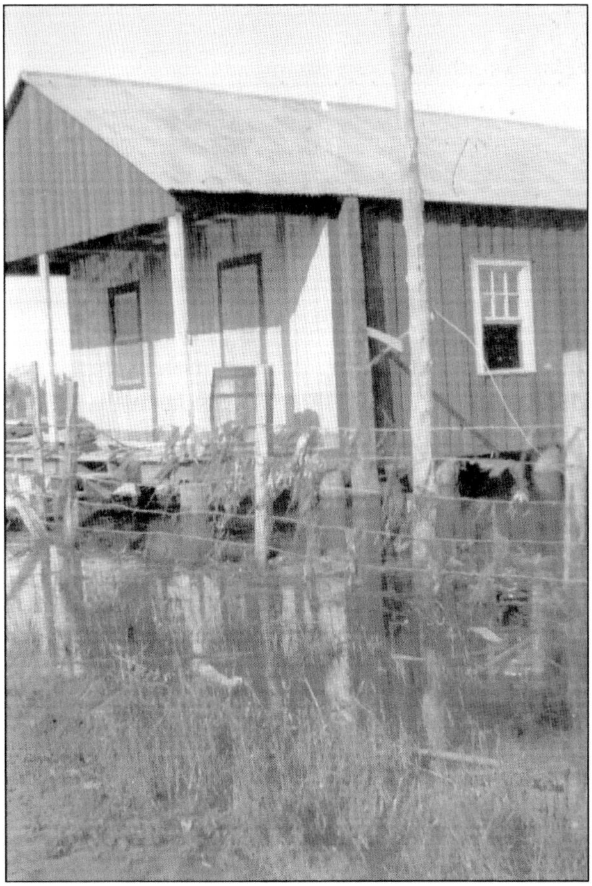

Pictured at left is a house that withstood the winds but succumbed to water at Montegut. Some of these houses and structures were recreational camps. The newspaper reported, "The identified dead are Claude Dupont, prominent citizen of Houma, La.; Charles Dupont, his 5-year-old son; Mose Matthews, foreman of a Felicity Island shrimp platform, Matthews's two daughters, Edith, 16 years old, and Serita, 10 years old; and one of Matthews' two young sons; Mr. and Mrs. Joseph Naquin and their 4-month-old baby Wilfred, natives of Felicity Island. The two members of the party who have been given up for dead but whose bodies had not been located tonight are Mrs. Mose Matthews and the other son who were at Felicity Island." (Both, THACS.)

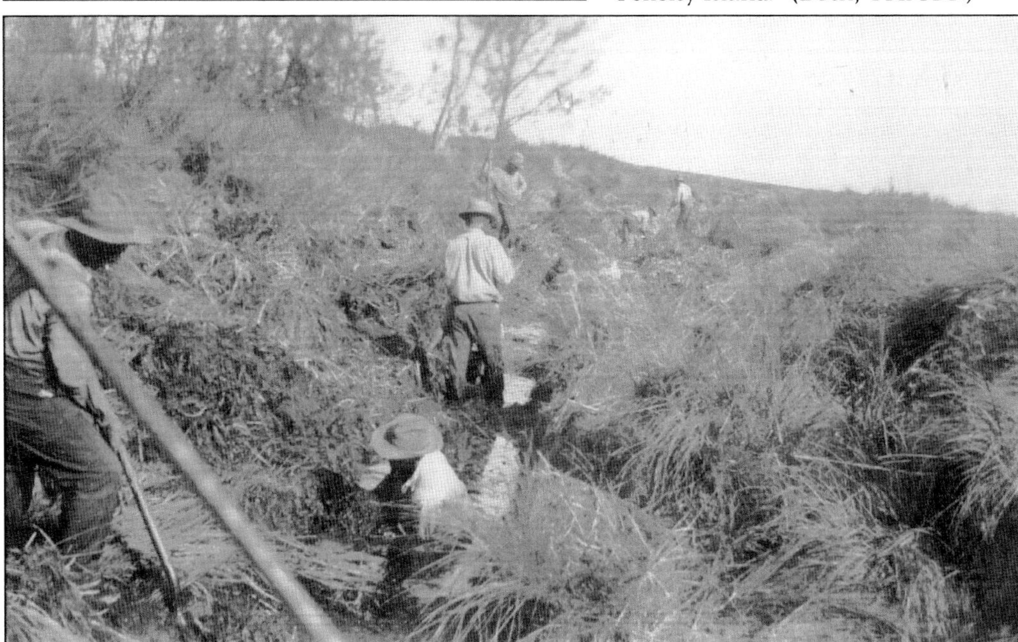

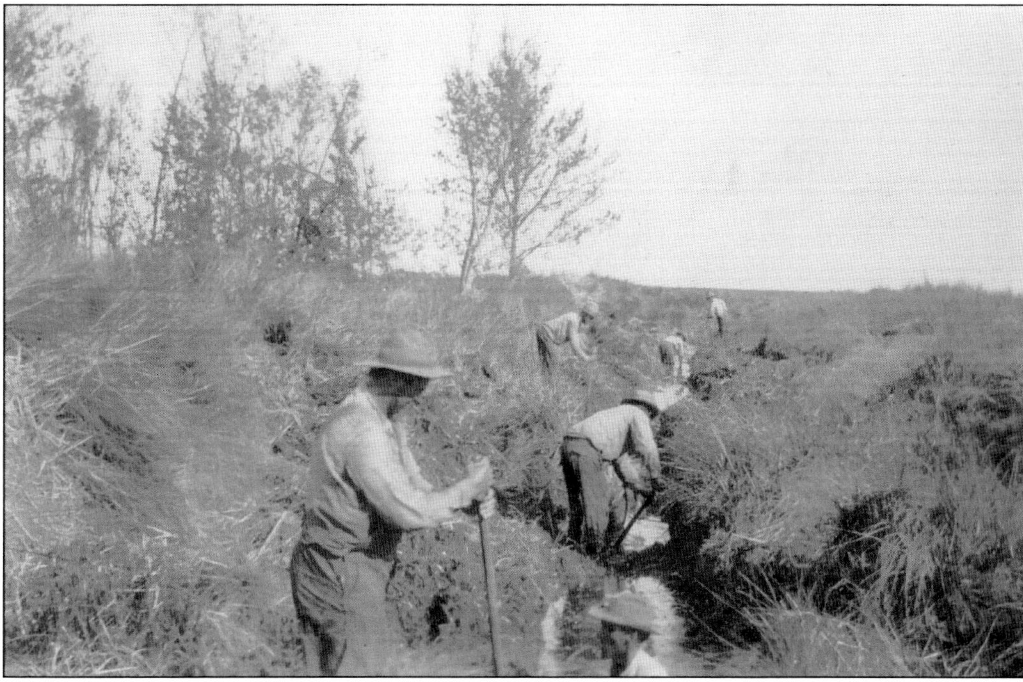

"The location of the bodies [at Felicity Island] and marks on the floor of the shack . . . showed the occupants of the camp tried to chip a hole in the floor to let water in so the cabin would not float out to sea convinced searchers that all eleven . . . were drowned like rats in a trap." When workers could begin the search and rescue, they utilized the so-called floating prairies. All along the Gulf Coast, a large border of marshland floats on the surface of the water. The mass of fallen timber and grasses gradually accumulates dirt and becomes firm enough to hold men or even a vehicle, as pictured. (Both, THACS.)

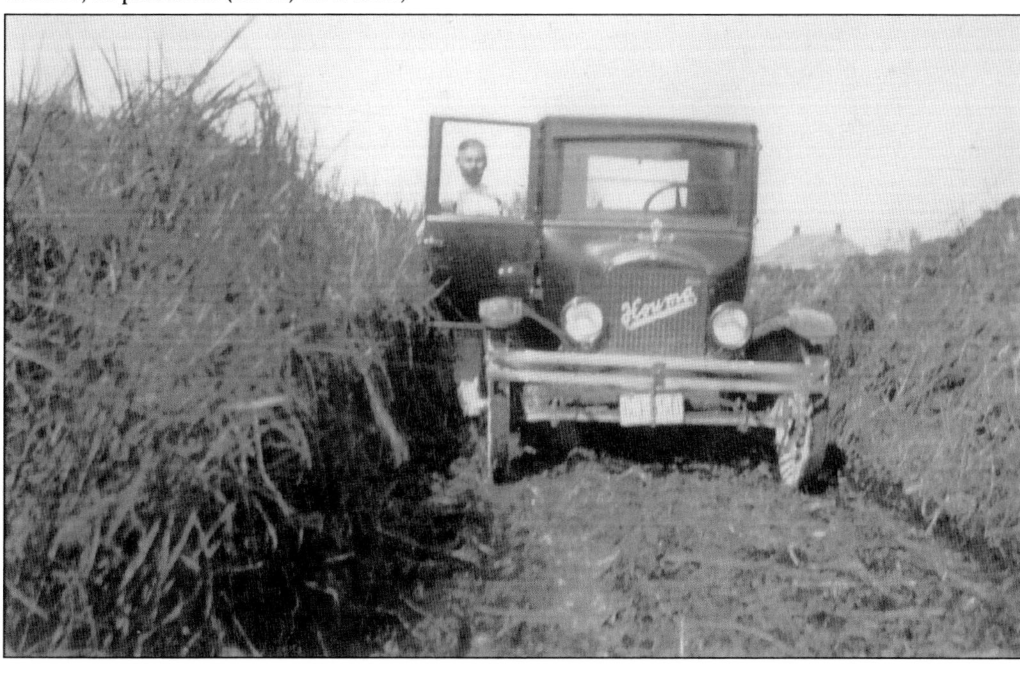

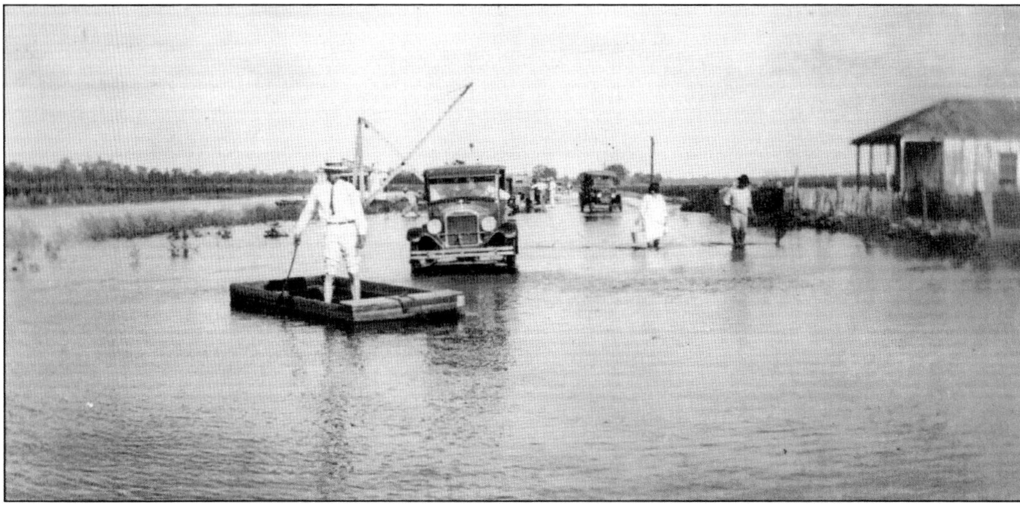

Nine members of the Leo Naquin family had been on the platform with Dupont and the others. Naquin and his family left the shrimp platform Wednesday afternoon and asked the other 11 members of the group to leave with them. Dupont and those who remained insisted it would be wiser to wait for a 45-foot lugger, which was expected to arrive soon to take the party inland. Naquin disagreed and set off across the island waterways. The storm caught them when the skiff was at about the middle of the island; Naquin and all of his family except the three who were drowned left before the hurricane reached its height and were saved after fighting the waves all night. Two men clung to thorn trees and kept the open skiff with the seven others aboard upright. (Both, THACS.)

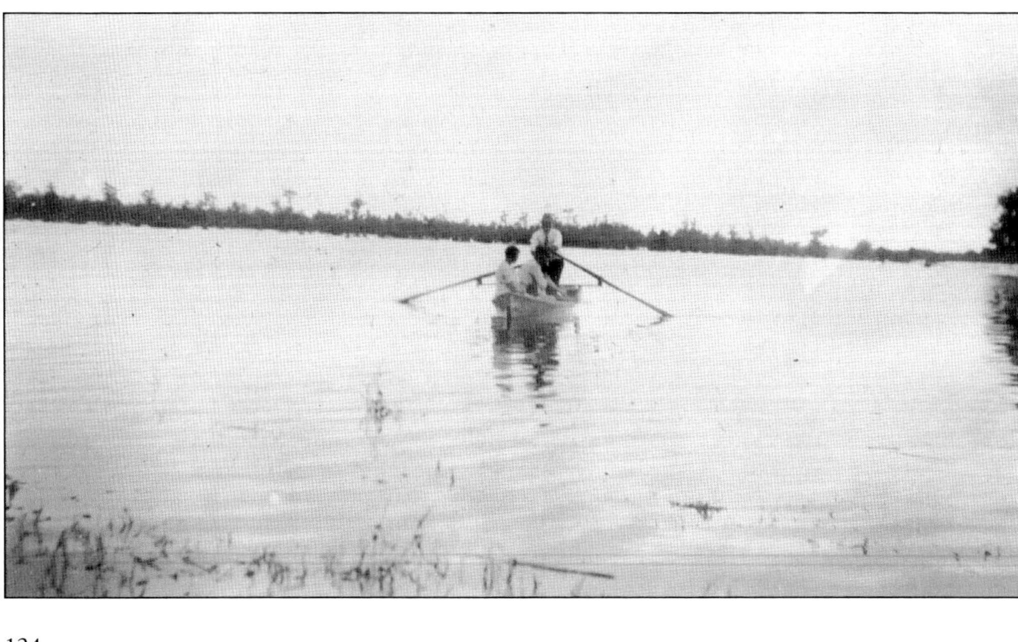

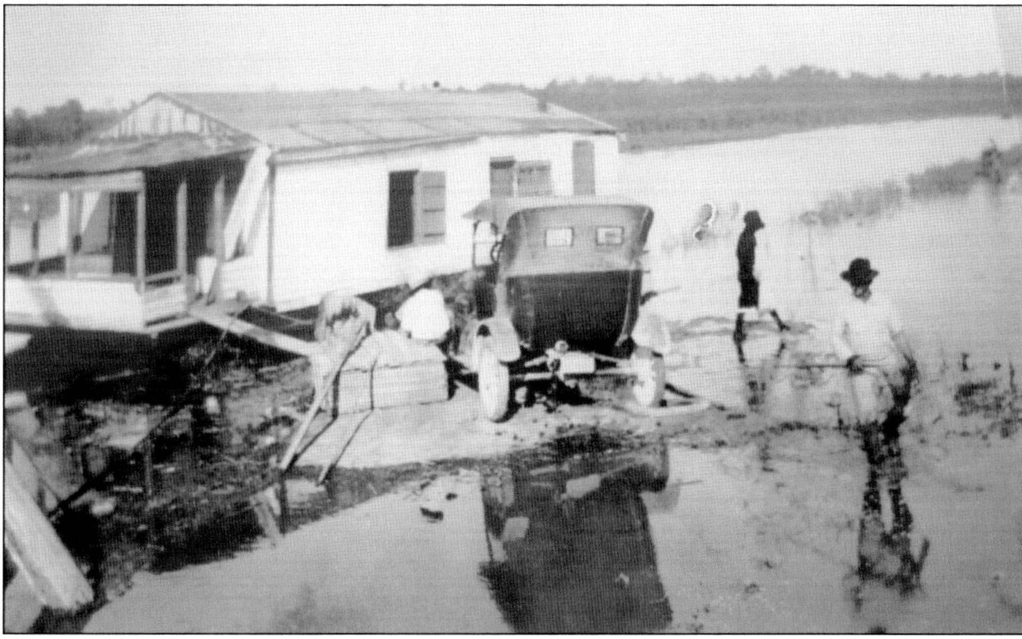

The 1926 hurricane and the flooding of the Mississippi River (as pictured above in 1927) devastated much of the parish. Industries struggled to come back in the aftermath of so much death and destruction in Houma, but they persevered, and Houma was again the hub of activity in the oil and gas as well as the fishing and tourism industries. Some areas have struggled to rebuild after subsequent hurricanes, but areas like Four Points, south of Dulac (pictured below), have weathered the storms and come out the other side. Hurricane protection will always be an issue for the people on the Gulf Coast, but the rugged men and women who carved this section of the United States for centuries will continue to battle for their homes and way of life. (Both, THACS.)

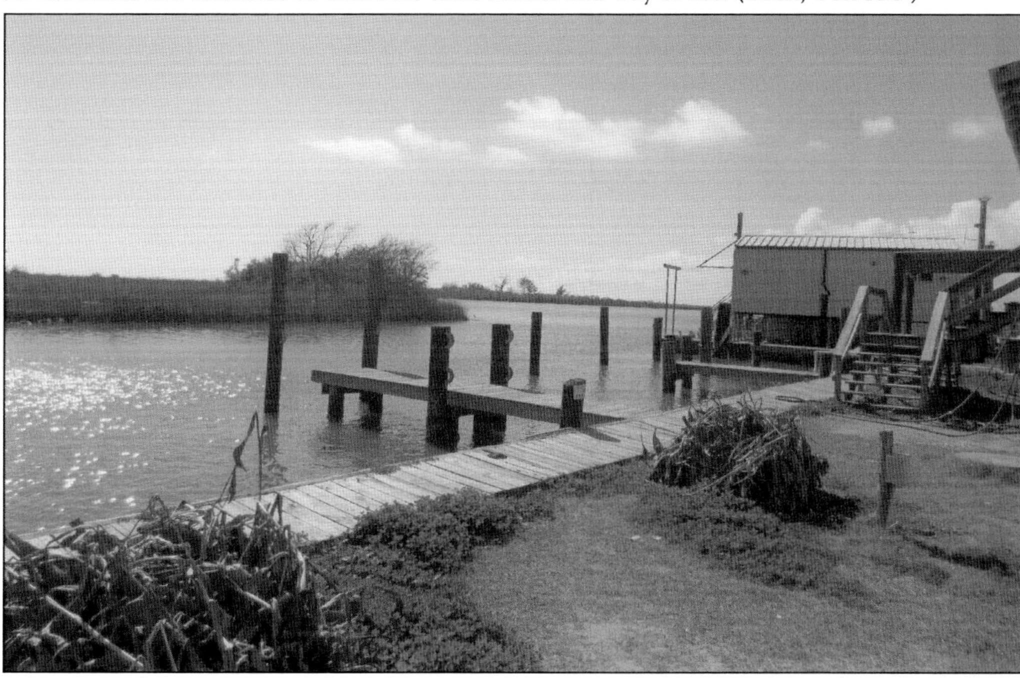

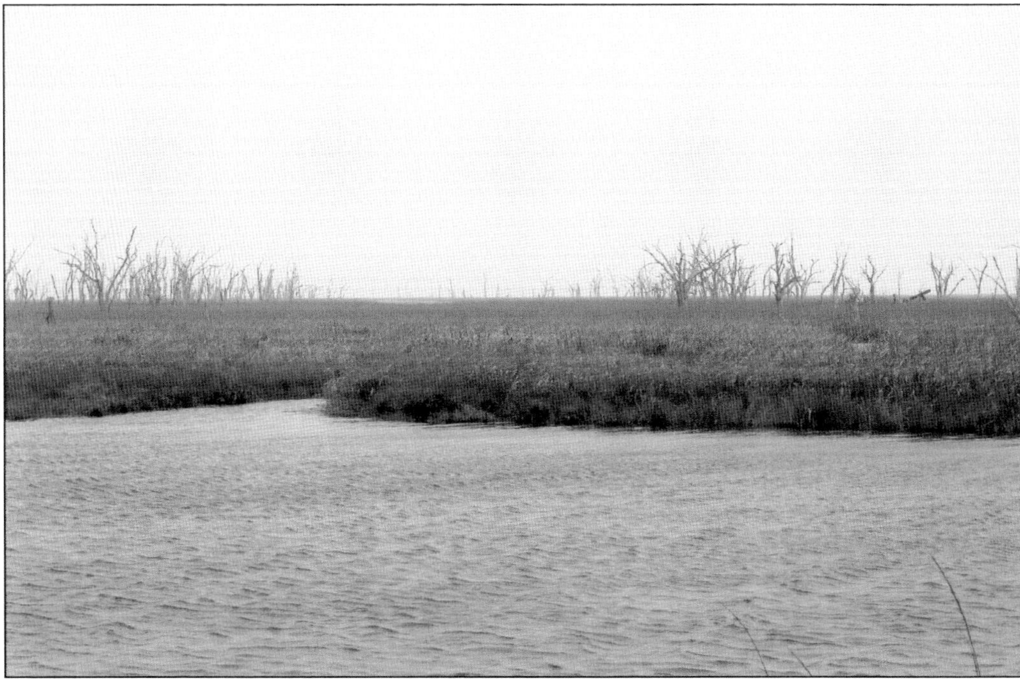

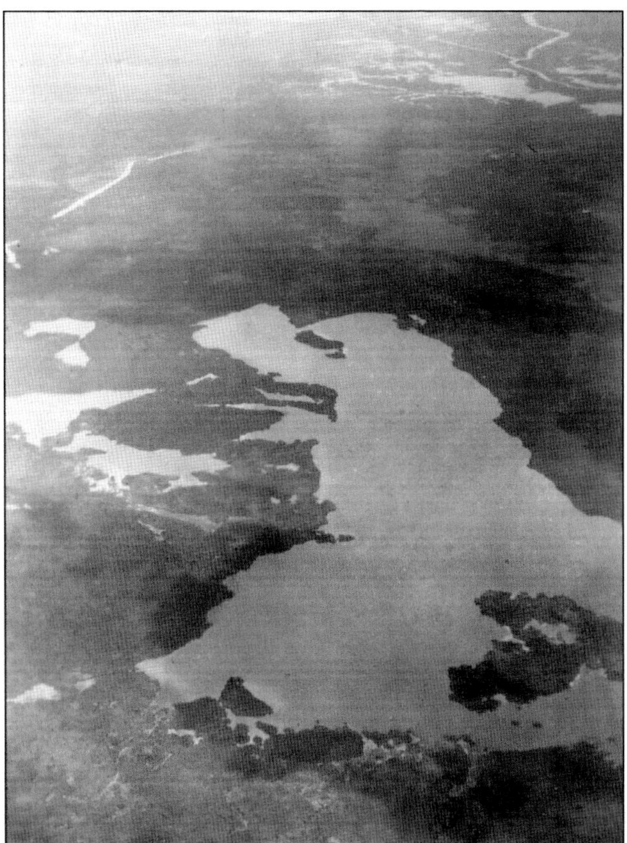

The crisis is that Louisiana contains approximately 40 percent of the nation's wetlands and experiences 90 percent of the coastal-wetland loss in the Lower 48 states. Of Louisiana's land loss, 60 percent occurs in the Barataria and Terrebonne Basins. The coast is losing 25–35 square miles of wetlands per year, with the Barataria and Terrebonne Basins losing 10 and 11 square miles per year. At current land-loss rates, nearly 640,000 more acres— an area nearly the size of Rhode Island—will be under water by 2050. Eighteen percent of US oil production and twenty-four percent of US natural gas production originates, is transported through, or is processed in Louisiana coastal wetlands. One-fourth of the nation's energy supply depends on the support facilities in south Louisiana. (Both, THACS.)

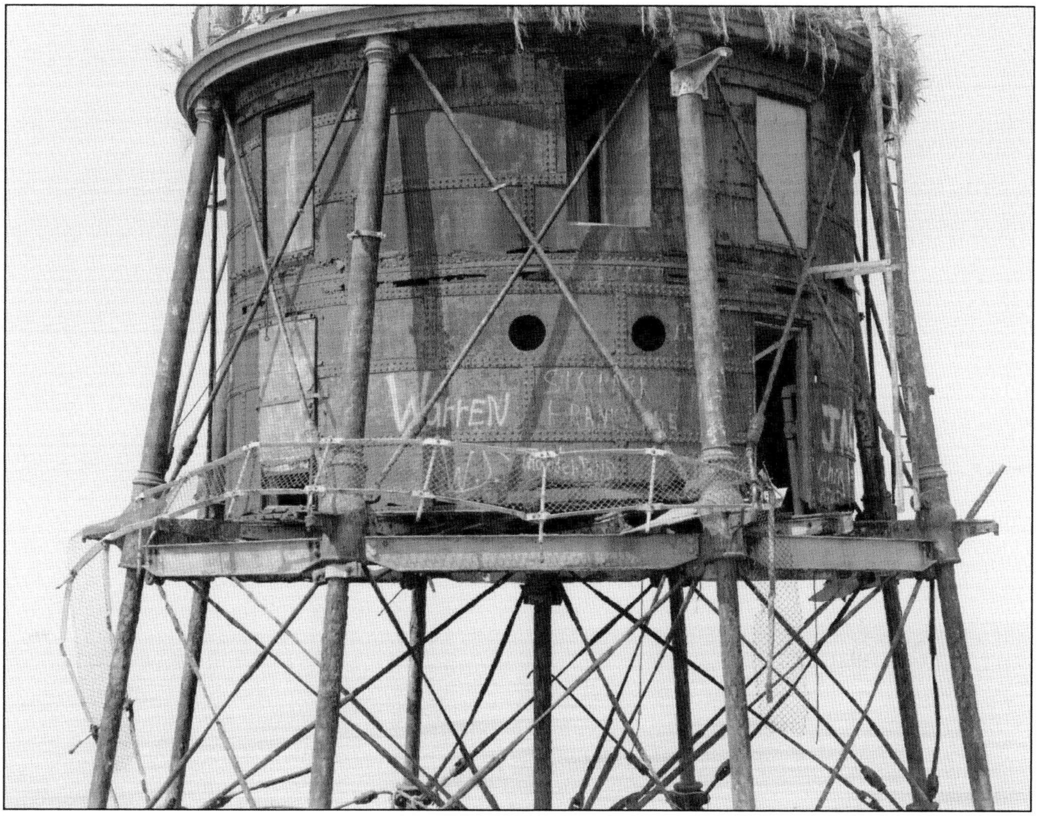

Like the lighthouse at Ship Shoal in Theriot that suffered neglect and vandalism and eventually disappeared, the coast of Louisiana is in the process of vanishing. For years, coastal communities have continued to shrink before eventually being wiped off the map. Names that used to be dots on the map are gone. Houma, a new community in 1822 and an area with unlimited possibilities for food, industry, and culture, is growing exponentially as people flock to a city with one of the lowest unemployment rates in the country thanks to oil and gas exploration, but just how long will it be until vanishing Terrebonne Parish is forgotten? (Both, THACS.)